Disrupting Kinship

THE ASIAN AMERICAN EXPERIENCE

Series Editors
Eiichiro Azuma
Jigna Desai
Martin F. Manalansan IV
Lisa Sun-Hee Park
David K. Yoo

Roger Daniels, Founding Series Editor

A list of books in the series appears at the end of this book.

Disrupting Kinship

Transnational Politics
of Korean Adoption
in the United States

KIMBERLY D. MCKEE

**UNIVERSITY OF
ILLINOIS PRESS**
Urbana, Chicago, and Springfield

Publication of this book was supported by funding
from Grand Valley State University.

Library of Congress Cataloging-in-Publication Data
Names: McKee, Kimberly (Kimberly D.), author.
Title: Disrupting kinship: transnational politics of Korean
    adoption in the United States / Kimberly D. McKee.
Description: [Urbana, Illinois]: University of Illinois Press,
    [2019] | Series: The Asian American experience | Includes
    bibliographical references and index.
Identifiers: LCCN 2018032358| ISBN 9780252042287 (cloth : alk.
    paper) | ISBN 9780252084058 (pbk. : alk. paper)
Subjects: LCSH: Interracial adoption—United States. | Interracial
    adoption—Korea (South) | Intercountry adoption—United
    States. | Intercountry adoption—Korea (South) | Adoptees—
    United States. | Korean Americans—Ethnic identity.
Classification: LCC HV875.64 .M35 2019 | DDC
    362.734089/957073—dc23
    LC record available at https://lccn.loc.gov/2018032358

Ebook ISBN 978-0-252-05112-8

To my parents,
all of them

Contents

transnational adoption industrial complex emerged in my course with Morgan Liu, and thank you to Shannon Winnubst, whose comments on adoptive families as queer kinship formations strengthened this project. Thank you to Martin Joseph Ponce and Jian Neo Chen whose work along with Lynn Itagaki and Judy Tzu-Chun Wu formed the core of my experience with the Asian American Studies program.

Research funding at the Ohio State University from the Asian American Studies program, Diversity and Identity Studies Collective, Office of Diversity and Inclusion, Council of Graduate Students, Arts and Humanities Graduate Research Small Grants, and G. Micheal Riley International Academic Fund in the College of Arts & Sciences supported the refining of arguments and analyses discussed in this project. Thank you to the Council of Graduate Students' Edward F. Hayes Graduate Research Forum for recognizing the contributions of my arguments concerning adoptees' racial, ethnic, and cultural identities. Funding from the Department of Women's, Gender, and Sexuality Studies' Elizabeth D. Gee Award supported my visit to the University of Minnesota's Social Welfare History Archives. Thank you to Linnea Anderson for her assistance and guidance as I navigated the archives.

The community I formed at Grinnell College as a Consortium for Faculty Diversity postdoctoral fellow supported the drafting of the manuscript and book proposal. The mentoring from Carolyn Herbst-Lewis and friendship with other non-tenure-track junior faculty including Erin Cowling, Nabeela Alam, and Laura Burrack created a generative intellectual community. Special thanks go to Karla Erickson for providing feedback on my book proposal.

Thank you to my Asian American Studies family. I am indebted to Cathy Schlund-Vials's comments on my book proposal. This project benefited immensely from the East of California Junior Faculty retreat. Thank you to Nitasha Sharma and Min Hyoung Song for organizing the retreat in 2015 and Crystal Parikh and James Kyung-Jin Lee for leading my small group. Karen Leong has offered important advice over the years. As I finished this manuscript, the comments and suggestions from those at the American Studies Association Korea conferences in recent years strengthened my interventions concerning adoptee citizenship and cultural productions. Meaningful conversations with colleagues at the Association of Asian American Studies, American Studies Association, and National Women's Studies Association conferences provided feedback and encouragement as I presented portions of this manuscript. Special recognition also goes to the International Korean Adoptee Association Korean Adoption Studies Symposium and the Alliance for the Study of Adoption and Culture. And to Patricia P. Chu, thank you for sparking my interest in Asian American literature and the field of Asian American Studies when I was an undergraduate in your English courses.

Thank you to my colleagues at Grand Valley State University. A warm thank you to Melanie Shell-Weiss, who provided valued feedback on later versions of the manuscript. Additional thanks to Anne Hiskes, Wendy Burns-Ardolino, Sarah King, Marion Mathisen, and Courtney Sherwood. The support I have received from the Center for Scholarly and Creative Excellence cannot go unrecognized. Thank you for the countless mini-grants that allowed me to strengthen my manuscript, benefiting from the keen editing eye of Anna Genoese, as well as support from the Book Publication Subvention Fund. My gratitude to the Fred Meijer Center for Writing and their faculty writing retreats—those spaces have been invaluable. Michelle Sanchez's attention to detail supported manuscript revision for clarity. Funding from the Pew Faculty Teaching and Learning Center facilitated generative conversations with colleagues at conferences.

Parts of this book have been previously published. Earlier versions of my discussion of the transnational adoption industrial complex's origins appeared in "Monetary Flows and the Movements of Children: The Transnational Adoption Industrial Complex," *Journal of Korean Studies* 21, no. 1 (2016): 137–178. Earlier versions of chapter three appeared in "Real versus Fictive Kinship: Legitimating the Adoptive Family" in *Critical Kinship Studies*, edited by Charlotte Kroløkke, Lene Myong, Stine Wilum Adrian, and Tine Tjørnhøj-Thomse (London: Rowman and Littlefield International, 2015), 221–336. I am appreciative of the editors and external reviewers' comments on these essays.

This book is indebted to the scholarship of those adoptee scholars in Korean Adoption Studies. A special thanks to Kim Park Nelson, Eleana J. Kim, and Tobias Hübinette, whose work profoundly shaped the field, and to Elizabeth Raleigh, Lene Myong, Kelly Condit-Shrestha, Jenny Wills, Sara Docan-Morgan, JaeRan Kim, and Jennifer Kwon Dobbs; our conversations over the years remain generative and affirming. Liz, thank you for your willingness to read portions of this project. Cynthia Callahan, Emily Hipchen, Margaret Homans, and Catherine Ceniza Choy, thank you for your incredible work in Adoption Studies to enrich the field and complicate narratives of adoption. My deepest thanks to Sarah Park Dahlen, who introduced me to a dynamic community of scholars engaged in Korean American Studies at my first AAAS. Thank you for your support and community over the years.

I appreciate and am grateful for close friendships over the years. Writing can be solitary, which is why I am continually grateful for long-lasting networks of scholars and friends, including Douglas Ishii, Krupal Amin, Anne Jansen, Denise Goerisch, Shannon Gibney, Meghan Cai, Sarah Clark, Andrea

Riley-Mukavetz, Juwon Lee, Stacy Schroeder, and Louise Leon. Krista Benson, thank you for being my sounding board when I bring together inchoate ideas and weave them together. You often are the first and second reader on my work. Thank you to Sai Isoke, for providing feedback and assistance on this project. Laura Smith, Laura McMaster, and Emily Sauls, you three have seen what this project looked like in its infancy, and Laura Smith's keen eye supported copyediting of the manuscript in its early days. Thank you to Ed Andrews, whose friendship over the years continues to bring joy. And to my KAAN family, much gratitude to you over the years.

To my mom and Steve, thank you for believing in me and your encouragement along the way. This manuscript would not be here today if you didn't encourage me to go back to pursue my PhD when you did. I also thank my dad and Abby. Bob, thank you for your support as I wrote and finished this manuscript while you visited us throughout the years. To my sisters and brothers, your lives have touched this manuscript in ways that you don't realize. To my omma and appa, sa-rang-hae. I ch'aek-ŭn u-li-ka ham-kke-han yŏ-haeng-ŭl pan-yŏng-hap-ni-ta. Finally, to my yobo. Your cooking fueled me along my writing journey. To Ashley and Max, follow your dreams.

Disrupting Kinship

Introduction

Adoption privileges a narrative of love and family. Rhetoric of child-saving rescue overshadows concerns for family preservation and ignores how adoption is
not a discrete, isolated event. Rather, adoption has transnational, institutional,
and commercial implications. Far too often, adoption focuses on the creation
of families and the transcendent nature of color-blind love and multiculturalism and overlooks the losses experienced by birth families. Society lacks a
sustained understanding of the everyday practices of adoption. And yet it is
through mundane, daily operations that transnational adoption became a *de
facto* social welfare mechanism for many sending countries and persisted into
an international form of family making and unmaking from the mid–twentieth
century onward.

At the same time, it is because adoption became naturalized within the global
landscape that the long-term impact of the process is overlooked, even as these
families—birth and adoptive—find themselves marginalized for disrupting notions of biologically related kinship. Naturalization of adoption is contingent
and inherently messy. On the one hand, adoption is celebrated and touted as
an opportunity to provide children "good" homes. On the other hand, this
naturalization cannot and does not erase adoption's psychic and real losses.

To better understand the ordinariness of international adoption and how
it became established in the global landscape, *Disrupting Kinship: Transnational Politics of Korean Adoption in the United States* explores the phenomenon
of international adoption between South Korea (henceforth Korea) and the

United States, interrogating the intersections of the macro- and micro-levels of adoption.[1] Unlike adoptions of children following military conflicts, such as World War II and the Vietnam War, Korean adoption never ceased, even as the nation rose to become one of the top fifteen world economies by the end of the twentieth century. This monograph exposes the growth of the transnational adoption industrial complex (TAIC)—a neocolonial, multi-million-dollar global industry that commodifies children's bodies.

As an assemblage formation, the TAIC reflects the intersections and con-nections of the Korean social welfare state, orphanages, adoption agencies, and American immigration legislation. These components facilitated the de-velopment of transnational adoption between the two nations. Assemblage theory exposes how the mechanisms forming the TAIC remain directly and indirectly linked to multiple processes of nation-state and nongovernmental organization (e.g., adoption agencies, orphanages) control.[2] My deployment of assemblage theory is imbued with a feminist intersectional approach to ac-count for instances where power and subordination operate simultaneously, and sometimes asynchronously, to impact the macro- and micro-levels of the adoption industrial complex.[3] Precarious and always in process, the interactions of multiple components may not occur synchronously, even if they operate simultaneously across space.[4] *Disrupting Kinship* elucidates the ways in which Korea's systematic adoption pipeline exemplifies a model of monetary success and a how-to formula regarding adoption as a de facto social welfare option for other countries.

Adoption participation not only absolves Korea—as well as other sending countries—from building a stronger social welfare state to aid the care and education of their future citizens, but it also provides the United States—along-side other receiving countries—future productive members of society. More than 200,000 Korean children were sent abroad, two-thirds of whom entered the United States, the largest receiving country of foreign adoptees worldwide. Three-quarters of these children grew up in white families, making these kinship units not only transnational but also transracial. Korean adoptees are a distinc-tive subgroup of the Asian American population, representing a significant one in ten Korean Americans.[5]

The TAIC reveals how an intricate system operates to create and sustain the continued abundance of children available for adoption. My interest in the commodification of bodies joins recent scholarship exposing the monetary values placed on the bodies of children and the limited impact of national and international legislation on adoption practices.[6] *Disrupting Kinship* reveals how children are produced as objects available for adoption. Diana Marre and Laura Briggs note, "Since the end of the Cold War, most children circulating in adoption are social orphans; they have living parents but have been relinquished by them or taken by the state and declared legally abandoned; they are only legally 'orphans.'"[7] Distinguishing between *real* orphans—those with no living parents to care for them—and *social* orphans uncovers the manufactured falsities predicating contemporary adoption. Acknowledging that the majority of adoptees are not orphans disrupts long-standing beliefs of rescuing parentless children. Fabrications of a child's origins originate in what Shellee Colen terms *stratified reproduction*—"a transnational system of power relations that enables privileged women to bear and nurture children while disempowering those who are subordinated by reason of class, race, and national origin."[8] Building upon this understanding, I argue that stratified reproduction reveals the inconsistencies about *who* may parent and exposes how adoption relies upon deeming who is worthy to parent. Parenting is no longer tied to one's procreative capabilities; rather, parenting becomes politicized. My interest in who is allowed to parent is in conversation with Laura Briggs's explorations of broader socioeconomic and social welfare failures generating the conditions of the adoption economy.[9] Briggs connects adoption to its increasingly neoliberal construction as a privatized venture.

The recognition of power differentials produced by adoption requires grappling with the absence of an altruistic relationship between sending and receiving countries because adoption always involves caring and consumptive exchange.[10] Disentangling one from the other overlooks how adoption cannot be seen as only a benevolent act of saving because it is a form of family making and unmaking. Adoption's humanitarian ideals operate in tension with the racialized and gendered hierarchies produced as a result of transnational, transracial adoption.

Invested in elucidating adoption's impact on individuals, this project engages Barbara Yngvesson's examination of what it means to *belong*—in the adoptive family, the receiving country's culture, the biological family, and the country of origin. Troubling notions of *belonging*, she reveals the discontinuities that rhetorics of belonging produces when understanding identity and adoption. Yngvesson also elucidates the implications for sending countries when transnational adoption becomes normalized as a child welfare policy.

Issues of belonging are intrinsically tied to reproductive and affective labor. The TAIC—like other industrial complexes—relies on the commodification of bodies and the purchasing of such labor. For example, the prison industrial complex resulted in companies from a variety of industries (e.g., healthcare, food service, surveillance) benefiting from the growth of for-profit prisons and the exploitation of prison labor by companies.[11] Prisoners' bodies become modified under a neoliberal regime whereby for-profit companies emphasize their status as objects to be counted to meet private prison lockup quotas and deployed as unfree labor. This monetization of bodies results in a decoupling of prisoners from being seen as individuals instead of a systematized mechanism to facilitate corporate growth. Directly linked to the prison industrial complex, as Dorothy Roberts demonstrates, are practices involving the fostering and adoption of children of color, whereby children are taken into state custody under pretenses of parental (un)fitness.[12] Furthermore, I contend that the wedding industrial complex's investment in monetizing reproductive labor remains rooted in a similar neoliberal framework concerning capitalism and consumption.[13] The logics of industrial complexes rest upon the creation and maintenance of neoliberal regimes rooted in markets and profit.

Due to its investment in unearthing the broader connections between various institutions aiding the growth of international adoption as a social welfare mechanism and tool to aid stratified reproduction, *Disrupting Kinship* explores the various facets of adoption in conversation with one another. In doing so, it reveals how these seemingly isolated nodes interact with one another to give rise to the TAIC. This interdisciplinary project examines the interconnected nature of adoption's military origins, Christian Americanism, and Korean social welfare policy with understandings of citizenship, belonging, and family. I build upon Soojin Pate and Arissa Oh's scholarship that renders the origins of Korean adoption visible and articulates how the initial organizations operating during the post–Korean War period laid the groundwork for the growth of a six-decades-long business.[14] Yet, examinations of the adoption program's origins often privilege narratives of Harry and Bertha Holt and the birth of the Holt Adoption Program (currently Holt International). I caution against this hyperfocus, as an emphasis on the Holts individualizes Korean adoption to underscore only one program, when in fact multiple agencies facilitated placements from South Korea to the United States, Australia, and a host of European nations. In 1953, the earliest adoptive parents were affiliated with the Seventh Day Adventist Church. Other agencies operating in these initial years of adoption also included Catholic Relief Services, Child Placement Services, International Social Services, Pearl S. Buck Welcome House, and National Catholic Welfare Committee.[15]

The valorization of the Holts leads to reductive understandings of how Korean adoption became cemented as an institutionalized force in South Korean society as it overlooks agencies' integral role in facilitating early Korean adoption. Thus, even as the Holts contributed to the expansion of Korean adoption as the narrative of their adoption of eight mixed race orphans touched American hearts and minds and their use of proxy adoption allowed for greater numbers of Americans to participate in adoption, the family cannot be seen as the sole reason for Korean adoption's success and continuance. After all, the institutionalization of international adoption as the de facto alternative to Korea's development of a strong social welfare state raises questions concerning adoption participation's long-term impact on the nation.

Korea holds the unique distinction of maintaining the world's longest engagement in transnational adoption as a sending country. The nation's persistent involvement in adoption results in Korea's centrality in shaping contemporary adoption practices. Instrumental to this positioning is the rise of the TAIC, which offered methods of standardization to be replicated in other countries. The fact that Korea did not cease to participate in adoption while other countries ended their international adoption programs immediately after the initial need was met (e.g., the adoption of mixed race children in the immediate post–World War II period) indicates the embedded nature of adoption in everyday society even as Korea became a global economic power.[16] This large-scale adoption project is rivaled by no other international adoption scheme. As a result, Korean adoptees' self-expression and activism cannot be overlooked, as their voices are leading conversations in flipping the script of mainstream understandings of adoption that render adoptees as perpetual children.

To strengthen our understanding of adoption's impact on adoptees and their families, this book foregrounds the voices of adult adoptees, exploring how their lives remain deeply intertwined with the transnational adoption industrial complex. The proliferation of adoptee-authored texts (e.g., documentaries, memoirs, poetry, theatrical performances, music) challenges the singular narrative of adoption as a form of child-saving and rescue. This line of inquiry builds on recent work that positions adoptees as experts of their experiences and explores transcultural, transracial adoption as a form of diaspora.[17] My analyses of adoptees' negotiation of racial, ethnic, and cultural identities in print and online media engages Tobias Hübinette's investigation of adoptees' reincorporation into the Korean state and the role of white privilege in their racialized lives.[18] In doing so, it joins Kim Park Nelson's ethnographic examination of adoptees' identity exploration in multicultural America and considerations of what being Korean means in the lives of adoptees upon return to South Korea.[19]

I build upon Hübinette and Park Nelson's discussions of adoptee identity and community with Eleana J. Kim's discussion of adoptees' online and offline networks that formulate the adoptee counterpublic.[20] Yet, I delineate between the adult adoptee counterpublic and the wider adult adoptee community. This counterpublic challenges the TAIC and the fetishization of their bodies that occurs within mainstream adoption discourse. However, members of the broader adult adoptee community may be disengaged from wider criticisms of the TAIC. These individuals forge kinship with one another based on their singular shared experience: adoption. This project elucidates how the TAIC explicitly and implicitly shapes the ways in which adult adoptees not only form community, but also negotiate what it means to be simultaneously American and an overseas Korean diasporic subject.

Where other projects examine discrete arms of the transnational adoption industrial complex, *Disrupting Kinship* attends to the ways adult adoptees co-exist within and outside of the TAIC and exposes how the reincorporation of adoptees into Korea arises in tension with adoptees' disruption of normative conceptualizations of adoption. Existing studies do not interrogate how various components of the adoption process—the origins of adoption, inclusion of adoptees into the overseas Korean diaspora, adoptee adjustment, and negotiation of identity—operate in conjunction with one another.[21] For example, even as domestic Korean social welfare policy may influence the nation's adoption participation, American immigration policy works simultaneously to encourage transnational adoption. A central objective of *Disrupting Kinship* is to expose the concrete ways in which multiple sites—the Korean social welfare state, the orphanage, and adoption agencies—facilitate the growth of transnational adoption culture. This macro-analysis elucidates how adoption became a tool to supplement child welfare and socioeconomic supports to unwed mothers and low-income families.

Disrupting Kinship makes evident the costs to maintain a regenerating market of children for the purposes of creating loving, forever families at the expense of destroying existing, loving, biological ties. Conceptualizations of nation, citizenship, and family are intertwined in the production of transnational adoption as an extension of the American imperial project. I articulate the ways in which Korean adoptees and their families disrupt generalized notions of Asian America and the Korean diaspora. As part of this analysis, *Disrupting Kinship* elucidates the complexities of reimagining adoption as more than a humanitarian project of child rescue.

The Cold War Origins of Korean Adoption

To understand the transnational adoption industrial complex's origins, one only needs to look at the role of American Cold War politics in providing the foundation for what is now an extensive system of transnational adoption between Korea and the United States. At the outset of the Korean War, President Harry S. Truman framed "all U.S. involvement in Korea as a defense against the threat of Communism."[22] The United States spent an estimated $200 million in

Korea to help rebuild the country during the immediate postwar period. This was in addition to funds expended to maintain an American military presence. As General James A. Van Fleet explained in a 1954 statement, "Our support of Korea during this period is more than humanitarian, it is more than giving from the heart. It is giving from the 'head' as well, for contributions toward the rebuilding of Korea are an investment in the future security of America and the free world."[23] American military and humanitarian interest in the region aided existing Cold War goals of promoting democracy abroad.

The interconnected nature between adoption and U.S. military involvement on the peninsula reflects the TAIC's origins in the military industrial complex, a phrase initially used by President Dwight D. Eisenhower to describe the rise of American defense industry during the Cold War.[24] Spurred by fears of communism, the military industrial complex entangled itself in all aspects of American domestic and international life. An interconnected system that links military expenditure, infrastructure, and social welfare, the military industrial complex offers a lens to consider the TAIC's emergence and persistence as a successful child welfare model. After all, the mixed race progeny of Korean women and American GIs stationed in Korea due to the Korean War (1950–1953) were a direct outgrowth of American militarism. These children were the initial orphans placed for adoption to the United States. They were particularly vulnerable for adoption because they lacked access to both Korean and American citizenship and faced societal stigma as a result of assumptions concerning their mothers' promiscuity. More broadly, families' economic precarity due to the devastation brought by war facilitated the relinquishment of children. The first wave of adoptees—war orphans and mixed race children—are direct products of Cold War militarism.

The emergence of the TAIC allowed everyday Americans to participate in the containment of the Communist threat and, by extension, join an ancillary arm of the military industrial complex by supporting the human effects of militarism on the Korean peninsula in the name of democracy.[25] Jodi Kim writes, "To conceptualize Korean transnational adoption as a militarized diaspora is to gesture to the pervasive force of militarization as a logic that structures not only international geopolitical relations but also the intimate scales of adoptee kinships and subjectivity."[26] Elucidating the linkages between the two industrial complexes is the documentary, *Geographies of Kinship*, by Korean adoptee filmmaker Deann Borshay Liem, which locates adoption as a project of neoliberalism and postindustrialization.[27] Liem offers a sociohistorical critique of the Korean and American nation-states, disrupting narratives of "winning" South Korea and containing communism as well as turning the gaze of adoption back to the complicity of the South Korean government.

Transnational adoption established Americans' investment in Asia and, by extension, in American foreign policy's promotion of freedom and opportunity. For example, American-Korean Foundation (AKF) members viewed charitable aid as a way to directly help Korean children. Leonard W. Mayo, an AKF board member, found, "The children of South Korea are truly a symbol of [South Korea's] plight and by the same token they offer the free world a receptive soil for a fruitful demonstration of democracy."[28] International adoption provided individual Americans a chance to participate in spreading democracy abroad, or so they believed. The TAIC as an extension of the military industrial complex remains intertwined in neoliberal patterns of reproductive care and labor concerning social welfare systems and assumptions of *good* families.

Adoption policy at this point drew directly out of Cold War thinking in regard to constructing a strong and robust Korean state. This unspoken relationship created a meticulous pipeline that transformed children from orphans to adoptees. Yet this conduit could function only with the aid of orphanages and adoption agencies. Monetary support from individuals, volunteer aid groups, and religious organizations (e.g., Save the Children's Fund, World Vision, and Catholic Charities) allowed these organizations undue influence to construct early Korean adoption policies because the nation lacked sufficient funds to create a strong social welfare infrastructure.[29] Participating in the caring of Korean children allowed religious organizations the opportunity to fulfill the Biblical call from James 1:27 to save orphans. Yet, these individuals overlooked the second half of the Biblical verse—"to look after orphans *and widows in their distress*."[30] Adoption was favored over family preservation. The TAIC examines the methods deployed by orphanages to erase adoptees' personal sovereignty and adoption agencies' complicity in rendering adoptee bodies as objects available for purchase.

The Demand for Gratitude

Adoption is inherently political. Yet the politics of adoption too frequently reduces a person's stance on adoption to a narrow binary: Are you "pro" or "against" adoption? A more comprehensive understanding of adoption is needed for many reasons, not the least of which is the fact that adoption is a reproductive justice issue concerning who has the right to parent.[31] Such an inclusive understanding recognizes what Kit Myers terms the *violence of love*. This concept complicates adoption, exposing the repercussions of adoptive parents' love and good intentions and recognizing the lifelong implications of adoption in the lives of adopted persons.[32] The loving act of adoption cannot be discussed without examining its interrelationship with the multiple losses associated with the internal and external reasons fueling relinquishment, the adoption process, and post-adoption experience. *Disrupting Kinship* demonstrates how various institutions, organizations, and individuals operate in conjunction with one another to generate and sustain the conditions of the TAIC.

In the case of adoptees, the TAIC continually transforms and impacts their lives from childhood to adulthood. *Disrupting Kinship* situates itself in conversation with the emergence of adoptees as agents of their own experiences. Adoptees find themselves in continual negotiation with binary logic that characterizes adoptees' as either "grateful, happy, and well-adjusted" or "ungrateful, angry, and maladjusted" individuals. The rhetoric of happiness renders adoptees as forever unhappy and embittered individuals. Yet this notion of adoptees limits and elides adoptees' ability to be agents of their own experiences and histories, overlooking how criticism and critique are modes of self-representation. The dichotomy originates in how adoptees encounter expectations of gratefulness by the outside world.

For adoptees to be "happy," they must reflect an image of gratefulness concerning their adoptions. Happiness is linked to accepting the narrative of adoption promulgated by mainstream adoption discourse—the notion that adoption is the best option. Happiness and gratefulness mark a specific type of experience—the mythic, saved orphan. Those who adhere to this trope are invariably labeled as well-adjusted. Distinguishing between the terms "happy" and "grateful" voids the interchangeable deployment of the terms by mainstream discourse to label adoptee experiences.

I draw upon erin Khuê Ninh's discussion of gratitude and filial duty within the Asian American family to understand rhetoric of the affective nature of gratefulness. While Ninh's analysis focuses on second-generation daughters and their immigrant Asian parents, I argue that her discussion of filiality is applicable when considering the ways in which assumptions regarding the model minority implicitly influence adoptive parents' selection of Korea for their future children. In other words, assumptions concerning the alleged intellectual capabilities and the ease in which persons of Asian descent assimilate into white American culture provided the groundwork for prospective adoptive parents to contemplate the inclusion of the Korean child into their families. While I further discuss this conceptualization of race and racial difference in chapter 3, my interest in Ninh rests in her understanding of familial obligation. She writes, "The construct of 'filial obligation' defines the parent-child relation as a debtor-creditor relation, but within this system without contract or consent, the parent-creditor brings into being a child-debtor who can never repay the debt of her own inception and rearing."[33] In the case of the adoptee, they can never return the actual amount spent on their adoption. The myriad of fees can never be recovered. Adoption cannot in this sense be conceived of as a "gift" when premised on the notion that the child is in perpetual debt to one's parents. This concept must be viewed as part and parcel with the language of child saving; without the purchase of adoptees, they would only be in metaphorical debt to their biological parents.

Yet, adoptees are also in literal debt to their adoptive parents, even if this priceless act cannot be recovered in the form of monetary payment. Adoptees incur this debt via subjection to problematic assumptions concerning their gratefulness over their rescue. Even as Ninh argues that this construction of the child as both priceless and with relentlessly calculable worth is an ideological fabrication, I maintain that any reference to the adoptee's cost is linked to the neoliberal pro-adoption regime that facilitates the actual buying and selling of children.[34]

Assumptions of gratitude and filial piety are magnified when payment is no longer an intangible point of discussion. When one can enumerate the real costs of not only the act of adoption but also the monetary amounts associated with adoption beyond the actual fee, we cannot assume the debt of adopted children is comparable to biological children. Adoptees encounter the weight of the financial expenses in combination with the incalculable load of savior narratives.

At the same time, rhetoric of ungratefulness minimizes adoptees' overall experiences to promote a more positive narrative. These individuals are characterized as "angry" due to this reductive framing. Discussing the concept of "anger," Sara Ahmed notes, "Your anger is a judgment that something is wrong. But in being heard as angry, your speech is read as motivated by anger. Your anger is read as unattributed, as if you are against x because you are angry rather than being angry because you are against x."[35] If they conceal their anger, adoptees risk complying with the moral distinctions associated with happiness. The adoptee thus "work[s] to support the belief that everything is fine—when it isn't."[36] This erases unarticulated moments in one's lived experiences and obscures the silence of what is not said. If adoptees even slightly intervene in mainstream understandings of adoption, they disrupt an unspoken contract between adoptee and adoptive parent. Such an either/or framework illustrates how happiness is subjective and predicated upon, what Ahmed terms, "being happy 'in the right way,'" whereby those who find themselves aligned against adoptive parents and adoption practitioners are labeled unworthy.[37]

The good, happy subject, or in this case, the happy, grateful adoptee, must then employ a particular affect conveying their joy. To fail to do so results in the adoptee's positioning as both unhappy and ungrateful. This sets the stage for the emergence of the *adoptee killjoy*, building upon Ahmed's discussion of the feminist killjoy. Troubling notions of what it means to be a "good" subject, the feminist killjoy, according to Ahmed, "is a spoilsport because she refuses to convene, to assemble, or to meet up over happiness."[38] She fails to be in agreement with the rest of the community, unnerving moments of perceived solidarity. In doing so, the feminist killjoy "function[s] as an unwanted reminder of histories that are disturbing, that disturb an atmosphere."[39] Discussing what it means to kill joy, Ahmed writes:

> Feminists do kill joy in a certain sense: they disturb the very fantasy that happiness can be found in certain places. To kill a fantasy can still kill a feeling. It is not just that feminists might not be happily affected by the objects that are supposed to cause happiness but that their failure to be happy is read as sabotaging the happiness of others.[40]

This understanding of the feminist killjoy offers a lens to locate adoptees that fail to adhere to normative requirements of what it means to be a grateful adoptee. As seen in campaigns for policy change in Korea to protect the rights of biological mothers and support for adoptee rights, the adoptee killjoy disrupts adoption narratives of child rescue through political activism. When an adoptee unsettles discourse concerning adoption as an act of humanitarianism, she becomes "angry." Adoptees' responses demonstrate their engagement in a politics of refusal—refusal to engage an affective performance of gratitude. In the eyes of mainstream society, ungrateful adoptees are failures—unfaithful betrayers of the nation for *failing and refusing to* embrace humanitarian narratives of adoption.

Adoptees *kill* joy when they fail to adhere to the adoption fantasy—where adoptive parents save the orphan from poverty and degradation. Not only is the joy of adoptive parents killed, the adoptee killjoy also outwardly scrutinizes and troubles narratives promulgated by orphanages and adoption agencies concerning the benefits of adoption. They reveal the contradictions and violence of adoption including fraudulent creation of orphans and denial of rights to birth parents. The adoptee killjoy sabotages the potential futures of adoptable children as they advocate for more stringent adoption regulations to ensure ethical adoptions.

The discussion of the ungrateful adoptee cannot occur in isolation. The *every adoptee* operates in contrast to the adoptee killjoy. A twenty-first-century invention and, in many ways, borne from the dust of the "grateful adoptee" trope, the every adoptee is seemingly compliant and does not challenge adoption's practice. The every adoptee is situated as someone implicitly grateful for adoption in silence concerning issues of adoption fraud or malfeasance. The every adoptee exists as a separate entity operating outside of adoption discourse. The every adoptee belongs to the broader adoptee community that lacks engagement with the activist adoptee community. These adoptees do not explicitly question the conditions that generated their adoptions. The every adoptee presents adoption in digestible bites focused on the consumption of culture such as Korean food or viewing Korean dramas. These bites are merely quick, palatable insights into adoptee identity.[41] In comparison, the adoptee killjoy requires members of the adoption constellation to critically consider the legacies and implications of transnational adoption in the lives of birth parents and adoptees.

The every adoptee creates a new path for adoptees to see themselves in the adoptee diaspora and Asian American community. The every adoptee gives voice to the nuances of adoptee identity and underscores how adoptees do not exist within a strict binary framework. As a sympathetic figure, unlike the adoptee killjoy, the every adoptee may openly discuss return to South Korea and reunion because they do not challenge the system of adoption. The every adoptee symbolizes whom mainstream society wants to root for—the adoptee who negotiates Korean culture, potentially searching and reuniting with their biological parents, while simultaneously maintaining strong ties to the adoptive family. This positioning as the friendly, innocuous adoptee allows the every adoptee to enter the cultural milieu of grateful, happy adoptees.

The binary framework traditionally used to understand adoptees' perspectives on adoption locates the every adoptee as somewhat compliant with the status quo. Yet, the every adoptee is precariously positioned as neutral until criticism of adoption practices is voiced. The every adoptee resides in the articulation of an individual's minor affects, constructing a new avenue for adoptees to enact personhood.[42] These adoptees exist in the messiness of what it means to disrupt adoption narratives and operate within the middle registers of affect. They negotiate the politics of disappointment regarding their gratitude and create a rhetorical space for adoptees to complicate binary logics of what it means to be *good* and *grateful*.

Adulthood clarifies adoptees positioning as "guests" in the family expected to adhere to a specific script concerning the politics of adoption. Ahmed finds, "To be a guest is to experience a moral obligation to be on your best behavior, such that to refuse to fulfill this obligation would threaten your right to coexistence."[43] Although discussing unhappy queers, Ahmed's analysis of how recognition is "a gift given from the straight world to queers, which conceals queer labor and struggle" and requires individuals to "be grateful for the bits and pieces that [they] are given" reflects how other subjectivities beholden to gratefulness and gratitude live a tenuous existence.[44] There is an expectation for both queers and adoptees that they be grateful for their acceptance within their families, who often do not inhabit their subject positions. For adoptees, their membership in their families is conditional. Adoptees' disruption of dominant adoption discourse and criticism of the TAIC threatens their ability to peacefully coexist with adoptive parents and adoption practitioners. Adoptive parents may be explicit in their desires to ensure that adoptees are aware of their existence as guests. For example, Mi Oak Song Bruining notes: "My parents told me I should feel grateful and lucky to be adopted and should not feel sad about anything. . . . My adoptive parents believed that they rescued me."[45] The linkages between adoption and child-saving underscore how gratefulness is the automatic and default adjective many adoptive parents seek to apply to their children. The precarity associated with adoptees' positioning as guests is why the every adoptee is always at risk of disrupting the status quo of traditional adoption narratives.

Summary of Chapters

Disrupting Kinship initiates a new conversation concerning the competing stakeholders in transnational, transracial adoption from Korea—governments, orphanages, adoption agencies, adoptive parents, and adoptees. I locate adoptees' experiences within a broader understanding of the TAIC, exploring adoptees' critiques of Korea's continued participation in adoption, interventions in cases of adoptee deportation, and challenges to the dominant portrayal of the "grateful, saved orphan." This project makes three distinct interventions in its examination of the macro- and micro-levels of adoption.

First, I historicize the origins of the TAIC within American militarism and Cold War Era rhetoric shaping U.S. involvement on the Korean peninsula in the mid–twentieth century.[46] I trace how adoption became a naturalized method of family disintegration and creation. Focusing on adoption's evolution from humanitarian desire to save children and promote democracy abroad to a social welfare mechanism, I expose the complex ramifications of adoption. Archival research conducted at the University of Minnesota Social Welfare History Archives strengthens this analysis. I examined files from the Child Welfare League of America; the Children's Home Society of Minnesota; the International Social

Service–American Branch, including Korean adoption case records; and the Leonard Mayo papers.[47] The first three sources conducted international adoptions from Korea and facilitated the placement of children across the United States. Leonard Mayo worked with the International Union of Child Welfare and the American–Korean Foundation from the late 1950s to the early 1970s. His papers, articles, and letters provide insight into how the U.S. government and private sector actors conceived of and understood adoption from Korea. Taken together, these sources illuminate how adoptees were presented to adoptive parents and discussed by agency officials as well as the links between adoption and democracy within U.S. Cold War rhetoric.

Second, *Disrupting Kinship* denaturalizes and queers the normalization of adoptive families in American society. Adoptees' positioning as members of white, adoptive families led to shifting definitions of citizenship and kinship over the last sixty years. Families impacted by adoption are inherently contradictory as they expose the limitations of legal adoption and the constraints imposed by assumptions concerning biological relatedness. The transnational, transracial adoptive family visibly reveals how family making is performed as much as it is created. Through their navigation of immigration and naturalization law, which impacts them as much as shifting cultural and social norms, it becomes clear that adoptive families must secure political and social legitimacy. Legitimacy is not automatically given to them. *Disrupting Kinship* unpacks the language used to bestow legitimacy upon these particular families, interrogating the intersection of state and familial belonging. This monograph departs from other Korean adoption scholarship in its direct engagement with questions concerning Korean adoptees' access to citizenship, adoptees without citizenship, and calls for retroactive citizenship.

Finally, *Disrupting Kinship* troubles assumptions that a monolithic adoptee community exists by focusing on three distinct, yet overlapping, adoption populations. Notions of adoptees as perpetual children are disabused as I examine adoptees' efforts to reshape adoption discourse to recognize the inherent rights of birth parents and adoptees. In adulthood, adoptees construct a new type of public personhood, one defined by their autonomy and agency. Analyzing adoptees' print texts, oral histories, and online activism elucidates their interventions in popular culture's portrayal of adoption. Adoptee literature produced during the late 1990s reflects the first moment adoptees came together en masse as a collective voice. Oral histories capture the voices of individuals whose involvement with the adoptee community may ebb and flow, inhibiting their engagement with formalized modes of speaking such as print media. Online communications shift the existing adoption debates and increase adoptees' recognition as stakeholders in the larger conversations about international adoption. The incorporation and analysis of adoptees' interventions in adoption discourse underscores the importance of adoptees' utilization of a variety of platforms to engage with one another. In forging community and asserting their expertise on adoption, these individuals move conversations of adoption forward beyond a focus on their childhoods or adjustment within the adoptive family.

The first chapter interrogates adoptees' rendering as interchangeable objects ready to be bought and sold. Deeply held beliefs about nation, citizenship, and family become intertwined, extending the American imperial project into transnational adoption. This chapter provides the framework to elucidate how understandings of citizenship and kinship are disrupted by the entry of Korean adoptees into the United States and, subsequently, the white, American family.

The second chapter historicizes adoptees' admittance to the United States. I locate adoptees' access to legal and social citizenship within Asian American history. Race and racialization are critical dimensions of this conversation. Adoptees undergo racialization differently than other Americans of Asian descent even as they encounter barriers shaped by American Orientalism and Cold War rhetoric.[48] Previous research on adoptees within Asian American Studies focuses minimally on how adoptees' experiences differ from other Asian Americans in their analysis of the initial, post–Korean War period adoptions.[49] *Disrupting Kinship* suggests that adoptees serve as a harbinger for more lenient Asian immigration quotas alongside the migration of Asian war brides to the United States in the mid–twentieth century. At the same time, adoptees' vulnerability to deportation highlights the long-standing contradictions in U.S. immigration policy. These deportees are products of a failed system, undocumented because their parents or guardians failed to naturalize them as U.S. citizens once their adoption was completed.

Recognizing how adoptees' entry into the nation-state is predicated upon the act of adoption, the third chapter explores how traditional kinship structures grounded in genetic relatedness are disrupted.[50] The Korean adoptive family reinvents normative conceptualizations of Korean American and white families, which are traditionally conceived as same-race, genetically related units. I employ the term *Korean adoptive family* when discussing Korean adoptees and their adoptive families. This terminology reflects how these families are different than other adoptive families (e.g., Chinese adoptive families or families formed via transracial, domestic adoption). Korean adoptive families raise questions about the monoraciality of the family unit. They also highlight the paradox of sexual and social reproduction. Though these families unsettle the standard paradigm of the biological and monoracial family, they reify the notion that a "family" is comprised of married, heterosexual parents because only legally married, heterosexual partners may legally adopt from Korea.[51]

To deepen understanding of how the TAIC shapes adoptees' lives, the subsequent chapters direct our attention to their modes of self-expression and mediations on adoption. Chapter 4 examines how adoptees interrupt ideologies of the mythic adoptee by focusing on two adoptee edited anthologies, *Seeds from a Silent Tree: An Anthology by Korean Adoptees* (1997) and *Voices from Another Place: A Collection of Works From a Generation Born in Korea and Adopted to Other Countries* (1999), and the YouTube web-series *asianish* by Korean adoptee and hip-hop artist Dan Matthews. *Seeds from a Silent Tree* and *Voices from Another Place* are the first publications edited by adult adoptees and the earliest collections to include multiple adoptees' recollections of their transracial childhoods in the United States, return to Korea, and encounters with racism.[52] In contrast, *asianish* (2015–2016) signals adoptees' entry into the mainstream as the series disseminated via Asian American YouTube channel ISAtv (International Secret Agents TV). The channel also distributed Matthews's docu-series *akaDan* (2014), which introduced him to the adoptee community as it shared his experiences reuniting with his biological parents in Korea and attending the International Korea Adoptee Association (IKAA) Gathering in Seoul in 2013.

Chapter 5 draws upon oral histories collected from thirteen adult adoptees (nine women and four men) who ranged in age from twenty-three to fifty-two. Their responses provide insight into how adoption affects individuals at the micro-level, specifically concerning themes of national belonging, citizenship, and family. Typically, these experiences are overshadowed by well-known memoirs, anthologies, blogs, and documentaries. These oral histories deepen *Disrupting Kinship's* wider examination of how adult adoptees trouble mainstream adoption discourse following over sixty years of being infantilized and fetishized. Elucidating the similarities and differences of adoptees' lived realities adds dimension to how this community is viewed and disrupts routine, singular understandings of the adoptee community.

Building upon the previous chapters, chapter 6 interrogates how the adult adoptee counterpublic critiques members and/or mechanisms of the TAIC online. Adult adoptees object to portraying adoption as a humanitarian form of child rescue. This chapter examines adoptees interventions in the *New York Times* and Minnesota Public Radio adoption coverage in 2007 and 2012, respectively, and their deployment of hashtag activism to raise awareness about a new generation of Korean orphans in 2014. These examples illustrate a broader shift in adoption discourse—one where adoptees are increasingly seen as experts of what it means to live the adoption experience. In this way, adoptees' online communication reflects the ways in which adoptees are building effective coalitions with allies.

The conclusion returns to *Disrupting Kinship*'s investment in situating the macro-level of adoption within a discussion of the lived experiences of adoptees. Grappling with the advent and continuance of the TAIC evokes complex emotions on the subject of adoption. For members of the adoption constellation (e.g., adoptees, birth parents, adoptive parents), the notion of the transnational adoption industrial complex is deeply personal. To recognize adoption as an economy and a mode of consumption troubles widely held beliefs that adoption is a gift and positive mode of family making. As an adoptee and adoption scholar, I am embedded within this complex. This location makes me particularly sensitive to the emotional conflicts that arise in adoption discourse. *Disrupting Kinship* troubles singular narratives of adoption, adoptees, and adoptive families and inserts nuanced perspectives to locating adoption within broader conceptualizations of kinship. In doing so, I extend the existing conversation regarding how kinship ties are severed or created to justify the existence of one relationship: that of the adoptive family.

A Final Note

As adoptees engage publicly in recuperating stories of adoption, society must disabuse itself of the notion that all adoptees are open books ready to share their personal journeys with anyone. Scholars who study marginalized populations, including adoptees, employ ethnographic refusal as a method to ensure that we do not engage in exploitation, exotification, and othering. Here, I am reminded of the work by Kim Park Nelson. Rooted in the tradition of oral history, Park Nelson consciously privileges the voices of adoptees. She notes, "After obtaining human-subject consent from each narrator, I told them that the choice of what to include or exclude from their oral histories belonged to them. They were each told that they could stop whenever they wanted to and that they could structure their stories however they wished."[53] This investment in honoring and respecting adoptees reflects an intentional commitment to disrupt the tendency to treat adoptees as native informants who must always defend their adoptive families and experiences.

When the term *ethnographic refusal* was first employed, Sherry B. Ortner focused on how researchers may engage in practices of resistance to facilitate a particular narrative.[54] Ortner's investment in resistance highlights the role of scholars as gatekeepers to communities in that they control what is shared with noncommunity members. Yet, she does not fully examine community members' agency in shaping the knowledge generated and disseminated. Audra Simpson builds upon Ortner in her discussion of decolonized methodologies whereby ethnographic refusal occurs when participants fail to disclose information on particular topics to avoid misrepresentation. The participants are interlocutors into a community. Simpson notes such refusals are generative, as they require scholars to examine how representations arise and produce recognition as well as how the area's marginalized communities enter and exist legibly. To this end, she acknowledges how scholarship from within may produce new, generative knowledges that may not be produced by noninsiders.[55] Ethnographic refusal, thus, should be seen as occurring as part of a productive dialogue between researcher and participant—where decisions of what is said and what is told are made together. Alex Zahara writes, "Its purpose is not to bury information, but to ensure that communities are able to respond to issues on their own terms."[56] Resistance becomes active as a way to ensure that the community is depicted in ways that avoid overgeneralization and misrepresentation. Ethnographic refusal allows space for people who are too often the "subjects" of research the authority to say, "Not all stories are up for consumption."

Part of this engagement in ethnographic refusal includes the ability for me—an adoptee and Adoption Studies scholar—not to frame this monograph as a personal narrative.[57] Rather, *Disrupting Kinship* reframes historical approaches to adoption and rethinks how we understand adoption as a form of family making and unmaking through its discussion of the transnational adoption industrial complex. These interventions include the privileging adoptees' retelling of their histories as acts of refusal to maintain the status quo of the happy, grateful adoptee. It is vital that adoptees have the autonomy over when and where they discuss their adoption experiences. This becomes more evident when considering assumptions concerning adoptees' disclosure through the lens of ethnographic refusal. More importantly, amplifying the voices of adoptee scholars in the field as well as recognizing the nuances of adoptees' identities allows for intentional adoption conversations.

CHAPTER 1

Generating a Market in Children

Interacting with Cold War ideology, individuals' Christian Americanism supported the notion that adoptees would enter "good homes" in a democratic society. By linking domestic intimacy concerning kinship and family ties with Christian values, proponents of Korean adoption sought to build upon the legacy of Christian missionary work in U.S. territories abroad.[1] The work of Christian Americans in the post–Korean War period is an extension of early American Orientalism and the "sense of evangelical mission" in the nineteenth century.[2] The promise of the American dream positioned adoption as a better alternative to life in Korea.

Transnational adoption reveals the hypocrisy concerning wider issues of the American government and citizens' paternalism and racism. Tinged by Christian Americanism, individual Americans and the nation at large invoked claims concerning the need to "rescue" children from the "backward East" and bring them to the "progressive West."[3] This allowed white Americans, the primary adopters of children, the opportunity to assert the superiority of Western hegemony. Many children felt the brunt of this rhetoric as they were told adoption was in their "best interests" and that if not for the kindness and generosity from their parents, they would have fallen through the cracks of economic poverty and degradation in the land of their birth. In doing so, rhetorics of gratitude became cemented in international adoption discourse. The detrimental nature of this particular savior narrative affects not only adoptees, but also the adoption industry more broadly. Emphasizing adoption as rescue hyperfocuses on adoptive parents' actions—their decision to adopt—without systematized oversight on what occurs within the adoptive family postadoption placement. And, as we will discuss in the subsequent chapters, this lack of investment in adoptees' lives following their entry into the West is problematic and exposes adoptees to potential abuses within their new families.

Implicated in positioning adoption as a method of child rescue were adoptee social studies, which recorded the progress and history of the child, including knowledge of the birth family. These social studies allowed orphanages to promote the popular belief that adoption is the "best option" for mixed race children.[4] For example, in the late 1970s, an orphanage worker noted:

> The natural mother has worked at American army [since age 19]. She met the natural father, an American soldier and gave birth to this child, but she has never heard from the natural father after the natural father returned to America. . . . Although the natural mother works in American army, she is so poor that she can not bring up two children [who are mixed blooded]. . . . [T]he natural mother decided to have both children adopted by a stable and understandable family in America thinking [their adjustment would be easier].[5]

This characterization of the birth mother's economic constraints focuses it as a maternal deficit versus considering the ways in which paternal responsibility or the American military generated the conditions of her and her child's circumstances. Likewise, in an earlier case from the mid-1960s, the intake specialist wrote, "[The birth mother] was unable to give the child the care needed by a baby and that she was the child of an American soldier so thought that it would also be better for the child if she could go to an American home for adoption."[6] Adoption typically resulted after fathers returned to the United States and stopped supporting biological mothers and children. Focusing on the biological mother's poverty instead of the biological father's failure to care for his offspring, adoption agencies and orphanages promoted narratives of rescue. Such accounts absolve the American father from wrongdoing and pathologize Korean culture—and, by extension, birth mothers—for being unable to care for these fatherless children.

By advocating the adoption of mixed race children, Americans shored up notions of democracy and liberal equality even as the United States encountered domestic questions concerning de jure and de facto racial inequality. Immediately after the Korean War, Assistant Director of International Social Service–American Branch Susan T. Pettis responded to an adoption inquiry from the Child Welfare Supervisor of the Department of Public Welfare in Greenville, South Carolina, on March 26, 1956:

> The American-Korean orphans are not accepted in the Korean culture and are considered outcasts, even left to die. These are the illegitimate children of American serviceman [sic] and the small group of Negro-Korean children are the most needy. The dark skin is completely unknown in this country and carries with it a tremendous stigma. They have absolutely no future in this country and are often discriminated against in the sub-standard under-staffed orphanages.[7]

This communication not only demonstrates the construction of Americans as benefactors but also positions the United States as a place of racial tolerance. Studies and reports completed in the immediate postwar period throughout the 1960s supported the notion that mixed race children faced limited opportunities in Korea.[8] An estimated 5,546 mixed race children were sent abroad from 1955 to 1973.[9] Mixed race adoptees existed between the Black and white binary girding American race relations, subsumed into language discussing their "whitening" or "browning" of the nation.[10] The almost white status of mixed white-Korean adoptees allowed assimilationist beliefs to flourish. These children were assumed to seamlessly enter the white adoptive family. Orientalist assumptions of Korean culture validated the positioning of the United States as a site of racial tolerance.

Yet it would be remiss not to locate this rhetoric in conversation with American racial prejudice. Michael Cullen Green writes, "The Cold War imperatives that encouraged the cultural celebrations of the adoption of Asian orphans and abandoned white-Asian children . . . did not extend to Afro-Asians."[11] Anti-Black racism impacted the "adoptability" of mixed Korean-Black children by white adoptive parents as many of these children entered Black families and were considered "hard to place" by adoption agencies. Prospective adoptive parents' requests for children reflect anti-Black sentiment as parents noted their acceptance of any child regardless of race, except for Black.[12]

At the same time, the American government and prospective adoptive parents overlooked the fact that mixed race adoptees lacked their father's American citizenship upon birth unless the Korean mother could prove the natal father's citizenship. This practice was not new in the post–Korean War period, as Green notes, "The United States, beginning with its turn-of-the-century acquisition of the Philippines, had long refused to provide social welfare benefits or citizenship to illegitimate biracial children in Asia."[13] Such complicated access to citizenship led to at least one case of a father adopting his half-Korean child. As the father knew of his paternity, it is unclear why this child was not naturalized as an American citizen upon birth. In February 1958, a white American former serviceman residing in the southern United States wrote to International Social Service (ISS) inquiring about adopting his Korean child. Working with the father, ISS completed the adoption by May 1959.[14] Formal legal acknowledgement of paternity remained unattainable outside of the father's recognition at birth until October 1982, with the enactment of Public Law 97-359, which "[permits] the immigration to the United States of certain illegitimate Amerasian children of United States citizen fathers."[15] This legislation only covered children "born in Korea, Vietnam, Laos, [Cambodia] or Thailand after December 31, 1950, and before October 22, 1982" and not their mothers.[16]

To better understand how the discrete arms of Korea's adoption program laid the groundwork for the rise of the transnational adoption industrial complex (TAIC), this chapter investigates the ways in which the limited Korean social welfare state, in combination with the actions of orphanages and adoption agencies, generated the conditions for the nation's more than sixty-year participation in international adoption. The transnational adoption industrial complex contributes to the sustained, globalized nature of intercountry adoption. The TAIC also evolves in response to policy or legislative changes. As Kelly Condit-Shrestha highlights, the procurement of Korean children shifted from those abandoned due to war or mixed race status to children made available by unwed mothers in maternity homes.[17] Korea's adoption program departed from the other postwar programs of Germany, Japan, and Vietnam in that the Korea program sought out new adoptable children after the initial crisis was alleviated. Whereas the Hong Kong and Cuban adoption programs operated for short periods in response to perceived communist threats, communism was only a factor that spurred interested adoptive parents to join in against the fight against communism and not the reason behind the program's endurance.[18] The longevity of Korea's participation in the global adoption market reflects how Korea perfected a program that persists even as the nation is one of the world's global economic leaders.

The continual export of adoptable children reflects Korea's distinction in perfecting a program that standardized adoption practices. The TAIC offers a unique lens for other countries to model monetary success and a how-to formula regarding adoption as a de facto social welfare option. Standardization underscores how assemblages are also "capable of variable replication."[19] After reviewing the multiple mechanisms informing South Korea's TAIC, transnational adoption cannot be viewed as a static act without political, economic, or social impact within sending and receiving countries. Varying, and sometimes unequal, power arrangements between adoption agencies, orphanages, and nation-states are sustained and redeployed in other global instances of international adoption. Global attention and governmental limits at the global and nation-state level on transnational adoption encourage smaller assemblages of the South Korean TAIC to evolve into slightly different formations in order to preserve international adoption participation.

Failures in Family Preservation

Narratives concerning unwanted children and patriarchal Confucian culture obscure the other factors that fuel Korea's continued adoption participation. Decisions to place children for adoption are not only made by biological family members but are influenced by societal limitations reducing lone parents' and families' economic situations to raise children in Korean society. Low-income families' and unwed mothers' abilities to parent are also curtailed by androcentric legislation concerning children's access to Korean citizenship, societal stigma against unwed motherhood, and prevailing notions of the male breadwinner/female housewife dichotomy. The intention of this particular line of inquiry is not to elide the agency of Korean women and the societal impact of Korean women's organizations.[20] Yet, Korean women remain disenfranchised as the nation's overtures toward gender equity are given inadequate resources or personnel. Supporting women as social, political, and economic actors remains critical to ending Korea's adoption participation.

Even as the 1948 Republic of Korea Constitution established gender equality, a notable gap existed between de jure and de facto gender equality to prevent political equity. The Nationality Law of 1948 classified *patrilineal jus sanguinis*. While the biological children of South Korean men obtained citizenship regardless of their natal mother's nationality, "children born to Korean women and foreign men could not."[21] Only when the law was revised in September 1997 to cover bilateral jus sanguinis did the state grant Korean citizenship rights to children of Korean women.[22] Operating in conjunction with the Nationality Law is the Family Law, established by Parts Four and Five of the Republic of Korea's Civil Code. From 1948 to 1991, the Family Law denoted the husband as the family provider and granted a series of rights to the husband regarding family members in his *hoju* (family registry), including the ability to admit an illegitimate child he begot with another woman into his family without his wife's consent.[23] Korean women lacked the right to enter their children on their family registry. The importance of the family registry in providing legitimate status to the child underscores the gendered nature of citizenship. And as Hosu

Kim writes, "South Korea's patriarchal marriage law did not grant custody of a child to a divorced woman, unless the father was willing to agree to such an arrangement."[24] Children, regardless of sex, encounter the effects of women's oppression.[25]

Predicated upon a male breadwinner/female housewife dichotomy, Korean women's employment prospects construct a stratified economy due to limited opportunities for professional development and economic mobility. Even with high levels of education, women earned less in comparison to their male counterparts and had fewer prestigious positions in comparison to men with less education.[26] In addition, when the government sought to increase numbers of female workers, their policies historically have engaged single women and female heads of households and focused on training women in traditionally feminized occupations (e.g., embroidery, cooking, sewing, and other low-technical skills professions), which maintained women's economic marginalization.[27] During the end of Korea's height as an adoption sending country in the 1980s, studies found that although 90 percent of single mothers participated in the workforce, the majority had irregular work, were unskilled, or were self-employed.[28] The rise of Korea as an economic world power happened alongside its rise as an adoptive sending country and relied heavily on Korean women.

The reliance of Korean women's labor to contribute to the nation-state's economic growth in the latter half of the twentieth century is reminiscent of the economic contribution of Korean women's sexual labor in military camptowns following the Korean War.[29] Often, these women were mothers to mixed race children, some of whom were adopted. Hosu Kim notes, "Transnational adoption operated as a population removal policy that was essentially institutionalized violence against the sex workers' motherhood, and racism against their mixed race children."[30] This is not to say that all mixed race adoptees were products of sexual exploitation; rather, to call attention to the way in which Korean women's sexual labor is similar to the physical labor they expend as workers is integral to the country's economic growth. Yet, frequently, this labor goes unnoticed. Korean women are part of the backbone of the nation's growing economy—serving the state through their physical and reproductive labor, given the ways in which the adoption industry contributed to Korea's economic rise.[31]

Women's location in the part-time and irregular feminized-labor sectors penalizes their ability to bolster family income and inhibits family preservation. Reflecting on her efforts to safeguard her family, Noh Keum-Ju notes, "When I was eighteen and working in a factory, I gave birth to Seong-wook (thirty-five, living in South Dakota, United States) due to an unwanted pregnancy. My starvation was so serious that I was unable to lactate. My husband gambled and was never around, and the next year, while I was away for a month, I lost my child."[32] For women like Noh, adoption becomes the only feasible option to ensure their offspring's survival. A stratified labor market also means women are less likely to benefit from the state's social welfare programs, which remain limited to formal employment. Equitable access to benefits has not been available on a wider level to women because Korean industrial organizations provide numerous nonwage benefits to full-time workers in the formal labor market as a form of social welfare.[33]

The limited government engagement in social welfare reflects the East Asian welfare model—a reactive practice whereby welfare measures are implemented during times of economic distress.[34] Korea historically dedicated a negligible amount to social welfare and security in the Gross Domestic Product (GDP). For example, at the end of Korea's peak engagement with adoption, social security expenditures accounted for only 2.3 percent of the 1993 GDP and central government spending on welfare and social security amounted to 10.2 percent in 1995.[35] Social welfare expenditures continue to remain low. In 2008, only 10.9 percent of the country's GDP was spent on social welfare. Among Organization for Economic Co-operation and Development countries, the amount Korea spent on welfare ranked the second-lowest, only above Mexico's expenditure on social welfare (7.6 percent of the Mexican GDP).[36]

Even when women entered the formal, full-time employment sector, these opportunities failed to account for how women continued to bear the burden of taking care of the home and children.[37] Lack of childcare, in particular, acts as a barrier to women's entry into full-time employment. In 1990, only 2,323 day care centers were available. These numbers accommodated barely a fraction, less than 9 percent, of children requiring childcare.[38] Moreover, given that the minimum wage in 1991 was only $1.15 per hour, government- or company-subsidized childcare would alleviate financial burdens placed on low-income parents.[39] To address the gendered division of household labor, economic reforms must address basic private sphere needs, such as childcare and eldercare. This is not to say that the Korean government did not attempt to mitigate parental needs. From 1995 to 1997, an estimated 1.3 trillion won (USD 1 billion) was invested to create nearly 20,000 childcare facilities.[40] Nevertheless, these new facilities failed to meet the growing demand throughout the decade.[41] In January 2012, the Korean government announced that government-sponsored childcare would be provided for all infants and toddlers, regardless of parental income level, in an effort to support childcare. This proposal focused on providing free childcare for children under two years old. Yet by the end of 2012, the program proved untenable and costly at the local level.[42] As the Ministry of Health and Welfare sought to remedy the financial strain of the initial free childcare program, the ministry noted that a new program would take its place. A revised initiative did not come to fruition as Park Geun-hye assumed the presidency in 2013.

Not recognizing the discrepancies that exist between de jure and de facto gender equality inhibits a woman's ability to consider unwed motherhood as a viable option. As Korea achieved economic growth during the 1970s and 1980s, the nation's annual adoptions peaked to over 5,000.[43] During this time, unwed mothers received little financial or social support from the state, as government support did not begin until 2003. Even so, 78.6 percent of unwed mothers attributed financial hardship as a barrier to caring for their children in 2006.[44] Only in 2009 did support for unwed mothers increase from 50,000 won ($44) to 100,000 won ($89) per month.[45] When financial overtures occurred, a 2010 study conducted by the Korean Women's Development Institute still found that unwed mothers' priorities included securing adequate, permanent housing; gaining financial support; obtaining childcare; and the enforcing of gender equality policies to protect their employers from discriminating against them.[46]

While Korean policy makers propose changes to the status of unwed mothers and need for subsidized childcare, these acts do not mitigate the legal and economic barriers that render adoption (most often transnational adoption) as the only viable, yet constrained, choice. The stigma of lone parenting has yet to be erased in mainstream Korean society despite evidence that more women choose unwed motherhood over adoption.[47] Adoption will continue to serve as the de facto social welfare support due to the Korean social welfare state's historic reactive nature and lack of investment in women as mothers and workers in the formal labor sector.

This is not to say organizations and individuals are not working toward equality for unwed mothers. Organizations such as the Korean Unwed Mother Family Association (KUMFA), Mindullae (Dandelions, an organization of birth parents of overseas adoptees), and Korean Unwed Mothers Support Network (an organization founded by an adoptive father) formed to support the rights of unwed mothers.[48] Recent work of KUMFA includes advocating for single mothers' access to the government allowance given to new parents as part of efforts to combat the nation's low birthrate.[49] Adult adoptee organizations in Korea, the Truth and Reconciliation for the Adoption Community of Korea

(TRACK) and Adoptee Solidarity Korea, also work with Korean unwed mothers to enact social change concerning international adoption and domestic single-parent policies. As part of this advocacy, in May 2011, unwed mother advocacy groups renamed Adoption Day to Single Mom's Day.[50] These two populations—single mothers and adult adoptee activists—are making inroads into a landscape dominated by government and adoption agency officials in changing discourse around adoption in Korea. Those adoptees engaged in activism find themselves positioned as adoptee killjoys for participating in what some adoptees and nonadoptees alike deem behavior that is *too political*. Being apolitical marks a *good* adoptee—one that adheres to scripts of gratitude. To be outspoken and critique the absence or presence of supports for biological parents or adoptees marks the adoptee killjoy.

Manufacturing Orphans, Interchangeable Children

Orphanages and adoption agencies bolster the notion of "unwanted" children who are merchandise available for purchase. Adoptees' commodification arises from their social death—the dissolving of biological/familial ties to Korea. Not only are they estranged or displaced from their birth countries and families, any link to their ancestries are eliminated. Through the erasure of connections to their biological origins, adoptees witness their Korean cultural capital slip away as they lack access to their cultural and social histories. Social death prevents adoptees from maintaining connections to their birth culture and creates orphans in name only as many adoptees have living biological parents.[51] Natal alienation operates in conjunction with this social death and results in social and cultural isolation due to the inability to integrate ancestral lived experiences to inform present-day social reality.[52] This overall process affirms that the child's *real* parents are the adoptive parents. Similarly, in her discussion of Korean birth mothers, Hosu Kim articulates their experiences of social death. Kim writes, "The misrecognition of birth mothers and their rightlessness is useful for maintaining the status quo in the transnational adoption practice. The omission of birth mothers from the child's postadoption life serves to appease the adoptive parents' prevalent fears or anxieties that the birth mother might one day show up to reclaim the child."[53] By rendering both the birth mother and adoptee as socially dead, orphanage and adoption agencies create the conditions for unattached, adoption-ready children and facilitates the continued erasure of the birth mother's labor.

The mechanism of social death erases adoptees' histories and manufactures new identities. Communication between the Korean and American branches of the International Social Service (ISS) indicate that the invention of birth dates and names was not an uncommon practice. In a letter dated May 23, 1960, Anne M. Davison of ISS Korea wrote to the American Branch, stating that Korean social workers are "afraid now to make or accept a guess in age" until the orphans are seen by a doctor. "One other case this week had three birthdates for the same child," Davison recalled.[54] This uncertainty over when a birth date may initially seem like a clerical error; however, I argue it reflects the ways in which biographical details are seen as fungible and mutable as part of the orphan manufacturing process.

Adult adoptees also recount the creation of information, noting that their Western birthdays are not representative of their physical birth date. Only upon returning to South Korea do adoptees learn their correct birth dates after reuniting with birth families and/or acquiring their adoption files from orphanages.[55] For example, Hope Huynh notes that she thinks she was born in 1976, but she's not sure as her adoption documents were falsified.[56] Huynh learned of this deceit upon moving to Korea in 2004 and completing a DNA test with the individuals listed on her birth records, who ended up being strangers.

Providing another perspective on the significance of this fraudulence, Kimberly Hee Stock writes, "Doctors *estimated* my age like I was a stray dog at an animal shelter, I was given a new *generic* name and a new *generic* birthday."[57] One must wonder whether orphanage and adoption agency practitioners considered how, as adults, adoptees would react to this duplicity. Discussing the effect of this misinformation on her identity, Leah Kim Sieck notes, "I feel like these little details that everyone uses to anchor their existence with, like birthdays or home towns, grow into big floating question marks."[58] In altering and fictionalizing biographical details, the orphanage demonstrates what many nonadopted children take for granted—correct birthdays and birth names. For adoptees, this information is deemed replaceable, even as individuals in the West increasingly conduct genealogy searches and seek to document their family histories.

Falsifying names and birth dates raises questions about the value of identity. The adopted experience reveals how key markers of self become irrelevant in the lives of some infants but not in others. Minimizing adoptees' alternative realities and possibilities dismisses their rights to personal sovereignty. Adoptees' social death and natal alienation underscores this disregard of adoptees' rights. The absence of critical natal details reveals how adoptees become commodities available for purchase similar to Cabbage Patch dolls—products designed to allow children to adopt "orphaned children." Discussing the normalization of transracial adoptive motherhood vis-à-vis the purchase of Cabbage Patch dolls, Hawley Fogg-Davis critiques how the commodification of fictional, inanimate dolls directly reflects how we understand their animated, human counterparts.[59] Each doll could take on any identity based on what young child adopted them. Similarly, depending on the nationality of one's adoptive parents, Korean adoptees found themselves pliable objects ready to gain cultural identities bestowed on them based on the arbitrary nature of adoption.

Orphanages also construct adoptees as being interchangeable. Reflecting on her adoption, Kelly Neff notes that when the baby her parents expected to adopt died, the adoption agency exchanged the child with Neff.[60] The orphanage as a site where adoptable children are produced is best demonstrated within the documentary *In the Matter of Cha Jung Hee* directed by Deann Borshay Liem.[61] A follow-up to her documentary exploring her adoption to the Borshay family (*First Person Plural*, 2000), Liem explores how as a child in Korea, the orphanage sent her in place of another girl, Cha Jung Hee.[62] Orphanage workers told Liem not to reveal that she was not in fact Cha Jung Hee prior to her airplane journey to the United States. As a result, Liem lives her life with Cha Jung Hee's birth date and adoption case history as her own.[63] Searching for the "original" Cha Jung Hee, Liem meets multiple women named Cha Jung Hee and wonders what happened to the young girl in the photo sent to her parents. Three different photos of Cha Jung Hee emerge in orphanage documents magnifying the possibility of duplicity. One photo is of Liem and the other two are young girls who were also once named Cha Jung Hee. The three photographs illustrate how the child's body is rendered as an interchangeable object of exchange. The orphanage renamed two other young girls as Cha Jung Hee to fulfill the fantasy of the original Cha Jung Hee as a young orphan in need of Western humanitarian aid. When children become identical objects instructed not to speak of their actual names and birthdays, they are implicitly told that their original identities are immaterial.[64] They are told to be grateful and apolitical simultaneously as their identities are built upon fraud.

This is not to say that adoptive parents did not question the veracity of their adoption paperwork during or after the adoption process. For example, upon their adoption's completion in 1961, one set of adoptive parents contacted the adoption agency, orphanage, and Christian Children's Fund (CCF) concerning inconsistencies involving the child's birth date and orphan history. The history provided by the adoption agency and orphanage conflicted with information given to the adoptive family by the CCF, when the family first began supporting the child through the CCF's Foster Parent's Plan. An April 1961 letter between

International Social Service-Korea to the American branch reveals that it was possible that the orphanage confused records of female orphans and that the original child requested was not available for reasons unknown and another child was substituted in that child's place.[65]

While these above-mentioned incidents may not be representative of all international adoption practices, one cannot overlook how the disingenuous practices of orphanage officials and workers facilitated the trading of children. The "marketing" of adoptees via the social studies provided to American adoption agencies and adoptive parents reinforces the belief of adoptees' interchangeability. Yet this language to express the "uniqueness" of adoptees was not actually distinctive. Similar language was used to discuss all orphans. Many of these reports adopted the following template to describe the child's origins:

> According to the official report, she was found abandoned on [date], and was referred to our [City] branch through the magistrate of [City]. She was placed in our [City] baby home. On [subsequent date] she was taken to our headquarters in Seoul and was placed in a foster home of our agency. Her date of birth was estimated by the clinic's director. Her name was given by our agency. Further information on her background is not known because she is an abandoned child.[66]

Variations of this account may note the child's date of birth as written on a slip of paper with the child's belongings. The language used to describe the children once they entered the orphanage complements these similarities in "origin stories." Children were routinely given the following characteristics: cute with round face, well-shaped nose, medium mouth and ears, double eyelid, normal complexion, good appetite and digestion, good health, medium black eyes, round ordinary eyes, healthy.[67]

The malleable nature of adoptees' identities is only one facet of how the TAIC objectifies adoptees. American adoption agencies contribute to this objectification by attaching monetary value to children's bodies in their use of "country" fees for children. These pricing schemes are tied to the adoptee's country of origin and are available on adoption agency websites. As of January 2018, Holt International's country fee for Korea remains one of the highest at $22,500. This cost increases to $32,250–$33,150 when including the miscellaneous agency fees associated with the adoption. These separate charges include an agency registration fee; program service fee; travel fee; and medical, legal, and translation fees. Agencies also charge professional service fees, which cover the expense of home study visits; parent preparation; processing of the adoption application and required paperwork for local, federal, and foreign governments; a child referral and placement; and support and guidance through the adoption process, including postplacement and postadoption services.

Country fees demonstrate how adoption agencies implicitly rank children's bodies.[68] Price differentials reflect the country program's various reputations. The program cost for Haiti is the only Holt International country fee that rivals in price at $25,000—the fee increases to $34,350–$35,250 when accounting for additional Holt fees. In comparison, the country fee to adopt from Thailand is $12,360—and nearly doubles ($20,910–$22,060) once other Holt fees are considered.[69] The rapid increase in program cost is most remarkable when looking at Holt International's Haitian adoption program. The adoption agency estimated their Haiti program fee as $8,690 in October 2011.[70] For context, Korea's program fee in October 2011 was $20,365.[71] The total adoption cost in January 2018 for Holt International to adopt a child from the Korea ranges from $38,785–$53,980. The total costs associated with adopting from Korea would cost the average American at least 44.55 percent of the year's salary in 2016, as the real median average income for a married family was $87,057.[72] However, if we're looking at the complete dataset from the last full census in 2010, the total costs associated with adopting from Korea would cost the average American at least 53.31 percent of their year's salary in 2010, as the real median average income for a married family was $72,751.[73]

Because the notion of buying children makes many parents uncomfortable, adoptive parents and agencies discuss this process as a "gift" exchange.[74] This misnomer—adoptee as gift—generates the logics of gratitude circulating within adoption discourse. Considering the financial realities of adoption magnifies the filial obligation discussed by Ninh in the Introduction. The gift metaphor frames adoption as not only an act by which the adopted children must be grateful, but also requires adoptees to be grateful for the gift of adoption. After all, another child could easily be in their place. The latter is important to consider because of rhetorics that frame the adoptee as *chosen* by their adoptive parents. This consumeristic construction of choice is what simultaneously positions the adoptee as object and as subject—the recipient of the gift of adoption.

More importantly, the actual cost of adoption outside of the costs associated with parenting serves to regulate which class of parents may adopt. Prospective adoptive parents often are encouraged to take advantage of the Federal Adoption Tax Credit, State Tax Credits, and examine whether their employer offers assistance.[75] And while the Federal Adoption Tax Credit is helpful, for example, the tax credit is affected by income and dollar limitations. The amount a family may receive as a tax credit—the maximum amount in

2017 was $13,570—reduces for those whose income is between $203,540 and $243,540, with families exceeding $243,540 ineligible to receive the tax credit. In the case of what the Internal Revenue Service (IRS) calls "foreign adoptions": "Qualified adoption expenses paid before and during the year are allowable as a credit for the year when it becomes final. Once an adoption becomes final, and subject to the dollar limitation, qualified adoption expenses paid during or after the year of finality are allowable as a credit for the year of payment, where the adoption is foreign or domestic."[76] When considering the case of Korean adoption, this tax credit would alleviate at minimum an estimated 35 percent of the total cost to adopt from Holt International's Korea program in 2018. The prohibitive cost of adoption results in families turning to their churches, friends, and even the internet to raise funds to support adoption-related fees.[77] Financial assistance is available for parents if adopting special-needs or waiting children, who may be infants or toddlers with medical conditions or older children.

International adoption did not always exist as a classed form of reproduction. For example, in 1972 the International Social Service–American Branch operated a sliding scale based on gross family income. A family earning below $15,000 was charged $200 in comparison to a family earning above $35,000, which was charged $650.[78] Four years later, this sliding scale increased. Families earning below $15,000 were charged $800 in processing fees, while households earning above $35,000 paid $2,500.[79]

With prices attached to these children's bodies, adoption agencies use photographs of waiting children to entice adoptive parents' interest. Contemporary internet photographs from adoption agencies' websites allow families to gain instant access to a plethora of waiting children from Korea and other "sending" nations. As spectacles, adoptees are considered based on their physical features and accompanying descriptions. Regardless of prospective adoptive parents' intentions, I argue photographs of waiting children are mere objects for spectators—prospective adoptive parents—to consume. This is not to discount the emotional ties adoptive parents have with their children; rather, these photographs serve as lures to entice parents to adopt from a particular agency.[80]

These internet sites are modern incarnations of earlier print advertisements in magazines such as the *Saturday Review* or *Life*, which "seared the idea of 'adoption' into millions of Americans' minds as an effective means to fight the Cold War."[81] Advertisements in the post–Korean War period demonstrated how American humanitarian and religious organizations framed adoption not only as part of American exceptionalism, but also as a way to position "Korea's children [as] the true victims of Communist aggression."[82] Reflecting on how this first generation of adoptees promulgated exceptionalist discourse, Kim Park Nelson writes, "These initial adoptees were powerful symbols of American superiority in the cultural Cold War, and their hypervisibility as Asian foreigners quickly transitioned as these children became a Cold War success story as all-American children in loving American families."[83] Adoptees signified the triumph of democratic values and erroneously allowed Americans to believe that they transcended racial difference, dividing the nation at the peak of the Civil Rights movement. American multicultural liberalism imbued itself on discourses of gratitude girding adoption. Americans were positioned as waiting with open arms for children Korea was casting out into the streets.[84] At least this is how humanitarian rhetoric shaped international adoption narratives at the time.

Figure 1 shows one of the early sources of how orphans were marketed to prospective American parents. While not from one of the well-known sponsorship organizations (e.g., Christian Children's Fund or Foster Parent's Plan), the form from the Everett Swanson Evangelistic Association, Inc., captures the ways in which images were used to encourage Americans to support children from overseas.

The bottom-right corner of the advertisement requests interested parties to select which child from the image they desired to sponsor or note whether they sought to support a girl or boy with financial and material goods. The association asked for $8 per month for the child. The form also provided an option for individuals to receive additional information about sponsoring Korean orphans. These advertisements greatly impacted adoption (e.g., the Borshay family's adoption of Cha Jung Hee). Prospective adoptive parents would write to their adoption agencies with a deep interest to formally adopt the children they sponsored. As part of their inquiries, it was common for interested parties to include the child's sponsorship case number, orphanage, name, and even the birth date.[85]

Photographs succeeded the initial written requests by adoptive parents for specific children. Adoptive parents clearly articulated whether they were interested in infants, toddlers, and adolescents, as well as male or female children. Parents provided racial preference (e.g., full Korean, Korean-white, Korean-Black) and whether they would accept children with disabilities. Communication between Mrs. Hong Oak Soon, director of Child Placement Service in the Ministry of Health and Social Affairs at Seoul, Korea, with social welfare agencies and lawyers in the United States revealed that parents placed "orders" for children.[86] Correspondence between local agencies and ISS–American

Figure 1: "Help Heal a Child's Broken Heart" Sponsor Advertisement from the Everett Swanson Evangelistic Association, Inc. Advertisements similar to this one were used as a method to increase American engagement in Cold War humanitarian efforts. Courtesy of Social Welfare History Archives, University of Minnesota (Box 10, Folder 28, International Social Service, American Branch Records).

Branch also contains concise language concerning preferences adoptive parents had for children. Families strongly asserted their racial preferences, sometimes indicating that they could not accept a mixed race Korean-Black child due to prejudices within extended family.[87] In a case from 1977, the social worker noted "The [family] would like a Korean child of either sex, between the ages of 1 and 3. An alert child with no physical or emotional handicaps would be most acceptable to the family."[88] A second case file from 1977 reveals that a family prefers: "Either sex, up to two years of age, but preferably a boy. . . . Minor correctable medical handicaps okay. Open to any racial mixture but Black. Could handle a diabetic problem."[89] This "ordering" highlights the construction of adoptees as products for consumption. The requirements and specifications of adoptive parents concerning age, race, sex, and ability status highlight the ways in which children become commodities in this system of international trade.

Contemporary Realities of the TAIC

The prolonged success of Korea's adoption program must be considered part and parcel with the nation's economic and geopolitical growth within the last quarter of the twentieth century. The nation saw the numbers of children sent abroad for adoption increasing as Korea gained economic prominence. While the nation experienced an influx of monies due to international adoption, the Korean state did not use these funds to provide financial supports for unwed mothers and low-income families. Rather, these monies contributed to the overall growth of the national economy. Pastor Kim Do-hyun, the director of KoRoot, an organization that provides assistance to adoptees in Seoul, contends that adoption was "part of [Korea's] economic development strategy."[90] This financial investment reveals the economic losses that would result if adoption ceased because adoption served as a de facto social welfare safety net. Decreasing adoption participation requires the Korean government to support low-income families and unwed mothers. Yet as Korea reached its height sending children for adoption in the late 1970s and 1980s, the 1980 total budget listed 0.06 percent as the budget for child welfare.[91]

This is not to say that Korea was unaware of the double-edged sword of adoption participation. Even as it has become heralded for its streamlined and mechanized approach to the exchange of children, the nation faced an image problem as children became the face of Korea's exports by the 1970s and 1980s. The number of children sent to the West reached its height of 6,597 children in 1976. North Korea condemned its southern neighbor, leading Korea to proclaim that it would promote domestic adoption and discontinue its involvement in transnational adoption.[92] By the end of the 1970s, the South Korean government "established a goal of reducing the number of intercountry adoptions by 1,000 annually while concurrently increasing domestic adoptions by 500 annually."[93]

Nevertheless, adoption participation persisted. Korea became synonymous with adoption. As the nation hosted the 1988 Summer Olympic Games, Korea encountered American media scrutiny over its adoption practices.[94] In many ways, this was an ironic accusation given the United States' role instituting adoption as a de facto social welfare policy in Korea nearly thirty years prior. Adoption was accepted when positioned as a method to aid the most needy, yet when it became a consumptive practice concerning the exportation of children, adoption became denigrated.

The negative coverage prompted the Korean government to ask the four operating agencies to "temporarily suspend all intercountry adoptions . . . during the Olympics."[95] A year later, the Korean government issued new guidelines to regulate transnational adoption and promote domestic adoption.[96] These guidelines specified reducing transnational adoption by four to six hundred children annually and "placing only racially mixed or disabled children internationally after the year 1995."[97] When the self-imposed deadline loomed ahead, the government passed the Special Law on the Adoption Promotion and Procedure, encouraging domestic adoption without examining the existing goal to gradually end transnational adoption.[98] In 1997, the Korean government announced a new twenty-year plan to progressively end transnational adoption by the year 2020.[99] One year later, an estimated 2,180 children were placed for international adoption, while domestic adoptions lagged below 1,500.[100]

While domestic adoption was encouraged, overseas adoption participation did not slow. Nearly two decades after the initial controversy over "exporting" children, in July 2006, the Ministry of Health and Welfare announced new measures to encourage domestic adoption, including monetary incentives for domestic adoptive parents, government subsidies for orphanages, and allowance of single adoptive parents.[101] The Ministry of Health and Welfare also introduced a quota limiting overseas adoption.[102] In 2008, the Korean government announced its new goal of terminating international adoptions by 2012.[103] Government overtures to end the nation's nearly sixty-year engagement with transnational adoption have yet to come to fruition. Korea sent 627 children to the United States in 2012.[104] The extent that transnational adoption exists as a naturalized institution highlights the fact that the onus remains on the country of origin to improve the social welfare system in order to disengage from the practice.

On June 29, 2011, the Special Adoption Law was passed in the legislature and provided new adoption guidelines. Effective January 2012, the legislation aimed to shift Korea's previous emphasis on adoption promotion to focus on family preservation. The *Joong Ang Daily* reports, "The new law will also expand rights for single mothers and adoptees. Under the law, adoptees gain greater access to birth records and women will have a seven-day period to deliberate on whether to keep or relinquish their child. Korea currently has no such limitation."[105] Even as the Korean state makes news overtures to focus on family preservation, the state's actions are reminiscent of years past when the government attempted to lower and even end Korean intercountry adoption beginning in the last decade of the twentieth century.

As Korea sought to terminate its participation in international adoption, the government simultaneously reincorporated adoptees into the nation. President Kim Dae Jung apologized to adoptees in 1998, reflecting a shift from labeling adoptees as Korean outcasts to "overseas Koreans." Adoptees reenter the Korean nation without connection to Korea, Korean culture, or the overseas Korean diaspora. They gain access to a national Korean identity that was once possible only to ethnic Koreans raised by Korean parents. This shift is buttressed by adoptees' ability to obtain the F-4 visa for overseas Korean residents and dual citizenship as a result of revisions to the Nationality Law in April 2010. The F-4 visa applies to persons who initially were Korean nationals but acquired foreign nationality.[106] Incorporating adoptees as "Korean" subjects transgresses the boundaries established by the TAIC and ignores their new national identities as Americans, for example.

The Korean government's invitation to adoptees to return to the nation that previously cast them out provides an additional template to other sending countries that may seek to reincorporate their adult adoptees. Government and nongovernment organizations' initiatives aimed at adoptive families and/or adult adoptees (e.g., motherland tours, scholarships to study at Korean universities) complements this change in rhetoric. Interrogating the various ways adoptees are reinserted into nationalist discourse provides a new lens to examine their access to claiming a Korean identity that is imbued with assumptions concerning ethnic and cultural homogeneity. In the next two chapters, I shift our focus to the United States where I clarify how the final component of the TAIC, American immigration legislation, is inextricably linked to the white heternormative family.

CHAPTER 2

(Un)documented Citizens, (Un)naturalized Americans

Adoptees' entry to the United States represents a marked departure from the heavily regulated migration of individuals from across Asia into the nation from the period of 1875 to 1965. The transnational adoption industrial complex (TAIC) facilitated avenues to citizenship unbeknown to other immigrants from Asia. In this sense, adoptees serve as a harbinger for immigration legislation changes occurring from the mid–twentieth century onward. And they remain outliers in U.S. immigration policy, as seen in the renewed efforts to limit the entry of immigrants and refugees to the nation under the Trump administration and the debates concerning undocumented immigration that gained momentum during the Obama administration.

Adoptees' continued position as acceptable foreign aliens is critical given the ways in which the treatment toward nonwhite immigrants and diplomatic relations with North Korea rapidly declined since the November 2016 election. While the latter issue may seem unrelated at first to the adoption of children from South Korea, the rampant move toward the nuclear option, as well as Americans' conflation of the two Koreas as interchangeable, often results in anti-Korean or anti-Asian sentiment being experienced by Asian Americans, including Korean adoptees.[1] This game of brinkmanship underscores how easily the lives of adoptees' birth families are seen as undervalued, if holding value at all.[2] Furthermore, in the case of international adoptees from countries in Africa and the Caribbean, media outlets widely reported in January 2018 that President Donald Trump referred to these nations as "shithole countries."[3] To overlook the contemporary political landscape elides the imperial and military histories that generated the conditions for these children to be adopted as well as the ties that these individuals have with the countries of their birth. Adoptive parents, adoption practitioners, and others who excuse this rhetoric participate in the denigration of adoptees as well as other immigrants and people who hold connection to those places. In the case of adoptive parents, their tacit support signals a tolerance for xenophobia.

Yet, we should not forget that adoptees' status as migratory exceptions is predicated upon their position as dependent children to predominately white American citizens. Adoptees are derivative citizens. They meet requirements for naturalization because of their adoptive parents' American citizenship.[4] Due to their representation of future Americans, adoptees gain access to American naturalization vis-à-vis their *as if* kin status. The next chapter discusses adoptees' status as biological surrogates within the white family; for the purposes of interrogating adoptees' citizenship, it is important to note that this affective labor relies upon locating adoptees as *children*.

The following sections explore how adoptive parents and adoptees circumvented restrictions governing Asian immigration in the late nineteenth and early twentieth centuries. This line of inquiry is in conversation with scholars examining the processes of racialization that discipline Asian bodies to fit into American conceptualizations of race.[5] The large-scale, transnational adoption of Korean children marks a significant exception to more than 70 years of legislation that either barred entry of Asians in the United States altogether or rendered Asians, and those of Asian descent, ineligible for American citizenship. Not only granted exceptional status, these children become objects used to bolster the ideal of the heteronormative white family. Exploring the politics of adoptees' naturalization reveals how, in adulthood, adoptees find themselves constructed as persons of color without the white privilege of their childhood. Nowhere is this racial difference clearer than when adoptees become undocumented as a result of their parents and guardians' failure to naturalize them as children. By juxtaposing the experiences of undocumented adoptees against their naturalized counterparts, this chapter exposes the tensions produced by activism supporting adoptees' retroactive citizenship when considering adoptees' experiences against other undocumented minors. As part of this analysis, I interrogate how rhetoric of the forever family becomes deployed as a way to link adoptees to the nation in ways not accessible to the broader constituency of undocumented Americans.

Before I go further, it's imperative to note that I use the term *undocumented adoptees* versus *adoptees without citizenship* because the former term—undocumented adoptees—aligns the experiences of noncitizen adoptees with other noncitizen Americans. I contend that the term *adoptees without citizenship* privileges noncitizen adoptees as "good" undocumented immigrants, while others who lack citizenship are rendered "bad" immigrants. This binary creates an "us versus them" logic and relies on assumptions that those who arrived vis-à-vis adoption are somehow *better than* children whose parents may have brought them to the United States through other means. The term *adoptees without citizenship* links adoptees to the nation and the American family. In doing so, it exposes white privilege's role in facilitating adoptees' entry into the nation. Transnational adoptees become *Other*—another voiceless, undocumented person of color—in adulthood.[6]

American Immigration Legislation and the Acceptable Asian Body

Migration from Asia into the United States was largely unregulated until the end of the nineteenth century when the U.S. Congress enacted multiple laws that severely restricted Asian immigration.[7] The Page Law (1875) was the first. Ostensibly focusing on limiting vice, the law's real intent was to curb the immigration of Chinese women, many of whom were trafficked into prostitution if they entered the United States unmarried or were economically vulnerable.[8] Over the next three decades, a series of additional laws prohibiting entry of Asian immigrants followed. The 1882 Chinese Exclusion Act and its subsequent iterations in 1892 and 1902 provide some examples. The 1907 Gentleman's Agreement and 1919 Ladies Agreement, which affected Japanese migration, signaled the U.S. government's commitment to regulating migration of foreign Asian bodies.[9] These initial measures also marked the first time in national history that the United States passed immigration laws targeting specific nations or global regions.

Xenophobic fears over Asian migration generated the conditions for additional restrictive measures regulating their entry into the United States. Nativists invested in protecting white America found the U.S. Congress sympathetic to their concerns, which led to the passage of legislation that impacted the migration of Asian bodies broadly. The 1917 Asiatic Barred Zone Act (Immigration Act) banned Asian Indian migration and prohibited immigration of persons originating from "a geographical area that included South Asia from Arabia through Southeast Asia and the islands in the Indian and Pacific Ocean."[10] Only the Philippines and Guam—U.S. territories acquired in the wake of the

Spanish-American War—were exempt from the ban. Four years later, the Quota Act of 1921 ensured these limits would remain in place for nearly half a century more. Using the 1890 census as a baseline, these laws capped the number of immigrants who could enter the United States from sending nations with the goal of encouraging more immigration from northern and western Europe while minimizing the influx of southern and eastern Europeans, Africans, and Asians.[11] Finally, in 1924 the door closed altogether. The 1924 Immigration Act included reduced quota limits and barred those migrants who would be ineligible for citizenship, "a euphemism that barred virtually all Asian immigration."[12]

The federal government also took steps to prevent the growth of subsequent generations of Asian Americans in the United States. Under the 1922 Cable Act, U.S. women who married foreigners ineligible for U.S. citizenship were stripped of their own citizenship as well.[13] Sucheng Chan highlights: "Women of European or African ancestry, who were eligible for naturalization, could regain their citizenship should they divorce or if their alien husbands died, but women of Asian ancestry could not since they themselves were racially ineligible for citizenship."[14] A 1932 amendment to the Cable Act allowed any woman, regardless of her race, to restore her natal citizenship. The act was repealed in 1936. Nevertheless, women of Asian descent married to men ineligible for citizenship could not reestablish citizenship.[15] By heavily curtailing immigration and prohibiting the naturalization of Asian immigrants, the U.S. government made clear that Asians existed outside of the national body politic as Americans, even though these individuals lived within the nation's borders and parented U.S. citizen children.

Racist political sentiments positioning Asians as an economic and social menace fueled anti-Asian sentiment and led to a more explicit restriction under the Tydings-McDuffie Act of 1934. This legislation excluded Chinese, Japanese, Korean, Asian Indian, and Filipino immigration.[16] The racial category of Asian was redefined.[17] For the first time, Filipinos became classified as "aliens." Previously they existed as U.S. nationals following the Spanish-American War. Their change in status is unsurprising as the Act also established the transition for the Philippines to become an independent nation over a ten-year period. Nearly ten years later, the U.S. government further complicated the understandings of birthright citizenship with the forced internment of first- and second-generation Japanese Americans.

Opportunities for naturalization did not arrive until the close of World War II. As Japan positioned itself as the enemy, the U.S. government forged an alliance with China in an effort to achieve success in the Pacific Theater. The geopolitics of the Second World War impacted domestic racial politics. The Magnuson Act, passed in 1943, provided citizenship to Chinese people already living within the United States and overturned the exclusion of Chinese immigrants by establishing a quota system.[18] This signaled the proto-liberalization of immigration policy. Naturalization rights were subsequently granted to Asian Indians and Filipinos in 1946 and Guamanians in 1950.[19] Ultimately, the 1952 Immigration and Nationality Act provided naturalization rights to all ethnic Asians. At the same time, however, it included immigrant quotas restricting the number of individuals migrating from Asia to a mere 2,990 people.[20] Not until the Civil Rights Era were immigration restrictions eased for the Eastern hemisphere, and the previous exclusionary laws were repealed with the passage of the 1965 Immigration and Nationality Act.[21] This context is critical to understanding the ways adoptive parents sought to mitigate any restrictions or delays to their child's naturalization as a U.S. citizen and the exceptional standing of Asian adoptees. While their wider Asian brothers and sisters were labeled foreigners, adoptees became Americans.

Individual laws sponsored by adoptive parents' congressmen coupled with federal refugee acts facilitated Korea-U.S. adoptions as well as other international adoptions.[22] This American exceptionalism cannot be overlooked. Without this legislation, adoption would never have become naturalized as a legitimate family-making process. Parents advocated for bringing home *their* children. By moving adoptees outside of existing immigration quotas, the U.S. government positioned adoptees as remarkable, acceptable Asians. Such rhetoric immediately situated the Korean adoptee into the American national body politic, distancing them—and other Asian adoptees—from other prospective migrants.

In August 1953, the U.S. Congress passed the Refugee Relief Act (or Public Law 203). This Act "allowed for 4,000 orphans, younger than 10 years old, from any country with oversubscribed quotas, to be adopted in the United States by American citizens."[23] While Korean children accounted for 12.2 percent (460) of orphan visas, this number was four times Korea's annual immigration quota of 100 people.[24] Orphans were defined as those who had suffered the "death or disappearance of both parents, or because of abandonment or desertion by, or separation or loss from both parents, or who has only one parent ... [who] is incapable of providing care."[25] This standing also provided consent to adoption. Under Public Law 203, American families were limited to two eligible orphans per family. Individuals exceeding this number in their adoptions required special legislation to secure the adoption of their Korean children—as in the case of Harry and Bertha Holt. There are other examples from this era as well. Subsequent iterations of the Refugee Relief Act extended the availability of nonquota visas and "raised the age limit from ten to fourteen, until a permanent immigration law for 'eligible orphans' was enacted in 1962."[26] This legislation allowed adoptive parents to adopt their children sight unseen, with the legal work, selection of children, and international transfer handled by a third party.[27]

After the end of the Korean War, multiple pieces of legislation were enacted to make it easier to adopt foreign children, even as the federal government reduced the cap on the number of foreign-born adoptees by half with the passage of the Orphan Bill in June 1959.[28] In 1961, when international adoption regulations were placed under the auspices of the Immigration and Naturalization Services of the Department of Justice, Korean children received a quarter of all orphan visas issued since 1953.[29] This shift in jurisdiction meant that rather than being treated as immigrants, adoptees became "immediate relatives" of U.S. citizens, freeing them from quotas or other numerical limits. As Soon Ho Park has underscored, adoptive children were thus able to enter the United States freely, without waiting for an opening under existing immigration quotas.[30]

While immediate relative status made it easier for adoptive parents to move children across national borders, it eradicated any legal standing adoptees had with regard to their own birth families. Adoptees experienced the social and legal death of their birth families in order to facilitate their rebirth as Americans. Without legal standing, adoptees cannot sponsor birth relatives for immigration if reunited with them in adulthood under family reunification measures.[31] These restrictions remain in place to this day.

Such adoption-related legislation can be viewed as some of the first steps toward liberalizing American immigration policies in the Cold War era. As Americans worked to end segregation at home, the ideology of fighting for democracy and human rights abroad loosened national borders under the auspices of saving the world's most needy people—orphans. Much of this work had distinctly Christian overtones. Christian Americanism contributed to adoptees' ability to access derivative citizenship and their subsequent location as honorary whites.[32] This early iteration of adoption solidified adoptees' location within the national body politic as Americans, ensuring the pipeline of adoptions from Korea to the United States would not be disrupted due to anti-Asian immigration laws. Their exceptional status also guaranteed the link between the logics of gratitude and adoption as discussed in the previous chapter.

American in Name Only

Even as the legal barriers to importing foreign children were erased, adoptive parents were ultimately responsible for naturalizing the child upon adoption finalization in the United States. American agencies believed adoptive parents would not overlook naturalization. In a 1962 letter to Ann Davison (ISS Korea), ISS–American Branch Associate Director Susan T. Pettiss writes:

> There's no reason for us to think that adoptive parents do not follow through on naturalization procedures. We have found that they are generally most eager to achieve this, as it has many practical advantages in terms of obviating the yearly alien registration procedure, simplifying travel arrangements for the family when going abroad and consolidating the homogeneity of the family unit. However, it would be impossible for us to follow up on each case to see when this naturalization has been completed.[33]

Her comments represent prevailing beliefs concerning adoptees' naturalization. Yet as Pettiss notes, agencies lacked the resources to follow up with all adoptive families to ensure that naturalization took place. Over a decade later Joan M. Crinnion, case consultant for Travelers Aid International Social Service of America (TAISSA), reiterated these constraints in her January 1976 letter to Social Welfare Society, Inc. president, Tahk Youn Taek. Describing the office's limitations, Crinnion notes, "Adoptive parents do not report to TAISSA about the child's citizenship since it is so long after the child's legal adoption when the case at TAISSA has been closed."[34] As part of their efforts to ensure children's citizenship, many adoption agencies provided information concerning naturalization and other legal procedures related to transnational adoption. For example, the 1972 ISS–American Branch handout, "Procedures Affecting Foreign-Born Children Adopted in the United States," urged parents to naturalize their children as soon as possible as an additional method of legal protection.[35] The two-year wait period between adoption finalization and naturalization was eliminated in 1978. This meant that upon adoption finalization, adoptive parents could apply for naturalization immediately.[36]

Additionally, adoption agencies lobbied congressional representatives in the late 1960s to better support adoptive parents and adoptees' access to citizenship during the early wave of international adoptions. International Social Service–American Branch President, Mrs. Michael M. Harris wrote to Senator Edward Kennedy (Democrat-MA) in 1967 and 1969, for example, as Sen. Kennedy introduced revisions to the 1965 Immigration and Nationality Act. In the first letter dated October 30, 1967, the president of ISS–American Branch wrote:

Our experience indicates that it would benefit all concerned if naturalization proceeding could be initiated at the time the adoption is completed. This would facilitate the complete integration of the child into the family, which is the purpose of adoption. Most of the children arriving for adoption will be in their new homes for some time before the adoption application is filled. ... [D]uring the two year period following adoption they are in a somewhat ambiguous position: legally the child of American citizens but still under the "protection" of a foreign country which is not in a position to exercise any responsibility. ... The logical time for adoptive parents to apply for the naturalization of the child is when legal adoption is being completed. Too often the waiting period results in postponing the naturalization for years. If, in the meantime, the circumstances change or the adoptive parents die, the child finds himself in a precarious situation without the protection of American citizenship.[37]

A version of this text was also sent to the Representative Michael A. Feighan in the House of Representatives (Democrat-OH). The ISS–American Branch was invested in the inclusion of "a provision enabling the early naturalization of citizen children adopted in the United States by American families."[38] Unfortunately, despite these dedicated lobbies for immediate naturalization of adoptees once adoptions were finalized, this practice would never become a reality within the twentieth century.

To ease the naturalization process for adoptees and their families, the U.S. Congress enacted the Child Citizenship Act of 2000 (Public Law 106-395). While some may wonder why this legislation did not occur earlier, it is important to recognize how this legislation directly reflects the belief that adoptees are part of the *American* body politic. This act affects the naturalization of transnational adoptees under the age of eighteen. Effective February 27, 2001, eligible adoptees may obtain citizenship if "at least one of the child's parents is a United States citizen" if the child: 1) lives in the legal and physical custody of the American citizen parent; 2) is admitted into the United States as an immigrant for lawful permanent residence; and 3) the adoption is final. However, the Child Citizenship Act of 2000 applies only to children who entered the United States on IR-3 or IH-3 visas.[39] The IR-3 visa is for children whose birth countries are not signatories of the Hague Convention, while the IH-3 applies to countries that are a party to the Convention. Both the IR-3 and IH-3 visas are issued if the adoption was completed overseas and "the adoption is recognized and final both in the child's country and in the United States."[40] Adoptees who entered on IR-4 or IH-4 visas do not acquire automatic citizenship and receive a permanent resident card.[41]

American policy makers appear to be cognizant of the fact that knowledge gaps persist concerning the adoptive parents' duty to naturalize their children. They clearly delineate the process for obtaining citizenship and offer prospective and current adoptive parents information concerning visa differences. The Child Citizenship Act does not necessarily mean all adoptions finalized since 2000 will be granted immediate citizenship. The government warns, "Please be aware that if your child did not qualify to become a citizen upon entry to the United States, it is very important that you take the steps necessary so that your child does qualify as soon as possible. Failure to obtain citizenship for your child can impact many areas of his/her life including family travel, eligibility for education and education grants, and voting."[42] For parents who misunderstand the laws governing visas for their adopted children, the ramifications will be just as damaging as the impact undocumented status has for those individuals adopted prior to 2000.

In 2013 with the passage of the Korean Special Adoption Law, Korean adoptees became eligible for the IR-3 visa, which grants automatic American citizenship.[43] This shift from IR-4 visas, which necessitates adoptee's naturalization in the United States, requires adoption finalization to occur in Korean court. However, not all adoptees necessarily agree with this IR-3 stipulation. Stephen C. Morrison, founder of the Mission to Promote Adoption in Korea, seeks to excuse adoptive parents from appearing in court, which would also mean these parents would not have to travel to Korea. Parents who decline to travel to Korea will find that their children will receive the IR-4 visas. This continues the system that places naturalization in the hands of adoptive parents. In contrast, adoptive parents who utilize the IR-3 visa option ensure their child does not become one of the current adult adoptees deported back to Korea.

Nevertheless, the contemporary changes to U.S. and Korean law easing access to U.S. citizenship fail to protect those adopted prior to 2000 that were over the age of eighteen. In these earlier instances of adoption, adoptees lacked the knowledge and resources to obtain naturalization as children/minors. Instead, their adoptive parents were placed with this responsibility. Yet those individuals failed to fulfill one important legal need for their children and propelled their children into legal statelessness—sometimes even furthering the legal limbo that adoptees experienced in their birth countries (e.g., mixed race children who lacked access to Korean citizenship upon birth). The U.S. government, adoption agencies, and adoptive parents failed to remove the precarity in their lives with adoption finalization. These supposedly "rescued" children lack the stability of citizenship. This new reality disrupts the logic of gratitude as narratives of gratefulness presume that adoption saved children. Lack of citizenship contradicts some of the security allegedly brought by adoption. The gift of adoption no longer exists—undocumented status erases the supposed gifts of American exceptionalism accrued via adoption.

Failure to naturalize adopted children has deep ramifications, leaving adoptees undocumented and eligible for deportation to a birth country virtually unknown. While this scenario may seem like a far-fetched nightmare, for some adoptees it became all too real. Lim Sang Keum, for example, was adopted in the late 1970s from South Korea. He was twelve years old at that time. Lim was also biracial, the son of an American soldier and South Korean woman. For over thirty years, he lived his life as an American named Russell Green. Unlike the idealized stories of saved and rescued orphans, however, Green's story is marked by a failure of the American government, the adoption agency, and the prospective adoptive parents to protect his rights when he was still a child. A few months after his arrival, his adoptive parents returned him to the adoption agency. The prospective parents had not yet finalized his adoption. The disrupted adoption pushed Green down the road to becoming an undocumented immigrant in the American foster care system when he was still a minor.[44]

Shin Song Hyuk found himself in a similar situation. Adopted in 1979 into a Lutheran family, Shin and his biological sister did not find themselves adopted into a loving family so often depicted in discussions of adoption. Rather, the pair entered a dysfunctional home already containing five biological children and a Korean adoptee where physical and sexual abuse were commonplace.[45] After six years of living with this family, the adoption was disrupted when his adoptive parents divorced. Shin and his sister were surrendered to the Oregon state child welfare agency. It is unclear what happened to the couple's existing biological children and previously adopted child from South Korea.

Separated from his biological sister, he was placed with the Crapser family in Salem, Oregon, in 1987. The family adopted him in 1989, and he became Adam Crapser. He was roughly eleven years old at the time. Crapser did not fare much better in this new home. During the five years that he lived with the Crapsers, it was commonplace to be beaten, burned, and abused. Although Tom and Dolly Crapser faced charges of rape, sexual abuse, and criminal mistreatment in 1991, he was not removed from their home.[46] What does it mean when adoption is heralded as the best option for children, even though not all adoptive families are created equal?

For Crapser, his placements in abusive, dysfunctional families (his first placement and the Crapser family) generated the conditions for his failed naturalization proceedings. Kevin Vollmers, the founder of *Gazillion Strong*, an organization dedicated to supporting marginalized communities, contends,

"It's a travesty that the promise hasn't been kept for individuals like Adam Crapser, who in my mind is a victim of the inadequacies of the broken U.S. adoption system that doesn't necessarily serve the individuals it says it cares about the most."[47] For many citizen adoptees who speak out on behalf of their undocumented counterparts, the implicit social contract between adoptee and adoptive parent, adoptee and adoption agency, and adoptee and receiving country is ruptured when adoptees find themselves undocumented. Adoption's positioning as the *better option* is voided when adoptees are not guaranteed citizenship. Crapser was made aware of his precarious situation as a result of his status as a felon for crimes unrelated to his undocumented status, when he obtained his adoption paperwork from Tom Crapser in 2012 and applied for a green card.[48]

Adoptees convicted of crimes lack the protection of naturalized American citizenship and risk deportation.[49] The federal government is allowed to deport noncitizen immigrants who are found guilty of a whole range of crimes from using forged checks or minor shoplifting offenses, to driving without a license, or to selling drugs or committing aggravated felonies.[50] For example, labeled a "criminal alien" as a result of conviction for attempted forgery and forgery, Indian adoptee Kairi Abha Shepherd was eligible for deportation due to her undocumented status. Shepherd's adoptive mother died when she was eight years old, prior to completing Shepherd's naturalization.[51] This case makes evident that it was not only adoptive parents of Korean children who failed to naturalize their children. In fact, Mike Frailey, a Vietnamese Babylift–era adoptee, notes that some individuals who entered the United States during Operation Babylift in April 1975 failed to gain citizenship.[52] As additional cases of undocumented adoptees surface, increased attention is required to examine how these once "saved" children are once again being cast out to the world.[53]

Deported adoptees are unaware of what to expect when they return to a country virtually unknown to them. And in the case of Korea, the nation is often unprepared. The deficiencies in supports for adoptees in their transition were exposed with the death of Philip Clay, who ended his life on May 21, 2017. Although Clay arrived in the United States legally, his parents never naturalized him as a U.S. citizen. A judge ordered Clay's removal from the United States in 2012 following multiple criminal convictions spanning nearly two decades, according to Immigration and Customs Enforcement.[54] The attention Clay's death garnered in the United States and Korea underscored the lack of mental health and addiction resources in Korea. Minimal provisions have been made to successfully aid deported adoptees' transition into a country where they lack cultural competency and language fluency. And while adoptee formal and informal networks seek to provide support, strategic government aid that accounts for the particular needs of this community is necessary. After all, these individuals—ostensibly members of the Korean diaspora—were children upon their adoption and now lack the cultural fluency to navigate Korean society in adulthood. Deportation and the failure to naturalize adoptees as children must be seen as a humanitarian issue similar to how the adoption of them as children was seen as part of humanitarian child rescue. To care for adoptees *only* when they are children highlights how their value is linked to their youth and perceived innocence.

Within this particular transnational adoptee subgroup—undocumented adoptees—it becomes obvious that Green and Crapser are not anomalies. The activism of Korean adoptees and allies continues to garner high levels of attention in comparison to the experiences of other internationally adopted individuals.[55] Although there is not a verifiable number from either the U.S. or Korean government of how many adoptees are not naturalized, adoptee activist Jane Jeong Trenka reports, "Korean adoption agencies did not receive the naturalization papers of 18,000 Korean children sent for adoption to the United States, even though this paperwork is required under Korean law."[56] For example, it was not until her husband died in 2014 that Ella Purkiss, sixty-one years old, learned that she lacked citizenship. Her adoptive parents never indicated that she was not a naturalized citizen following her adoption at age two in 1956. As an adult, Purkiss passed security clearance checks to work on Air Force and Army bases, voted, and fulfilled jury duty. Once she realized her status, Purkiss applied for citizenship, was denied, and sought help from her congressional representatives, as this might be her only form of recourse. She became a naturalized citizen in July 2016 after a journey that involved seeking support via the media and contacting congressional representatives.[57] Capturing the bewilderment of many adoptees concerning why so many lack citizenship, Purkiss comments, "It's sad to think that . . . people can take them [adoptees] from a foreign country, drop them into another country, and no one guarantees that they are a citizen of anywhere."[58] Her statement underscores how the social contract of adoption becomes broken when governments, adoption agencies, and orphanages fail to ensure adoptive parents secured citizenship for their transnationally adopted children.

Adult adoptee activists and their allies network online to raise awareness of the plight of undocumented adoptees and continue to advocate for retroactive citizenship. In 2011, the adult adoptee community and allies began a petition for undocumented adoptees' retroactive citizenship. The petition notes deported adoptees arrive to "countries unknown to them in every way: language, culture, family or friends."[59] The petition further states:

> One of the requirements of the Child Citizenship Act of 2000 (CCA 2000) was that the adoptee be under the age of 18 on its effective date, February 27, 2001. Transnational adoptees 18 and older were not granted citizenship under its provisions. Some, but not all, obtained citizenship through their own efforts or those of their adoptive parents. Of those who did not, many were unaware that they lacked this legal protection. . . . Strict immigration policies under the Illegal Immigration Reform and Immigrant Responsibility Act of 1996 have placed internationally-adopted individuals without U.S. citizenship at increased risk of deportation. This law does not allow adoption or the unique circumstances that led to an adoptee's lack of citizenship to be taken into consideration in determining outcomes.[60]

I highlight the petition at length to underscore how adoptees' entrance into the United States remains indelibly linked to the adoptive parents' white privilege. When these adoptees became aware of their tenuous immigration statuses as adults, this white privilege is revoked. It is at this point that adoptees forfeit their exceptional migrant status. And yet, even as the petitioners sought to raise awareness of the plight of deportees, the petition's demands simultaneously invoke adoptees' white privilege as exceptional immigrants as children. The petitioners seek immediate and appropriate action to grant all adoptees citizenship regardless of legal status or criminal history. This includes providing adoptees assistance to obtain proof of citizenship and allowing deported adoptees the opportunity to return to the United States. The stipulations require the American government to distinguish between adoptees and other undocumented persons of color deported to their native countries. These demands implicitly reflect adoptees access to derivative citizenship that facilitated their entry into the nation.

Arguments noting that international adoptions, like domestic adoptions, are premised on the promise of a forever family privilege the adoptive family over other types of family formation formed by both legal and illegal avenues of migration. The term *adoptees without citizenship* implies that these individuals are deemed *worthy* of automatic citizenship—solidifying adoptees' status as exceptional migrants. Thus, retroactive citizenship goes uncontested in contrast to the contentious nature of granting amnesty or citizenship to other individuals who arrived in the United States as undocumented minors, and even adults.[61]

To raise broader awareness of the plight of undocumented adoptees, adoptees employ hashtag activism. #CitizenshipForAllAdoptees became a widely used hashtag to garner support for legislation concerning retroactive citizenship. This hashtag bears the same name as the Tumblr Citizenship for All Adoptees that includes posts that are "stories by/about international adoptees who do not have US citizenship/discover they don't have US citizenship."[62]

While only seven accounts are provided on the Tumblr account, Citizenship for All Adoptees personalizes the experiences of adoptees whose parents failed to naturalize them as U.S. citizens during childhood. For example, in her June 19, 2013, post, a Korean adoptee woman—whose identity was kept anonymous—recounts how at age fifteen she discovered that her adoptive parents failed to complete her naturalization application. She obtained American citizenship after a ten-year ordeal that led to the completion of the naturalization process, including the English proficiency test.[63] In this situation, the adoptee in question was a minor who never was convicted of any crimes when she realized her American citizenship was never finalized. These two factors are central to understanding how her quest for legal citizenship was undeterred.

Another entry from Janine highlights how she and her twin sister learned that they lacked American citizenship.[64] Adopted in 1972 from Korea, it was not until her twin sister filled out college financial aid forms in 1990 that the pair discovered they were permanent residents. Nevertheless, Janine's sister did not realize this meant that they lacked citizenship. That revelation occurred in 1998 upon the marriage of Janine's twin, when their father informed them that he failed to complete the naturalization paperwork.

The experiences of these women—as well as others featured in the Tumblr posts—could be any adoptee. After all, there was no guarantee adoptive parents would complete the steps for naturalization. No safeguards were in place to protect the rights of these minors. These women are the every adoptee—albeit a different face of the same experience. In other words, the every adoptee trope becomes transferrable to understand how one's status as a citizen or undocumented citizen is arbitrary. The precariously positioned undocumented adoptees are individuals that the adoption community wants to root for, to ensure their naturalization occurs without issue. After all, given the arbitrary nature of adoption, any adoptee could be undocumented as citizenship remains precariously tied to adoptive parents' commitment to naturalize their children. The stories of Crapser and Green make clear that not only can we not assume citizenship is guaranteed for all, but also that adoption may not protect adoptees from harm. Under the call for "Citizenship for All Adoptees," the Adoptee Rights Campaign launched the *Family Is More than DNA* postcard campaign from September through November 2016. Featuring childhood photographs from internationally adopted children and their white American families, the postcard called for support of the Adoptee Citizenship Act (S. 2275, HR 5454).[65] A deeper examination of the links between adoptees' claims to retroactive citizenship, exceptional migratory status, and access to white privilege is discussed in the following section.

Revisiting Adoptees' Exceptional Status

Providing an avenue for adoptees to gain American citizenship upon entering adulthood raises questions of exceptionalism once again when considering their experiences against other individuals who arrived as involuntary, undocumented minors. This is particularly salient considering legislation introduced in the 113th (2013–2014) and 114th (2015–2016) congressional sessions. In 2013, Senator Mary Landrieu (D-LA) worked across partisan lines to include the Citizenship for Lawful Adoptees Amendment to S. 744 (The Border Security, Economic Opportunity, and Immigration Modernization Act). Senator Landrieu's press release notes, "The amendment provides technical but important fixes to the Child Citizenship Act of 2000 (CCA) and the Immigration and Nationality Act (INA) so that automatic citizenship provisions under these laws apply to all foreign-born adoptees of American citizen parents."[66] Specifically, the amendment:

> 1) Applies automatic U.S. citizenship provisions of the CCA, which currently only apply to children who were under the age of 18 at the time of its enactment in 2001, to all foreign-born children lawfully adopted by U.S. families who were ever lawfully admitted to the United States; 2) Clarifies language in the CCA so that eligible children need only be "physically present" in the U.S. versus "residing" in the U.S. for their citizenship to accrue. This clarification benefits adoptees of American families who live and work overseas, such as those serving in the military or at U.S. Embassies or Consulates; and 3) Modifies the INA so that only one adoptive parent—not both—must travel overseas to visit a child during the intercountry adoption process for the child to qualify for the type of visa that leads to automatic U.S. citizenship upon entry.[67]

While this was a first step to secure citizenship for undocumented adoptees, the broader bill lacked support from the House of Representatives after passing in the Senate. Consequently, undocumented adoptees lacked recourse to gain citizenship.

Regardless of the fact that this bill never became law, the amendment raises questions concerning which individuals who arrived into the United States as undocumented minors are "good" citizens. The amendment's simple introduction demonstrates how certain nonwhite bodies are seen as acceptable, exceptions in times of heightened fears of immigration. Kim Park Nelson addresses adoptees' removal from immigration discourse writing:

> The erasure of adoptees' immigrant pasts, like the erasure of many of their other pre-adoptive experiences, separates them (and their adoptive families) socially and culturally from important potential bases of identity in the United States by preventing them from identifying with other American people of color and/or other immigrant populations whom they might benefit from knowing and understanding.[68]

Adoptees are continually recognized as Americans regardless of natal origin. Underscoring adoptees' inherent Americanness, former U.S. Senate staff member and one of the individuals who drafted the 2000 Child Citizenship Act, McLane Layton contends, "Lawmakers and the public need to understand that these adoptees were adopted by American citizens, were brought to this country legally, were raised in American society."[69] Similarly, Maureen McCauley Evans, former executive director of the Joint Council of International Children's Services, notes, "It undermines the integrity of the adoptive family. These adoptees are genuinely family members, and then we have the government saying, 'No, they are not.'"[70] This appeal to the American public—that not only are adoptees Americans but that they are linked to the American family—should not go unnoticed.

The amendment attached to S. 744 paved the way for continued adoptee activism and the introduction of the bipartisan Adoptee Citizenship Act of 2015 (S. 2275) by Senator Amy Klobuchar (D-MN) and cosigned by Senator Dan Coates (R-IN) and Senator Jeff Merkley (D-OR) in November 2015.[71] The Adoptee Citizenship Act of 2015 would amend the Immigration and Nationality Act and provide retroactive citizenship to adoptees regardless of adoption finalization date. Passage of the Act would also allow those adoptees previously deported to their countries of birth as a result of involvement in minor crimes a pathway of return to the United States as long as their sentences were served.[72] On June 10, 2016 Representatives Adam Smith (D-WA) and Trent Franks (R-AZ) introduced a version of the bill into the House of Representatives, H.R. 5454 Adoptee Citizenship Act of 2016. Upon its introduction, H.R. 5454 was referred to the Committee on the Judiciary. Kelsey Yoon, an attorney working on S. 2275 and an international adoptee, notes, "The issue is simple: the bill ensures that adoption is the creation of a legal family, no strings attached."[73] She further comments:

It continues to befuddle me how members of Congress continue to promote adoption when the U.S. is unable to ensure the basic right of U.S. citizenship to those adoptees that have been legally adopted into this country already. It is shameful that those politicians who tout themselves as leaders in adoption advocacy on the hill are unwilling to lead the efforts in supporting the adoptees that they so eagerly sought to bring into this country for the purposes of adoption decades ago.[74]

In mentioning the inconsistencies and even hypocrisy of the rhetoric espoused by pro-adoption advocates, Yoon retools the language used by these individuals to bolster the argument for retroactive citizenship. In other words, if one is truly committed to seeing adoption as rescue, then the nation must do its due diligence to keep these once rescued children in the United States. To do otherwise fails the commitment promised by adoption. This language reflects how adoptees are repurposing the language of gratitude associated with adoption and reframing it so the gift of adoption is automatically tied to citizenship.

Emphasizing the Americanness of adoptees underscores the fact that they have *always* been part of the nation, even though this American identity is contingent upon adoption. And, this particular rhetoric links Americanness to whiteness and adoptive parents' white privilege. On the topic of whether accountability for naturalization rested with Crapser, Senator Jeff Merkley (D-OR) notes, "It was not [Crapser's] responsibility to fill out that immigration paperwork. He knows no other country."[75] Senator Klobuchar (D-MN) employed similar language as she sought support from her congressional colleagues:

These adoptees grew up in American families. They went to American schools. They lead American lives. Yet, adopted children who are not covered by the Child Citizenship Act are not guaranteed citizenship. Because of their lack of citizenship, adoptees have been refused admission to college and turned down for jobs. The constant threat to the life that they know is unjust, and this bill would simply ensure that international adoptees are recognized as the Americans that they truly are.[76]

Framing adoptees as someone who could be your son, daughter, neighbor, or friend reiterates adoptees' links to the future of the nation. These children, after all, would never have entered the United States if not for the Christian Americanism that facilitated their adoptions. This positioning distances adoptees from other undocumented individuals.

A group of adoption and Asian American organizations worked behind the scenes to encourage lawmakers to pass S. 2275. NAKASEC (the National Korean American Service and Education Consortium), 18 Million Rising, Gazillion

Strong, the Adoptee Rights Campaign, and Korean American Coalition organized the first Adoption Citizenship Act Day of Action in Washington, D.C., and across the United States on April 19, 2016. The Day of Action included a full day of visits to members of Congress, a press conference, a social media campaign, and use of the hashtag #CitizenshipForAllAdoptees. In her testimony at the Day of Action, Amie Kim recalls:

> I was 22 years old when I learned from INS [Immigration and Naturalization Services] that I was not a U.S. citizen. I had spent my life in Minnesota assuming I was. In my 30s, there was a period of about two years when I could not get an above the board job because my green card had expired and I couldn't afford the exorbitant renewal fees. . . . Adoption to me meant loss of family, language, and culture, but in exchange, I was promised a stable family life, better opportunities, and a welcoming country. So far, none of these have come true for me, but the passage of Adoptee Citizenship Act could right one of the wrongs.[77]

Her testimony creates a narrative of "what could have been" for other adoptees. All adoptees are raised believing that the United States is home. After all, adoptive parents, adoption agencies, and the state propagate this narrative. Kim's first-person perspective again reinserts these undocumented adoptees into the every adoptee trope.

For many, Crapser represents a worst-case scenario, given the abuse he suffered at the hands of his adoptive parents. He is thus treated as an aberration even though adoptees routinely disclose psychological, physical, and sexual abuse. Consequently, when narratives—such as the ones proffered by the #CitizenshipForAllAdoptees Tumblr, Purkiss, and Kim—arise they present a more transferrable narrative because no one wants to believe that adoptive families are abusive.

Nonetheless, Crapser remained at the center of the legislative push in the 114th Congress. His story garnered the most attention of adoptees and their allies in recent years even as Green's case projected the issue of citizenship on their radars initially. Even as the other undocumented adoptees' experiences continue to surface, Crapser's experience of abuse and dysfunction underscore how adoption cannot be seen as the be-all end-all of creating stability in children's lives. This is not to say that his supporters do not recognize that he seems an unlikely candidate for becoming a face of a movement. Acknowledging that Crapser served time for his crimes, his attorney Lori Walls asserts, "Punishing him further with deportation would be a terrible injustice. It would separate him from the only family he has ever known. It would devastate not only him but his wife and children."[78] In his court declaration prior to an April 2, 2015, deportation hearing, Crapser wrote, "America promised me a home. I implore this country to keep its promise. If not for me then for my children, so they won't have to grow up without a dad."[79] On February 8, 2016, he was detained by Immigration and Customs Enforcement and held at the Northwest Detention Center in Tacoma, Washington. Supporting Crapser, the Seattle Human Rights Commission wrote to the Honorable Judge John C. O'Dell of the Tacoma Immigration Court asserting that his detainment was unjust and violated Article 10 of the International Covenant of Civil and Political Rights. The Seattle Human Rights Commission also asserted that the failure to naturalize Crapser fell to both sets of his adoptive parents and the State of Oregon.[80]

After an October 24, 2016, immigration court in Tacoma sentenced Crapser for deportation, he found himself returning to a country he did not remember less than a month later.[81] His arrival to Korea marked a reunion as well. After viewing a documentary on Korea's MBC-TV, his birth mother Kwon Pil-ju discovered the son she relinquished all those years before.[82]

Adoptees' assertion of an exceptional status in matters of retroactive citizenship reflects a fundamental failure to connect their experiences as immigrants to other undocumented individuals. The rhetoric used to discuss why Crapser as well as other adoptees facing deportation should be granted a stay in deportation could be applied to children eligible for the previously touted Development, Relief, and Education for Alien Minors (DREAM) Act and President Obama's June 2012 Deferred Action for Childhood Arrivals (DACA) plan.[83] Yet unlike the legislation proposed to support undocumented adoptees, DACA does not offer eligible persons a direct path to residency or citizenship. Deferred action only provides individuals access to remain in the United States if they never ran afoul from the law (e.g., no felony or misdemeanor convictions) or posed a public safety or national security threat. The parameters of DACA apply to those persons who "were under the age of 31 as of June 15, 2012," and "came to the United States before reaching [their] 16th birthday."[84] These individuals' eligibility rests on whether they fall into one of the following categories: current school enrollment, high school graduate or GED certified, or Coast Guard or Armed Forces of the United States veteran.

I mention DACA not to engage in a debate over its merits; rather, my interest in DACA is the way in which it impacts individuals who entered the nation involuntarily as minors under the auspices of parental decisions. The language of DACA is similar to the United States Supreme Court ruling in *Plyer v. Doe* (1982), a case concerning undocumented students' access to public school education. In her analysis of *Plyer v. Doe*, Linda Bozniak writes, "Undocumented status should be treated as substantially irrelevant here because the undocumented status of these children was acquired involuntarily, and its consequences cannot, therefore, [be] fairly visited upon."[85] If their status as involuntary migrants as minors trumps their current undocumented status, one may wonder why these two groups are by design given separate and unequal treatment. Why are undocumented adoptees constructed as the more sympathetic subject? Is it because of their parents' status as American citizens? Or because transnational adoption is woven into the fabric for the nation vis-à-vis celebrity and evangelical Christian adoptions? Discussing issues of citizenship and deportation more broadly, Sunaina Maira writes:

> Deportation connotes a moral judgment of worthiness and desirability that differentiates between "good" immigrants who are not deported and "bad" immigrants who are, but this line is not as fixed and self-evident as it appears in mainstream discourse about "illegal" immigrants and "un-American" dissidents, both of whom presumably pose a threat to the nation. However, there is a moral economy deeply embedded in deportation that constructs the virtue of citizenship and helps to continually reinscribe the borders of the nation.[86]

Consider the dichotomy of good immigrant versus bad immigrant. Both the undocumented minor eligible for aid via the DREAM Act or DACA and the undocumented adoptee may have operated in the United States under the assumptions of their legality in the nation. Each population also obtained cultural citizenship as Americans during their upbringing. Yet, only one population is acceptable and considered "good."

The adoptee, unlike the child of undocumented persons, fulfills heteronormative aspirations of family. Their affective labor to reproduce the (white) American family—as three-quarters of adoptees entered white families—serves as a visible transference of white privilege and one's access to derivative citizenship. Reflecting the connections between derivative and retroactive citizenship, Vollmers asserts in a 2015 interview, "We're pushing to fix an adoption law, not an immigration law," even as "experts on Capitol Hill . . . insist that the CCA falls under the jurisdiction of immigration."[87] This link between retroactive citizenship and adoption law illustrates the deep connections between adoptees' derivative citizenship and white privilege to assumptions of who is *deserving* of citizenship—undocumented adoptees versus other undocumented Americans.

In the wake of the 2016 election, it's even more imperative to consider the ways in which the experiences of undocumented adoptees align themselves with other undocumented individuals. The current administration's stance on immigration hearkens back to a time of more restrictive immigration law and has witnessed the rescinding of protections for those previously holding protected status.[88] This is why it's vital to closely examine the language of the most recent Adoptee Citizenship Act (S. 2522; H.R. 5233) in the 115th Congress (2017–2018). Adoptees and their allies worked to revive the bill after it stalled in the previous congressional session. Passage of the 2018 version of the bill would ensure automatic U.S. citizenship to adoptees who meet the following criteria:

> a) The individual was adopted by a United States citizen before the individual reached 18 years of age; b) The individual was physically present in the United States in the legal custody of the citizen parent pursuant to a lawful admission before the individual reached 18 years of age; c) The individual never acquired United States citizenship before the date of the enactment of the Adoptee Citizenship Act of 2018; d) The individual was residing in the United States on the date of the enactment of the Adoptee Citizenship Act of 2018 pursuant to a lawful admission.[89]

It's important to recognize that this retroactive citizenship would not be bestowed to all undocumented adoptees. Excluded from the 2018 legislation are those who "committed a crime that was not properly resolved" following a background check, persons "found guilty of a deportable offense that has [as] an element the use, attempted use, or threated use of physical force against another person," and persons who have previously been deported.[90] I suggest that this shift from incorporating broad language concerning retroactive citizenship to more narrow language that leaves out a segment of adoptees is strategic and recognizes the political climate toward undocumented immigration under the Trump administration. Yet in doing so, advocates for the legislation become complicit in creating a *good* undocumented immigrant narrative, one that further emphasizes how *the every adoptee* could also be undocumented. While it's too soon to tell what will happen to the Adoptee Citizenship Act of 2018 at the time of this writing in May 2018, the alignment of retroactive citizenship and undocumented adoptees with a purported "good" immigrant narrative must be problematized.

Consequently, I maintain that a more explicit connection between adoptees without citizenship and other undocumented individuals is required. Disentangling adoption law from immigration law overlooks the fact that the former was implemented as a way to bypass restrictive and racist legislation barring Asian migration to the United States. Although the Child Citizenship Act of 2000 not only secures immediate naturalization for adoptees, it allows them to bypass existing immigration structures and fast-tracks their citizenship. Adoptees' derivative citizenship and the method in which they entered the nation propagates an exceptional discourse concerning their access to American citizenship. Any amendment addressing adoptee citizenship will always be tied to issues of immigration and adoption. To uncouple retroactive citizenship from both immigration and adoption law obscures and overlooks the long history of adoptees' entrance to the nation. It also overlooks how white privilege operates in ways in which connections are not made to broader movements for citizenship for individuals who arrived as undocumented minors to the United States.

More importantly, to divorce these two issues—adoption law and immigration law—creates a false sense of worth concerning some immigrants over others. Even if not all adoptees see themselves as immigrants, they still are seen as immigrants under the auspices of naturalization law. The Child Citizenship Act of 2000, after all, does not apply to all adoptees—only those who enter the United States with IH-3/IR-3 visas. And, if one only considers the Child Citizenship Act of 2000, we risk ignoring the ways in which hundreds of thousands of adoptees entered the United States. This results in a failure to recognize how undocumented adoptees are treated as any other type of immigrant by the law. Intentional connections among undocumented individuals, regardless of how they entered the United States, are needed in this political moment, as these persons are part of a broader assemblage connecting diasporic movements, nation-states, and kinship units.

Both online and offline, adoptees critique arguments for retroactive citizenship that fail to situate the plight of undocumented adoptees within broader discourses concerning comprehensive immigration reform. These adoptee killjoys elucidate adoption's contradictions and failures. They highlight the multicultural fallacy of international adoption in aligning retroactive citizenship with other immigrants' rights. Yet, those offering a more nuanced discussion of undocumented Americans and retroactive citizenship lack the national platform of their retroactive citizenship activist counterparts. After all, those reporting about undocumented Americans find that adoptees are an easy, sympathetic target. They were brought here by white American parents and (allegedly) rescued. These individuals are seen as more deserving than other undocumented persons who entered the United States at a similar young age, as their parents of color are not seen as benevolent figures in the American imaginary. To align with communities of color on issues concerning citizenship also means that adoptees must recognize and acknowledge that although they have proximal whiteness due to their transracial adoptions, this whiteness does not extend itself into all facets of their lived experiences. Adoptee killjoys expose the tensions and complexities of transracial, adoptive families' kinship.

CHAPTER 3

The (Re)production of Family

Even as adoptees are derivative citizens aiding the reproduction of the white normative family, they also disrupt traditional notions of kinship.[1] The presence of Korean adoptees in the white American family reinvents heteronormative conceptualizations of white and Asian American families, which are traditionally conceived of as same-race, genetically related units.[2] Yet Korean adoptive families simultaneously reify the notion that families are comprised of heterosexual, married parents, as these are the only individuals who are permitted legally to adopt from Korea. Nevertheless, adoptive families' lack of genetic ties marks them as *fictive* due to their historical positioning as *less than* for deviating from biological, sexual reproduction.[3]

This chapter investigates the sexual and social reproductive disjunctures produced by international adoption as well as how this dissonance impacts the racialization of the family. Queer theory elucidates the contradictions found in the social reproduction of the adoptive kinship structure. I draw from David L. Eng and Alice Y. Hom's notion of queer as "a political practice based on transgressions of the normal and normativity."[4] While adoptive families contribute to the reproduction of the "family," this construction remains a mere facsimile of *real* kinship due to the obvious transracial composition of the familial unit. The desire for normativity renders the Korean adoptive family queer, even as it creates new avenues to redefine traditional conceptualizations of "family."

In its examination of adoptees' and their families' performances of "family" as queer, this chapter joins the work of David Eng and Shelley M. Park, whose monographs interrogate the interventions of nonnormative families in theoretical conceptualization of kinship.[5] Here, I build upon feminist and queer theorists' scholarship to situate Adoption Studies within these fields as a mechanism to rethink kinship and family outside of the boundaries of heteronormativity. A queer theoretical lens elucidates how the Korean adoptive family undergoes racialization as a non-monoracial unit. In doing so, queer theory illuminates the contradictions produced by these families as it relates to understandings of the family's desire for legibility as a normative kinship unit. Such an analysis reveals the latent normative desires of adoptive families as well as the ways that queer theory facilitates the disentanglement of racial difference within transracial adoptive families. This chapter investigates the racial performativity enacted by the adoptee and adoptive family to prove their normalcy within broader negotiations of whiteness and Asianness. My discussion of racial performativity originates in Judith Butler's work on gender performativity.[6] Performativity is an "act," recognizing the power of language and, subsequently, the "act" of doing as "a matter of reiterating or repeating the norms by which one is constituted."[7]

This analysis also is indebted to José Esteban Muñoz's discussion of racial performativity.[8] For Muñoz, racial performativity focuses on "a doing"—"a political doing, the effects that the recognition of racial belonging, coherence, and divergence present in the world."[9] He further contends, "To look at a race as a performative enterprise, one that can best be accessed by its effects, may lead us out of political and conceptual impasses that have dogged racial discourse."[10] My analysis of adoptees' performativity is rooted in how they are always *doing*, continually engaging assumptions of Koreanness, whiteness, and Americanness. Regarding the latter, it's important to recognize how whiteness and Americanness remain interchangeable similar to how Asianness and foreignness find themselves routinely linked. Discussing whiteness in relation to brownness, Muñoz writes:

> Whiteness in my analysis is also very specific: I read it as a cultural logic that prescribes and regulates national feelings and comportment. White is thus an affective gauge that helps us understand some modes of emotional countenance and comportment as good or bad. It should go without saying that some modes of whiteness—for example, working-class whiteness—are stigmatized within the majoritarian public sphere. Modes of white womanhood or white ethnicities do not correspond with the affective ruler that measures and naturalizes white feelings as the norm.

This conceptualization of whiteness is useful when considering, more broadly, the ways in which adoptive families seek to align themselves with the norms of *real* kinship and white, heteronormative families predicated upon biological relatedness. In their marked transracial nature, adoptive families desire to move from stigmatization as fictive into a legible category similar to *real* kinship. Operating outside legible understandings of kinship due to their circumvention of procreative heterosex, adoptive parents covet legitimacy provided by traditional kinship. Whiteness is thus used as a barometer to consider what families are valued.

The racial performativity undertaken by adoptees and, by extension, their adoptive families reveals the affective nature of what it means to *be* family. Adoptees are always engaged in processes of *feeling* as they desire to belong as members within their adoptive, white families, their predominately white communities in the United States, and within Asian America. Here, I want to be clear that these families and individuals are not engaged in a racial performance rooted in mimicry or yellowface (e.g., Rachel Dolezal's employment of blackface and exerting white privilege to pass as a Black woman).[11] Rather, racial performativity recognizes the ways in which these kinship structures "*do* family" in a way that transgresses the color line and assumptions of biology. A queer theoretical approach to performativity facilitates a deeper examination to understanding how this performative action is both transgressive and normative in adoptive families' desire for legibility.

Transnational, transracial adoption disrupts what Kimberly McClain DaCosta calls the racialization of the family, which accounts for "how racial premises came to be buried in our understanding of family, in which genetic-phenotypic sharing is coded to signify cultural sharing, intimacy, and caring."[12] I situate the examination of the racialization of the family in conversation with David Eng's discussion of the racialization of intimacy to locate nonnormative bodies, including the adoptive family, within kinship structures.[13] The racialization of intimacy highlights the erasure of race, whereby race becomes neutral and difference merely accidental in liberal constructions of citizenship. This results in the reinscription of racialized subjects "into a discourse of colorblindness."[14] Nevertheless, the racialization of intimacy overlooks how processes of racialization render the family deviant from real kinship due to how race is operationalized in society. The definitions of white and Asian American families must be reframed to account for transracial, transnational adoption. By understanding adoption's legacy concerning the redefinition of white and Asian American families, this study contributes to contemporary discussions of what it means to live in a postracial society.

McClain DaCosta's concept of the racialization of the family captures how racial blindness occurs within transracial adoptive families. Racial blindness describes how adoptive parents deploy colorblind rhetoric, as well as overlook the implications of racial difference in the lives of their children. My deployment of the term *racial blindness* is not meant to elide the fact that, according to Osagie K. Obasogie, "blind people understand race visually just like anyone else" in his comparison of sighted and blind communities' understandings of race.[15] Sighted people's deployment of race as an organizing tool for their lives implicitly and explicitly shapes blind individuals' perspectives on race. Often, friends and family members' racial prejudices and biases effect the racial socialization of blinded individuals. Yet even as blind people visualize race, the conceptualization of blindness has become constructed as a utopia where race is no longer salient.

A discussion of racial blindness aims to unsettle assumptions of how sight does and does not eliminate the ways in which sighted people's biases are transmitted to those within blind communities. Racial blindness in this sense can be seen as a method by which adoptive parents' colorblind rhetoric and ignorance over the legacy of racial difference in the United States impacts adoptees of color. Adoptive parents' racial blindness may also be a result of implicit bias or silent racism—"unspoken negative thoughts, emotions, and assumptions about [people of color] that dwell in the minds of white Americans."[16]

Racial blindness may be either passive or active. Adoptive parents passively deploy racial blindness by not addressing the racial difference, refraining from participating in activities related to the child's ethnicity, and living in a racially isolated area. Active blindness occurs when parents ignore their child's questions about their country of origin and operate as if the child had no other life prior to their adoption. To this end, Obasogie writes, "Sighted people are in a sense blinded by their sight: their visual perception prevents them from 'seeing' the social practices that produce the saliency and coherency of their visual understanding of race."[17] Adoptive parents' actively resist acknowledging histories of white supremacy in the United States in their willful ignorance toward processes of racialization.

By not acknowledging racial difference, colorblind ideologies seek to disentangle race from holding any meaning in social or legal decision making out of fear of being racist.[18] This ahistorical approach ignores how colorblindness is an active ideology that, according to Obasogie, "[is an] always present filter through which increasing numbers of people understand the social world."[19] In this regard, I draw upon Eduardo Bonilla-Silva, who discusses the notion of *white habitus* in relation to colorblind racism. He defines white habitus as "a racialized, uninterrupted socialization process that conditions and creates whites' racial taste, perceptions, feelings, and emotions and their views on racial matters."[20] When racial blindness is operationalized within the Korean adoptive family, white habitus and colorblindness are explicitly linked.

Adoptive parents' erasure of difference attempts to situate the family as transcending race, even while the failure to openly acknowledge race or racism exacerbates any tensions. Their proclamations of "we don't see color, we only see our child" or "we're all the same underneath our skin color" inform how gratitude and gratefulness in adoption circulates. Implied in such statements are assumptions that a person of color should be grateful for the opportunities brought by adoption into white families and that only someone ungrateful would focus on the family's transracial composition. Adoptees kill joy—or in this case the myth of a true melting pot—when they call attention to racism or the role of race in shaping lived experiences.

Positioning Adoption within Queer Theory

Locating adoptive families as queer formations creates new possibilities to understand nonnormative kinship structures.[21] A queering of the family demonstrates how non-normative families (e.g., adoptive, blended, or single-parent) enter/exit legitimacy and legibility against a cultural presumption of normative families—heterosexual, monoracial, and genetically related. Circumventing the heart of reproductive futurism—the notion that all human beings biologically beget the child—the nonnormative nature of Korean adoptive parents' heterosexual union renders the family as queer in their failure to engage in procreative reproductive sex.[22] I emphasize the nonnormative heterosexual relationship because only married, heterosexual couples may adopt from Korea.[23] Even if these adoptive families include biological children, the existence of nonbiological children still marks the family as abnormal because Korean adoptees visibly disrupt notions of families as *always* genetically related. Additionally, while adoptive parents may divorce and sexual identification may shift, the heterosexual nature of their marital union remains one of the strict criteria allowing these families in particular to adopt from Korea.

Queer theory exposes the reproductive disjunctures produced by the adoptive family. The importance of procreative sex in traditional kinship echoes Judith Butler's assertion that heterosexuality is explicitly linked with reproduction, and consequently the future.[24] With this understanding, I draw upon Lee Edelman's interest in reproductive futurism as synonymous with the continued heteronormative reproduction of society.[25] Not biologically reproducing renders the adoptive couple deviant. Adoption circumvents the heart of reproductive futurism, the notion that all human beings want to biologically beget the child, who "embodies the citizen as an ideal."[26] Yet Edelman does not integrate an intersectional analysis, focusing on white middle- and upper-middle-class children in the United States.[27] José Esteban Muñoz comments:

> The future is only the stuff for some kids. Racialized kids, queer kids, are not the sovereign princes of futurity. Although Edelman does indicate that the future of the child as futurity is different from the future of actual children, his framing nonetheless accepts and reproduces this monolithic figure of the child that is indeed always already white.[28]

However, it is precisely because of Edelman's failure to consider racial or class difference that I employ the concept of reproductive futurism to explore the white adoptive couple. The utilization of the implicit white norm mirrors how heterosexism permeates mainstream family ideology as seen in discussions of real versus fictive kinship. Transnational, transracial adoption is invested in the production of the "right" and white family.

Reproductive futurity provides a new lens to consider how processes of racialization are employed and deployed within the transnational, transracial adoptive family. While Muñoz's assertion that racialized children are not linked to the reproduction of the future, adoptees of color exist as a tangible means for white adoptive parents to participate in reproductive futurism. The framework of reproductive futurism allows for a deeper interrogation of kinship and family formation in adoptive families because procreative sex must be disentangled from notions of familial succession. And it is within reproductive futurism that the performative aspects of the adoptive family become evident. The adopted child is the literal embodiment of the adoptive family's future.

To understand adoptive parents' failure at biological reproduction, I suggest that we must account for the ways that adoptive parents seek to beget the child outside of procreative heterosex. I am concerned with how the alleged mutability of racial difference facilitates the incorporation of adoptees of color as the citizen ideal within their white, adoptive families, even as adoptee deportations make the fallacy of adoptees as citizens as ideal evident. Without the protections of their adoptive parents' white privilege, adoptees' status as persons of color is amplified and renders them outside of the future.

Reproducing the Future: Hierarchies of Kinship

Korean adoptive families are outliers that exist at what Butler describes as "outside the disjunction of illegitimate and legitimate."[29] Although legitimate under national and state laws, this legitimacy does not necessarily extend into the social realm, which emphasizes procreative heterosex to beget the child. The desire to mimic the meta-narrative girding common understandings of family reflects their interest in gaining legitimacy and legibility alongside genetically related families. Yearning for acceptance as a real kinship formation, the Korean adoptive family is as a site of repro-narrativity, which Michael Warner defines as "the notion that our lives are somehow made more meaningful by being embedded in a narrative of generational succession."[30] Repro-narrativity is directly tied to reproductive futurism. Warner expands upon these linkages in his discussion of reprosexuality—"the interweaving of heterosexuality, biological reproduction, cultural reproduction, and personal identity."[31] Rhetoric concerning the reproduction of a certain kind of raced and classed family linked via genetics shapes the ways in which adoption is an abnormal construction of repro-narrativity.

Due to the heteronormative aspirations of adoptive parents, these individuals embody deviant reproduction for achieving reproductive futurity outside of procreative sex. I suggest rethinking Warner's concept of reprosexuality to account for how the adoptive family exists on a continuum of deviant heterosexuality. Coined by Jennifer Ting in her discussion of Chinese bachelor societies, deviant heterosexuality accounts for how men in these communities were rendered deviant for their nonreproductive and nonconjugal composition.[32] Deviant heterosexuality lends itself to understanding adoptive parents' nonprocreative sex and social reproduction within the conjugal family. Adoptive parents participate in the values of reprosexuality, facilitating adoptees' access to white privilege and cultural whiteness.

Due to this complex negotiation of biology and culture, the Korean adoptive family—in particular the parents—embody what I term *deviant* reprosexuality. The concept of deviant reprosexuality expands the concept of reprosexuality to account for the family's social reproduction across racial, ethnic, cultural, and national borders whereby disruption of the parent and child "biological mirror" occurs.[33] This differs from the reproduction of the family within multiracial or mixed race households in that the genetic relationship shared between parent and child provides an opportunity for the continuance of repro-narrativity and normative reprosexuality. Aware that Shelley M. Park suggests that adoptive families resist Warner's concepts of reprosexuality and repro-narrativity,

I maintain that these families remain complicit in the reproduction of a particular type of normative family.[34] Adoptive parents participate in reproductive futurity vis-à-vis their investment in reproducing the white, heteronormative family. Due to these aspirations, the adoptive family desires legitimacy as a *real* kinship formation, reflecting their parental desires to beget the child. Their participation in queer futurism means both gaining access and attempting and often failing to gain access to a family structure that is read as normative. This particular family structure is predicated upon the fact that adoptees undergo social death, severed from their natal origins.

Even as Korean adoption complicates heteronormative reproduction, this set of kinship relations replicates existing beliefs regarding real kinship based on regulations concerning who shall be permitted to adopt children, as noted earlier. These regulations reflect the deviant reprosexuality occurring within the adoptive family as normative kinship standards are applied—the notion that parents must be married and heterosexual. Transnational, transracial adoptive families may be less illegitimate or postmodern than their remarried or single parent counterparts because adoptive parents of Korean children must adhere to normative family requirements. Prospective adoptive parents must be married at least three years, have less than two divorces between them, and "have an income higher than the U.S. national average."[35] These guidelines aim to ensure that Korean adoptive parents fit idealized assumptions of family.

The legibility provided to postmodern families cannot be universalized. Nonnormative families operate in tension with one another due to the ways in which legitimacy and legibility are bestowed unevenly to these kinship formations. Even as postmodern families are increasingly visible given the rise of divorced, blended, and/or queer families on mainstream television and film, assisted reproductive technologies (ARTs) and adoption impact common understandings of biological relatedness and family.[36] Families formed via ARTs may remain genetically tied, while also circumventing sexual procreation and even gestational motherhood.[37] This family simultaneously is rendered deviant, yet normative, for the parents bypass traditional hetero-procreative methods to biologically beget the child. Such processes underscore how biological and genetic relatedness becomes privileged in discourses of the reproduction of the family. Conversely, even as adoption raises concerns over the importance of genetic relatedness, their seemingly normative construction offers the Korean adoptive family access to legibility that may not be extended toward single and/or same-sex families who continue to be pathologized in mainstream "family values" rhetoric.[38]

The Impact of Transraciality
on the Adoptive Family

Due to the racialization of the family, adoptees examine their adoptive families until they realize that the family is *their* family and representative of who they are, because families are a social space for learned behavior. The concept of transraciality—the dislocation adoptees' experience in identity formation as racially Asian and culturally white subjects—is useful to understand adoptees' sense of self and nuanced perceptions of what it means to be an adopted person.[39] Transraciality offers a framework to critically examine how racial difference functions within the adoptive family as well as how issues of race, ethnicity, and culture impact adoptees' identity construction. Aware that Michael Awkward deploys the term *transraciality* to "describe the adoption of physical traits of difference for their purpose of impersonating a racial other," I argue that this emphasis on racial performativity is only one aspect of the ways in which adoptees gain access to cultural whiteness.[40] Awkward's definition of transraciality inadequately captures the complexities of attempts to traverse what appear to be static racial boundaries because of his emphasis on the constructedness of racial categories.

Transraciality addresses the continuous dialogue between processes of transculturalization and re/racialization in adoptees' hybrid identity construction. Transculturalization accounts for how adoptees, acculturated into the normalizing nature of whiteness, negotiate their relationship with Korean/Asian American culture and history. A. Irving Hallowell defines *transculturalization* as "the process whereby individuals under a variety of circumstances are temporarily or permanently detached from one group, enter the web of social relations that constitute another society, and come under the influence of its customs, ideas, and values to a greater or lesser degree."[41] Transculturalization occurs via the projection of "whiteness" on the adoptee due to the deployment of adoptive parents' racial blindness. This transference of whiteness underscores how adoptive parents' white privilege is extended in limited—but important—ways, as seen in my discussion of adoptees' circumvention of racist immigration laws and calls for retroactive citizenship to undocumented adoptees in the previous chapter.

At the same time, adoptive parents may have consciously grasped how racial or cultural difference may affect their child's life. Within their home studies, adoptive parents disclosed how racial and cultural difference would be mitigated upon adoption finalization. One family from the West Coast in the late 1970s was honest with their social worker, who recorded: "The child placed with them, though, probably will not have many opportunities to know other people of Korean background. The [family] will do what they can to help the child know about his own culture."[42] This family, aware of the prospective impact of racial and cultural difference, clearly desired to have open lines of communication about adoption. Yet this account cannot be seen as the standard for all adoptive families. Not all prospective adoptive families responded as progressively. For instance, discussing another family, a different caseworker noted: "In essence, [they] see adoption as the difference, not race. It doesn't matter to them if the child is Caucasian or Asian. They point out that with a brunette child, they will run the range of coloring with the three children."[43] The term *coloring* underscores how the parents are attentive to hair color and, potentially skin hue, not racial difference. In other words, race is just another "color," not a distinct social formation. Racial blindness may impede adoptive parents' comprehension of the fact that having brown hair and eyes like their white siblings did not mitigate being racially distinct from other family members. A parallel understanding of racial and cultural difference existed in the late 1960s. For example, a caseworker documented: "Some racial prejudice exists, but in most cases is not intense, and, when present, seems directed toward the Negro individuals rather than other non-American nationalities."[44] Based on this account, one can only assume that the family was unaware with how racism would affect Korean children because they were non-Black. While they may have also lacked an awareness of racism's effects on Black children, these prospective adoptive parents at least possessed competency concerning anti-Black racism unlike their limited knowledge of anti-Asian sentiments circulating in American society.

Adoptive parents further expressed a commitment to an open dialogue with the child concerning adoption. Considering a prospective adoptive couple, a social worker noted: "They feel it is important that the adopted child know of [his/her] adoption. . . . [The prospective adoptive parents] have traveled to other countries, are very interested in all cultures and traditions. . . . They also have friends who have adopted both local and Korean children."[45] Similarly, another family told their social worker that, "there are Korean children in the school and neighborhood."[46] Parents also articulated a desire to gain Korean cultural capital. For instance, the prospective adoptive parents of a child of elementary-school age expressed an interest in taking a Berlitz language course in Korean.[47]

Bearing this in mind, I want to return to my initial discussion of racial blindness. While adoptive parents recognize that their adopted children would benefit from interactions with other adoptees in their communities and express an interest in learning more about Korean culture, it is not clear how these parents acted on these interests following adoption completion. In other words, did these parents express their awareness to social workers to facilitate the adoption process with ease rather than complicate their home studies? Prospective adoptive parents' sentiments encouraging ethnic/racial identity negotiation contradict adult adoptees' statements regarding the lack of diversity and existence of racism in their local communities. For example, Korean adoptee Becca Higgins Swick notes, "I was raised as a Caucasian. By that I mean that when we talked about family things, we always talked about my mother's and my father's families, so my being Korean was never introduced into the picture."[48] Racial blindness ignores the history of racialization in the United States as adoptees encounter how race informs their lived experiences and interactions with institutions and society-at-large.[49] Even as awareness for multiculturalism is evident in the late 1960s and 1970s, this interest is mitigated by parents' inability to consider the impact of anti-Black racism on their adopted Asian children.

Moreover, transculturalization provides adoptees access to white privilege and a culturally white identity more broadly, something that is unavailable to many nonwhites in the United States and the West. The deployment of racial blindness occurs simultaneously with adoptees and adoptive families' racial performativity as part of their efforts to conform to a specific mode of whiteness and legibility. Their simultaneous *doing* and overlooking of race exist in tension with one another as part of a broader commitment for legibility as a legitimate form of family—one that is often denied to non-monoracial, nonbiologically related families. Transculturalization renders the adoptee as a "blank slate" ready for a new identity upon their adoption and ensures the continual emphasis of the adoptees' (white) Americanness vis-à-vis the nuclear family's racial blindness.[50]

Re/racialization occurs as adoptees explore their Korean heritage in adulthood as agents of this consumption versus as children responding to parental influence (e.g., attending culture camps or language school from a young age). Although adoptees are raced as Other based on societal presumptions concerning their phenotype, this involuntary racialization reflects the way in which adoptees do not willingly identity as Korean/Asian American. Such prescribed notions of identity do not reflect the adoptees' actual sense of self. Re/racialization thus follows the transculturalization that adoptees underwent during childhood and adolescence. Multiple opportunities are presented to adoptees as they enter the re/racialization process. Adoptees may engage with the adult adoptee population in local, national, or global adult adoptee organizations. Simultaneously, they may choose not to partake in a recognized community and instead learn more about Korea through other means, such as taking East Asian studies or Korean language classes at their local university. The abovementioned examples are not all encompassing and may not reflect all of the methods adoptees utilize in processes of re/racialization. Rather, these examples are meant to provide some understanding into how adoptees continue to negotiate their racial and ethnic identities.

Performing Race, Performing Family

Returning to the earlier discussion of the adoptive family's heteronormative aspirations, the deviance of social reproduction arises from the need to rethink what it means to be in a monoracial family.[51] Even as monoraciality of the family is disrupted, it is simultaneously upheld vis-à-vis adoptive parents' racial blindness and transculturalization. Korean adult adoptees routinely discuss how their parents were instructed to "raise them as their very own."[52] Adoptive families mimic normative kinship in their desire to emerge as an authentic family.[53] They actively "*do* family." In other words, they continually perform their kinship to be read as legible and legitimate parent-child and sibling-sibling formations.[54] When transracial adoptive families fail at *doing* family, society is quick to pass judgment and question the legitimacy of the relationships between parent and child and the safety of the children within these families.[55] Thus, I contend that adoptive families' attempt to pass as *real* is seen in other marginalized groups' attempts to pass in heteronormative society, whereby whiteness and heterosexuality are placed in as dominant discourse against Blackness and homosexuality. International, transracial adoption raises questions concerning the dissonance between the racialization of the family and the perceived monoraciality of the family.

In response to adult adoptees' reports of the negative effects of transculturalization processes, culture keeping emerged within adoptive families as an effort to partially replicate "the cultural education internationally adopted children would receive if they were being raised within a family of their own ethnic heritage."[56] This practice may provide only certain aspects of the culture to the adoptee. In her research on culture camps, Lori Delale-O'Connor finds: "These camps make explicit the types of culture that are valued in American society . . . [and] highlight those aspects of children's birth cultures that do not contradict or create dissonance with mainstream American culture."[57] While culture-keeping appears beneficial, ethnic commodification allows adoptive parents to explore and appropriate specific aspects of "authentic" Asianness into their families vis-à-vis tokenistic inclusion.[58] Recognizing how culture keeping involves the tokenistic inclusion of "diversity," Barbara Katz Rothman raises the following questions:

> And just what is this heritage we celebrate in our adopted children? What is it that the parents of the Chinese girls are celebrating with their pandas, that all of these adoptive parents, with the foods and music and folk tales and clothing, are bringing home with their children from all over the world? Is it culture? Does a baby have culture? We're doing this celebration of heritage for children who left their native lands long before they learned to speak, let alone developed food preferences for things Peruvian or Chinese. Where does this culture reside in the baby?[59]

Ethnic commodification allows adoptive parents to explore and appropriate specific aspects of "authentic" Asianness into their families. For adoptive parents such as journalist Karin Evans, culture-keeping is one way for parents to "[cultivate] respect for that culture and [impart] as much information as possible during childhood is a way to keep the doors open should the [adoptee] wish to step through."[60] Even as adoptive parents celebrate their multicultural families, it is unclear if these methods provide adoptees the tools to successfully navigate the world as a person of color. After all, eating kimchi does not magically vest one with the abilities to recognize and process racial microaggressions. The effects of such multicultural practices will not be seen until adopted persons raised at the turn of the twenty-first century enter adulthood en masse and recount whether processes of transculturalization impacted their lives.

Adoptees gain legibility within the white heteronormative family due to their access to a culturally white identity. In their access to cultural whiteness, adoptees participate in racial performativity as markers of whiteness become attached to their bodies. These bodies are disciplined from unassimilable forever foreigner to an "almost the same, but not quite" white. Adoptees must negotiate their racial/ethnic status—Asian or Korean—against the white normative framework produced by their transnational, transracial adoptions.[61] They gain subject status vis-à-vis cultivating what Frantz Fanon calls a *white mask.*[62] This mask reflects how adoptees can mimic whiteness, even though they never gain white subjectivity. Negotiating whiteness is central to locating adoptees' transracial and transcultural experience. The white mask transfers the adoptive parents' white privilege onto the adoptee as a child.

Yet this white mask remains an "inauthentic promissory note" as seen in the deportation of undocumented adoptees.[63] In their performance of whiteness, adoptees represent what Butler describes as "an ideal that no one *can* embody," as the parody of whiteness fails in its mimicry.[64] The adoptee can never be white in that they will never gain white physical countenance, even if they obtain cultural whiteness. Racial performativity is limited, as *doing family* cannot erase the ethnic/racial difference made visible in transracial, adoptive families. Nevertheless, when adoptees voice their concerns about the limits of their whiteness, they run risk of becoming labeled killjoys. Calling attention to their status as persons of color reveals the precarity of wearing the mask and marks them as ungrateful for raising awareness of the limited impact of proximal whiteness.

Korean adoptees' deployment of the white mask is rooted in their parents' desire to replicate the heteronormative family. The performative nature of the adoptive family underscores the importance of how racial difference renders the family fictive in a world predicated upon biological relatedness. These families fail to adhere to traditional scripts of whiteness in their departure from heterosex. No longer a monoracial unit, this new iteration of the white American family pushes the boundaries of traditional kinship, in that the culturally white identity bestowed upon the adoptee's body inscribes the nonwhite child into the white family. Whiteness can no longer be viewed in a binary construction of white versus nonwhite. Instead, whiteness becomes blurred, whereby the social construct of whiteness becomes broadened to understand how cultural white identities impact the white American family.

This mask takes a different color when critically interrogating adult adoptees' Korean language performance in Korea. Attempting to gain subject status as a Korean in Korea, adoptees' use of Korean language becomes clouded in their desire to speak like a native Korean. Legibility becomes revoked when the adoptee speaks accented Korean that could lead to misrecognition. Their legibility is also questioned if their flawless "an-nyŏng-ha-se-yo" (Hello) prompts a Korean national to respond in Korean. These exchanges leave adoptees in bewilderment as how to respond because their linguistic ability remains circumscribed by their limited knowledge to say hello, goodbye, and thank you, for example.

By not speaking Korean with the proficiency of a native, other Koreans mark adoptees as a deficient replication. The precarious mask of Koreanness renders the adoptee unreadable as "Korean," while at the same time, their raced body in Korea as Korean places them outside dominant understandings of "American" in the East. Even if adoptees note they are an "ib-yang-in" ("adoptee"), they actively locate themselves at once both inside and outside the nation. As a result, adoptees fail in their performance of what it means to be Korean—lacking access to Korean cultural capital.

An exploration of racial performativity underscores how transraciality is implicated not only in the life of the adoptee, but it is also inextricably tied to the family in its entirety. This familial formation—the adoptive family—pushes the boundaries of traditional kinship due to its disruption of the aesthetic continuity of whiteness and deviant reprosexuality. While Eng argues that these families embody the racialization of intimacy, this framework provides no recourse to account for adoptive parents' ability to impart a positive racial or ethnic identity on the adoptee due to an assumption that racial difference is silenced within the family. Eng suggests that adoptive families are incapable of being viewed as Asian American since many adoptive parents did not identify themselves with "their children's Asianness."[65] Nevertheless, the adoptive family *is* Asian American. By focusing only on whether adoptive parents view themselves as racialized subjects ignores the racialization of the adoptive family as a whole by society at large.

Because the involuntary racialization process continually categorizes the adoptee as Korean/Asian, the adoptive family is unable to pass as a real kinship structure. However, these families become part of Asian America.[66] Transracial adoptive families transform historic notions of what it means to be a member of nonwhite communities. By crossing the color line, these families require a rethinking of what it means to be part of the diversity of Asian American experiences. The lack of monoraciality propels the adoptive family to be reinscribed into an Asian American family.[67] The adoptive family expands definitions of what the Asian American family looks like—a family not bound by monoraciality or biological ties. And, as a reminder, this does not mean that adoptive parents literally become Asian American and acquire yellowface. Rather, adoptive families reflect broader definitions of Asian America whereby white adoptive parents must be attuned to and aware of the experiences of Asian Americans in the United States. To disconnect and live in isolation from Asian America means that adoptive parents implicitly disavow the importance of Asian Americans or Asian America in the lives of adoptees. Consequently, Korean adoptive parents must look inward and examine the ways in which white privilege affects the lived experiences of themselves and their children.

The notion of the Asian American family must evolve as the Asian American identity is reinvented to ensure that the experiences of adoptees are included to reflect the changing demographics of Asian Americans. If the child is reinscribed into understandings of who is Asian American within the nation, then it is only plausible that their families can be viewed as Asian American. These families, while not Asian American in the traditional sense in their deviation of monoraciality, embody the twenty-first-century Asian American family—a family that is not inclusive of two biological parents of Asian descent. Mixed race families join adoptive families, for both rewrite historical understandings of what it means to be authentically Asian American.[68]

Not only do adoptive families disrupt common understandings of the genetically related family, these kinship formations complicate the racialization of the family as a monoracial unit. The performative nature of the heteronormative family underscores the importance of how racial difference renders the family fictive in a world predicated upon biological relatedness. The adoptive family fails to adhere to traditional scripts of whiteness in its departure from procreative heterosex. Only through reading these families as queer and postmodern will new interventions be made to understand how sexuality, reproduction, and kinship remain intertwined.

Embodying deviant reprosexuality, adoptive parents desire to complete reproductive futurism even as their families transgress monoracial understandings of family. Adoptive parents demonstrate the dissonance created by the transracial adoption of Korean children into white families in their disruption of the traditional white family. At the same time, their desire for normativity obscures parent/child racial difference. This racial silencing accentuates how the adoptee and the family remain marked by their transracial existence. Nevertheless, dominant discourse does not inhibit the development of an Asian American identity for the adoptee or the family. Yearning to biologically beget the Child, adoptive parents also become Asian American regardless of whether they actively participate in the assertion of this identity. Marked as queer, adoptive families become racialized even if the parents do not embrace this racialization much like how the adoptee undergoes involuntary racialization.[69] The following chapter builds upon this analysis of belonging in its investigation of adoptees' negotiation of racial, ethnic, and cultural identities as Americans and Koreans.

CHAPTER 4

Rewriting the Adoptee Experience

To fully understand the large-scale impact of the transnational adoption industrial complex (TAIC) on adoption, an interrogation of its lasting legacy on adoptees' realities is necessary. Overlooking the TAIC's role in shaping adoptees' lived experiences means being complicit in one-dimensional narratives promoting adoption as a method of child-saving rescue. The most explicit and obvious example of how the TAIC influenced mainstream society's perceptions of adoptees is in the binary categorizations of adoptees discussed in the Introduction, whereby adoptees were historically positioned as either happy and grateful or angry and ungrateful. It is through understanding this continuum, which generated the conditions to make possible the adoptee killjoy and every adoptee, that the TAIC finally takes shape.

The adoptee killjoy and every adoptee are lenses through which the adopted experience becomes legible. While these concepts may seem constraining due to their roots in a reductive dichotomy, I suggest that these terms allow adoptees to assert their agency as subjects within the transnational adoption industrial complex. Historically, in discussion of adoptions, adoptees are the objects—ready to be bought and sold—or in more palatable language, the gifts of a loving transaction of family formation. As objects, adoptees undergo social death—severed from their natal origins. Yet as adults, adoptees make evident that they are in fact *real* persons. This occurs explicitly when adoptees' lack of gratitude makes evident the breaking of filial bonds and affections.

The real and imagined costs of a child illustrate the ways in which rhetoric of gratitude cannot be disentangled from the project of adoption. Not only are biological children framed within this discourse of gratitude, this is magnified for those individuals told how lucky they were to be adopted. These positionings reveal adoptees' ability to exist as active participants in speaking back to and challenging mechanisms of the TAIC. Questions are raised concerning what it means to be part of the broader Korean diaspora. Adoptees are both American and Korean, even though this latter identity is erased upon their social death.

Adoptees' print and online works provide a critical starting point for other adoptees as they negotiate their multiple, intersecting identities. The autobiographical narrative is a particular form of self-representation that encourages adoptees' assertion of what it means to be an adopted person. This chapter examines how adoptees moved from articulating their collective identities in the earliest published, adult adoptee-edited anthologies, *Seeds from a Silent Tree: An Anthology by Korean Adoptees* (1997) and *Voices from Another Place: A Collection of Works from a Generation Born in Korea and Adopted to Other Countries* (1999), to their deployment of social media to connect with one another and members of the broader Korean diaspora through an examination of adoptee hip-hop artist Dan Matthews's YouTube series *asianish* (2015–2016).[1]

The two anthologies highlight Korean adult adoptees' initial engagement with the public as experts of the adopted experience. These volumes represent the earliest engaged voices in the adult adoptee community who coalesced at the beginnings of the reterritorialization of adoptees as a result of nascent online engagement. While other adult adoptee memoirs were written during this period, the examination of a single-author text can obscure the multitude of voices found in such a heterogeneous community. *Seeds from a Silent Tree* and *Voices from Another Place* reflect my commitment to highlighting volumes edited and authored by adult adoptees themselves. Remember, adoptees historically were not seen as valid knowledge producers. They were illegible in conversations about adoption and were often spoken for by adoption practitioners and adoptive parents. Even as other edited volumes featuring adult adoptees emerged at the time (e.g., *After the Morning Calm*, 2002; *Once They Hear My Name*, 2008), they were edited by non-adoptees including adoption practitioners, adoptive parents, and non-adopted Korean Americans or they examined the experiences of domestic and international adoptees (e.g., *Outsiders Within: Writings on Transracial Adoption*, 2006). This project attends to the ways in which adult adoptees articulate and assert their personhood and expertise on the adopted person's experience.

Seeds from a Silent Tree and *Voices from Another Place* thus represent a watershed moment in Korean adoption history. Not only are they first two publications edited by adult adoptees, they opened the door to future works produced, edited, and authored by adoptees, including memoirs such as *The Unforgotten War (Dust of the Streets)* (1998), *Ten Thousand Sorrows* (2000), *A Single Square Picture* (2002), *The Language of Blood* (2003), and *Twins Found in a Box: Adapting to Adoption* (2003). Tonya Bishoff and Jo Rankin's *Seeds from a Silent Tree* includes thirty accounts from adopted Koreans who grew up throughout North America and Europe.[2] Featured adoptees describe a range of experiences including their struggles to find their place in the world, returning to Korea, and encounters with racism. The text is heralded for its assertion of adoptee agency to generate and represent a text reflective of the myriad of voices found in the overseas Korean adoptee community at large. The second anthology, *Voices from Another Place*, edited by Susan Soon-Keum Cox, was produced to coincide with the first International Gathering of the First Generation of Korean Adoptees in September 1999 in Washington D.C.[3] First-generation adoptees arrived in the West immediately after the post–Korean War period through the 1970s. The thirty narratives were selected by the Gathering planning committee.

While the two anthologies represent the earliest iterations of adoptees' engagement with popular culture, *asianish* and Dan Matthews exemplify how adoptees have claimed their positions in twenty-first-century American middle-brow culture, moving beyond niche releases as "adoption" films or books. For example, Netflix released the documentary *Twinsters* (2015), which follows the reunion of two Korean adoptee twins, Samantha Futerman and Anaïs Bordier, who were separated at birth and raised in the United States and France. The film gained popularity as news outlets featured Futerman and Bordier as a special-interest story because they are one of the only pairs of twins adopted to different families garnering media attention in Korea's over sixty-year history in adoption.[4]

Today, adoptees are seen through a holistic lens that captures their Asian American experiences. This incorporation reflects adoptees' status as experts of what it means to be adopted and their legibility as Asian American subjects. Unlike other adoptees that entered the American public's consciousness vis-à-vis adoption-focused productions, Matthews did so as a result of his career as a hip-hop artist under the moniker DANakaDAN and involvement with the Asian American YouTube channel ISAtv (International Secret Agents television), which was founded by the Far East Movement and Wong Fu Productions. Matthews has performed with other Asian American artists as part of

Kollaboration, "a platform for aspiring Korean American artists to share their talents and pursue those 'impossible' 'unrealistic' creative careers."[5] Unlike other adoptees known within the adoption community for their work, Matthews was known first as a Korean American or Asian American artist. He entered the adoption community's collective consciousness after the release of the docu-series *akaDan* (2014) on ISAtv's YouTube channel as well as DramaFever and Hulu.[6] This should not be a surprise as in *akaDan* (2014), Matthews reveals that the 2013 International Korean Adoptee Association (IKAA) Gathering was his first encounter with the wider Korean adoptee community, even though he previously visited Korea in his early twenties. Through a guided journey, Matthews reveals the intimacies associated with birth search and reunion. He facilitates a private-public narrative of an act once considered personal vis-à-vis his deployment of social media to live Tweet, Instagram, and blog on Tumblr about his time in Korea.

This chapter's examination of Matthews's follow-up project on ISAtv, *asianish*, reflects how he effectively leveraged his position as an Asian American internet icon to highlight what it means to be adopted and Korean American. *asianish* represents a new moment in adoptees' collective history. No longer are adoptees bound by text—in print or online. Rather, they strategically use new technologies, increasing their audience reach to individuals who might otherwise not engage in these conversations. *asianish* highlights how adoptees have become more vocal in verbalizing their existence at the interstices of white and Asian American cultures in everyday life and not in specific print texts or documentaries marketed to adoption audiences. Matthews's work crosses boundaries that previously saw adoption as ancillary to the Asian American community. Bridging two communities—adoption and Asian American—Matthews signals a shift in how adoptees and their experiences in transracial households are incorporated into Asian America. And, in many respects, Matthews represents the shift of the pre- and post-YouTube era that shapes how Asian Americans see themselves represented in popular culture.[7]

Examining these two moments—the publication of the edited volumes and the contemporary rise of Matthews—in concert with one another exposes the evolution of adoptees' acceptance in mainstream society as experts on adoption. Remember, prior to the last decade of the twentieth century, adoptees were often spoken for as a result of the routine infantilization of adoptees as perpetual children. This status renders adoptees, regardless of age, as incapable of being experts on adoption even though the act of family disintegration and formation directly affects their lived realities. Even today, adoptees continue to recount experiences where they have felt silenced and unheard.

(Un)official Histories: Validating Adoptee Voices

Feminist and Asian American literary criticism captures how adoptees' voices exist outside of "official histories" that locate adoption as an act of humanitarianism.[8] The rearticulation performed within these texts recalls how the feminist autobiographical project, according to Leigh Gilmore, "is concerned with interruptions and eruptions, with resistance and contradiction as strategies of self-representation."[9] Each adoptee's autobiographical essay provides a glimpse into their negotiation of concepts such as identity, family, and national belonging. Literature is one avenue for adoptees to reconcile the tensions in forming their identities as adopted Asian Americans.[10] Similar to other Asian American writers, adoptees repudiate Western constructions of "Americanness," while untangling the meaning of Asian American from assumptions concerning same-race biological/social parents.[11] Autobiography is a means by which Asian Americans reclaim "space for self-articulation and representation, against a history of external representation, stereotyping and partiality."[12] Adult adoptee writings expose an emergent and growing strand of the Asian American experience—the adopted person as an Asian ethnic in a transracial household.[13] It is through this lens—feminist, Asian American—that I use these narratives as sites to understand how adoptees disrupt traditional tropes of adoption and what it means to be Asian American. This chapter is in conversation with Mark Jerng and Kim Park Nelson, who carefully negotiate how adoptee writings run the risk of pathologization.[14] Jerng elucidates a need to disentangle adult adoptees from a pathology linked to a continued search for wholeness. Similarly, Park Nelson is attuned to how the voids and absences found in adoptees' lived experiences mark their writings.

Adoptee-authored productions engage in narrative repair and assert adoptees' agency as subjects.[15] Narrative repair occurs vis-à-vis the production of counterstories that seek to remedy the misinformation or mischaracterization of a marginalized community. Adoptees redefine a past that incorrectly characterized their experience in articulating their counterstories.[16] These new narratives are an act of resistance—"set out to correct what the master narratives get wrong."[17] In openly sharing their experiences, adoptees shift mainstream portrayals of adoption. They dislodge one-dimensional portrayals for multidimensional, nuanced realities. Master narratives, according to Hilde Lindemann Nelson, "characterize groups of people in certain ways, thereby cultivating and maintaining norms for the behavior of the people who belong to these groups, and weighting the ways others will or don't tend to see them."[18] She further argues, "The existence of a master narrative so powerful that it delegitimates all other possible stories produces serious amount of confusion and bad faith for the members of the group."[19] Thus, these counterstories ensure that other adoptees become aware of the multitude of reactions to adoption that are available to them. Adoptee narratives that challenge the mainstream rhetoric provide opportunities for other adoptees to envision a new articulation or vision of the significance of adoption in their lives.

These counterstories represent a form of what bell hooks terms as "talking back." By verbalizing their experiences, adoptees talk back to decades of being silenced by adoptive parents and adoption practitioners. Adoptees assert themselves as experts of the adopted experience and reframe what it means to be a knowledge producer. Talking back is a form of resistance, shifting an understanding of adoptees in the eyes of the public imaginary.[20] Through this mode of knowing, these works unearth previously silenced perspectives of adoption, highlighting the various ways that adoptees actively engage in processes of self-definition.[21] This resistance allows room for both the adoptee killjoy and every adoptee an opportunity to negotiate the minor affects of adoption by disrupting reductive narratives of gratitude.

Adoptees' critiques represent what Jodi Kim considers an unsettling hermeneutic, "generat[ing] a new interpretive practice or analytic for reading Asian American cultural productions, and the very formation of contemporary 'Asian America(n),' in new ways."[22] Their interventions spark new conversations of what adoption is and is not and who adoptees are—the filial children of adoptive parents or those who kill joy from their adoptive parents. Yet it is through celebrating the adoptee killjoy that we reframe mainstream perceptions of adoption. And, I suggest that even the every adoptee takes part in this unsettling. By contemplating what it means to be adopted even superficially, the every adoptee calls into question the invisible and implicit filiality that is assumed to take place between child and parent regardless of age. Adoptees' voices—both the adoptee killjoy and every adoptee—reshape the adoption narrative and rework understandings of what it means to be "happy" or "unhappy."

Locating the Self in Autobiographical Narratives

Interested in the nuanced and varied nature of the Korean adoptee experience, I interrogate adoptees' movement to/from the United States and Korea through two concepts—re/birth and inauthenticity—in my analysis of essays in *Seeds from a Silent Tree* and *Voices from Another Place*. Marking the start of adoption, re/birth signals the disruption of adoptees' lives as Korean nationals when they were reborn as Western subjects vis-à-vis the airplane journey from Korea to the United States. Adoptees encounter questions regarding their authenticity or inauthenticity as Asians or Americans. Exploring these tensions yields insight into how adoptees characterize themselves within broader understandings of Asian Americans living in the United States.

In my use of these two themes to analyze adoptee narratives, I depart from scholars deploying racial and ethnic identity measures to capture degrees of racial salience in the adoptee's life, as I find these categories place either/or constraints on identity.[23] The binary logic of positive or negative ethnic identity pathologizes adoptees as incomplete for lacking a perceived positive ethnic identity as an Asian American. This approach may also reward some parenting behaviors over others by linking a positive ethnic identity with parents who encouraged ethnic or birth culture exploration without accounting for the interplay between class and geographic location in shaping adoptees' identity exploration.[24] Rather, a holistic approach elucidates how ethnic and racial identities are negotiated over time by adoptees.[25] I situate this chapter in dialogue with scholars who explore adoptees' ideological investment in whiteness within their local communities, even as they are continually read as the Other due to visibility of racial difference.[26]

Critiquing adoptees' existence as guests of their adoptive parents elucidates the salience of racial/cultural passing and impersonation in adoptees' lived realities. In regard to passing, I refer to chapter 3's discussion of how adoptees and their families desire to pass as a *real* family. Adoptees operate as cultural whites with access to the privileges of whiteness vis-à-vis their parents' American citizenship. Passing within the family and immediate community, adoptees recall "forgetting" they were Asian/Korean within these localities. Tina Chen's concept of impersonation deepens our understanding of how, as Asian American subjects, adoptees negotiate notions of authenticity as Asians, Koreans, and Americans. Chen argues that Asian Americans commit acts of impersonation as they negotiate American racialization processes due to their historical location as inassimilable subjects, which inhibits access into the national body politic.[27] Impersonation is a form of resistance, for it recognizes the heterogeneity found under the umbrella term Asian American and provides room for the continued revision of the definition of "Asian American." I employ both passing and impersonation to capture the experiences evoked by their transraciality. In this respect, I depart from Chen, who differentiates passing and impersonation, locating passing within a specific mixed race experience of black/white. This project employs passing as something that also can be done by cultural whites.

RE/BIRTH: EXITING THE AIRPLANE

Korean American adoptees have pasts prior to their arrival to the United States. However, because this entry marks the start of their lives into their adopted families, they are reborn. Adoptees shed their Korean names and language for a new name and the English language. For example, they gain first names like Thomas, Adam, Rebecca, and Jennifer, and last names like Murphy, Smith, Robinson, and Marshall. Addressing the dissonance their names and faces create, Todd D. Kwapisz writes: "I am a person whose last name is correct, even though you believe it should be 'Lee,' 'Chang,' or 'Kim.'"[28] He captures adoptees' encounters with public confusion over their seemingly "American" last names. While the curiosity over adoptees' "American" names may seem genuine, looking below the surface, the racialized nature of the question emerges. If Kwapisz's last name really was "Chang," "Lee," or "Kim," no questions would be asked due to the association between "Asian"-sounding names and raced Asian bodies. The forever foreigner myth associated with Asian Americans may also result in the adoptee being asked: "What is your *real* name?"[29]

Not only do adoptees' encounter continual and constant questioning regarding why their faces and names do not "match," but also whether they know their *real* families. This persistent questioning remains distinct from other Asian Americans in that the binary of real and fictive kinship does not enter the equation concerning legitimacy within the family. Even if an Asian American is biracial, the biological and familial tie with their Asian genetic parent protects the individual from conversations associated with *real* parents. The cultural milieu in which these individuals are socialized remains markedly different from that of adoptees. A distinct contrast arises in that the adoptee's upbringing within an all-white family provides the adoptee with access to a cultural whiteness that may not be readily accessible to people of color more generally. Working in combination with these complex social encounters, adoptees face internal questions over their legibility as cultural whites because of the powerful image reflected back in the mirror. Discussing her upbringing, Loey Werking Wells aptly summarizes this difference between adoptees and other Asian Americans, "I knew by my looks alone, and my status as a Korean adoptee, I was not really the WASP I was being brought up to be."[30] For Ellwyn Kauffman, "the mirror was the inescapable reminder of where I had come from."[31] The mirror provided a visible reminder of the tensions between one's racial phenotype and cultural upbringing. Mary Lee Vance writes, "As long as I didn't look in the mirror, I could pretend that I looked no different from the rest of my family or friends, with an exception of a nonbiological sister who had also been adopted from Korea."[32] The mirror becomes an inescapable object—a continual reminder of what one is not, rather than what the adoptee believes.

And yet the importance of names is not only linked to creating moments of misrecognition and incongruity. Naming and renaming serve as an extension of social death to solidify adoptees' positioning as Western subjects. Such practices also are not limited to infants and toddlers. Children as old as eleven found themselves renamed upon adoption.[33] Capturing the impact of this practice, Crystal Lee Hyun Joo Chappell writes, "At the age of 4, Lee Hyun Joo was sent to America to be adopted. Her name became Crystal Chappell. Like thousands of other Korean adoptees, her birth family and culture were left behind. Not until she was a young adult did she realize that something was missing from her life."[34] Chappell's recollection reflects re/birth—the beginning of (a new) life in *becoming* American. Through the process of social death, adoptees are removed from their roots, history, and culture as Koreans en route to a new history and culture and the roots of their adoptive parents.

Transferred via airplane from Korea to the United States, adoptees disengage from the only life they knew. At the same time, during the initial airplane journey, adoptees may lack awareness of its significance. Only afterward may adoptees realize the profound impact of their first international flight. Confounded with a new name, language, culture, and family, adoptees are in flux, neither here nor there as this re/birth represents their positioning in the interstitial. Adopted at age six, Amy Mee-Ran Dorin Kobus recalls that she was unaware of what was happening upon her arrival, noting: "My escort pushed me toward a group of white people and said in Korean, 'This is your new family.' She then turned and walked quickly away."[35] This reflection is followed by her description of her adoption as an "uprooting and transplanting from Korea to America."[36] Pronounced language difference exacerbates the disconnect between familial belonging and nation. Thomas Park Clement notes, "Language was the most difficult barrier to my integration into my new wonderful world. I had a lot of trouble expressing my feelings and I didn't know that language was the problem."[37] With no forewarning or comprehension of the concept of adoption, adoptees exist as nonconsenting partners in the exchange of children. Re/birth supplants memories and histories for new realities and truths.

At the same time, re/birth obscures the fact that adoptees hold on to their pasts and memories. Sherilyn Cockroft's vivid recollections of orphanage life provide insights into how children became ready for adoption. Orphanage personnel asked her questions about her family, how she got lost, and her birth date.[38] Her memories corroborate case files documenting the experience of older children in orphanages.[39] Yet these details of adoptees' *becoming* adoptable subjects and then Americans remain hidden from view. Instead, mainstream adoption narratives emphasize the importance of life after their humanitarian rescue.

Families may celebrate or commemorate the adoptee's arrival with little to no acknowledgment of how this day marks the time when adoptees also left behind their country of birth, birth families, and orphanage communities. Chappell writes, "Culture shock and the trauma of gaining a new family, home and identity erased my memory. In essence, I came to believe that I had been born on that day I was adopted, at age four."[40] Representing arrival to the United States, "Airplane Day" or "Gotcha Day," obscures one of the many losses adoptees encounter as children. Airports and airplanes thus become the signifying source of adoption. However, if we overlook the significance of these celebrations in the lives of adult adoptees, we run the risk of delegitimizing their role in shaping adoptee identity. The arrival celebration emphasizes the quintessential Americanness of the child without consideration for any residual memories or relations from Korea.

Re/birth relegates names, birth dates, and birth years to the periphery in that they occur prior to adoption, even though these details are held to high esteem in the West. While accounts of a biological mother's pregnancy and birth process are valued and recounted, these same life events are overlooked as minor or unimportant in the lives of adoptees. Re/birth has utmost importance in the involuntary migration process tied to adoption, not the actual birth in Korea. This process works in tandem with adoptees' social death in Korea in that adoption only serves to emphasize the child's life as beginning on the day of arrival to the West.

THE MEANING OF "AMERICAN"

Given their re/births, the concept of family is central to understanding adoptees' transraciality, in particular when considering their discussions of childhood and adolescence. For example, seeking to "fit in" as an American, Dorin Kobus denied her ethnic heritage while growing up. Stereotyping Asians as quiet and passive, she desired to become "American" through her outspokenness. This internalized behavior is reflected in how she sought to perfect her American English accent, changed her style of dress, and utilized white face powder to construct physical whiteness.[41] Her performance of whiteness is symptomatic of what Nancy Caraway terms "aesthetic assimilation," which occurs when individuals of color internalize the belief that whiteness equates beauty.[42] In the case of women of Asian descent, double eyelid surgery and skin whitening creams are two methods utilized to embody the white, Western, feminine ideal.[43]

Many female adoptees engage in the same type of racial and ethnic beauty practices occurring within the broader Asian American community to conform to the white beauty ideal. While they may not seek cosmetic medical procedures to alter their appearance, these adoptees exist in a world where women of color routinely internalize racist perceptions of beauty.[44] For example, *Never Perfect* (2007) follows Vietnamese American, Mai-Anh, as it explores the extremes Asian Americans undertake to comply with this Eurocentric image of beauty. Aesthetic assimilation garnered mainstream attention in 2013 when CBS television personality, Julie Chen, publicly discussed her double eyelid surgery to Westernize her features and make her more physically appealing to viewers in her early career.[45] At the same time, the investment in Eurocentric standards of beauty may not lead to drastic procedures that permanently alter one's image. Some women may employ superficial practices that include taping their eyes to create the double eyelid without cosmetic surgery or lightening their hair.[46] Allison Lau, Sharilyn K. Lum, Krista Marie Chronister, and Lina M. Forrest note, "The discrepancy between American media images of attractiveness and an Asian American woman's perception of her own attractiveness may create a situation that is highly threatening to her body image and physical self-concept."[47] And yet these women simultaneously exist in a double bind, as they negotiate stereotypes concerning the "American" beauty ideal—white femininity—and Orientalist assumptions concerning what Asian women *should* look like.

The negotiation of the pressures produced by Eurocentric beauty norms and one's ethnic identity reveal the competing messages Asian American women encounter in popular culture. Further, Asian Americans in predominately white environments grapple with stereotypes concerning what it means to be "American" in isolation away from role models of color. Adoptees, including Dorin Kobus, had limited access to positive Asian role models in their nuclear families and local communities. They strove for acceptance and carried a strong desire to blend in and go unnoticed.[48] To this end, female Korean adoptees, like other Asian American women, may internalize these beauty norms as a result of their cultural identities as Americans and exposure to American media that promotes a narrow definition of beauty.[49]

These tensions underscore Tina Chen's discussion of how impersonation involves "a dynamic exchange between competing definitions of itself."[50] For example, recounting her obsession with her body image and her desire to be white, YoungHee writes: "I obsess over white women. I compare every inch of my body to theirs. . . . *Theoretically I was white*, my family is white, the community I grew up in was white."[51] YoungHee's desire for whiteness to complement her cultural identity reflects the internalized belief that the adoptee is white like any other person in their family. The struggles to fit in and look like the dominant ideal are not limited to Dorin Kobus or YoungHee. Many female Korean adoptees write about their desire to have larger, rounder eyes, non-coarse hair, and a more prominent nose. Similar to the Asian American community, more broadly, adoptees recognize that "looking a certain way was more valued."[52]

While adoptees' performance for whiteness bestows a hypervisible status, as seen in Dorin Kobus's use of face powder, the desire for invisibility reflects the yearning to be part of the dominant ideal. Whiteness is tied to invisibility because of its unmarked nature and existence as the norm in American society. At the same time, "Asianness" is tied to hypervisibility with racialized stereotypes of Asians as the Yellow Peril circulating within American popular culture. Even as Asians encounter stereotypes concerning their invisibility as linked to the model minority stereotype, female adoptees seek to erase the hypervisibility of physical difference by embracing whiteness. Adoptees undergo an act of impersonation vis-à-vis their attempt to constitute themselves as one type of Asian American subject—invisible, capable of "blending in" to their white, suburban surroundings.

The impact of aesthetic assimilation persists. Reflecting on her struggles in adolescence around self-confidence and self-esteem in 1970s Iowa, Kat Turner proclaims her shock when "learn[ing] that the adopted Korean daughter of one of [her] neighbors was living [her] déjà vu . . . in Minneapolis in the mid-1990s."[53] Turner writes: "I couldn't believe this generation of girls on the edge of a new millennium were not only faced with the same issues and insecurities, but to the same degree I had faced them almost twenty years before."[54] For Turner, realizing that many of the same issues from her adolescence persist in the most recent generation of adoptees is jarring. She assumed that twenty years between her and the subsequent generation would mean increased self-assurance about their racialized appearance. Instead, she discovers how racial difference continued to inflict its negativity in the development of identity for adolescent female adoptees.

Though the internalization of white beauty standards shaped female adoptees' assimilationist practices, male adoptee narratives focus more on their struggles to be "all-American" and recount the use of the terms "Chink," "gook," and "Jap" to describe them.[55] Even though these epithets appear gender neutral, the historical deployment of racialized stereotypes in the United States remains highly gendered. And the nerdy Asian man or the use of the racial slurs remain tied to origin stereotypes castigating Asian American men as either the "yellow peril" or "model minority."[56] For example, Todd D. Kwapisz lists numerous perceptions Americans have of him due to his ethnicity—"the one who started WWII or the Vietnam War," "martial art expert," and "the exchange student with [his] host family."[57] Jim Milroy echoes the need to assert his belonging in the United States, writing, "People will believe that stones are cars before they'll accept that my brother, or sisters, or father or mother is my real family."[58] For male adoptees, to belong does not require an aesthetic assimilation; rather, it necessitates an active negotiation of racist practice and rhetoric found in the United States concerning their national belonging.

When considering their cumulative discussions of displacement, adoptees articulated an overwhelming desire for overall belonging and acceptance. Wayne A. Berry comments that while growing up in a small Minnesota town, he *wanted to be* an American and how his only memories are of life in the United States after he was re/born as a Western subject.[59] It is important to note that for Berry, Americanness is implicitly conflated with whiteness. Similarly, Cockroft discusses her "desire to 'fit in' and be 'normal'" because she "always felt different and inferior"[60] Cockroft notes how growing up in the Midwest around individuals with limited contact to other races or cultures caused awkward situations. She writes: "Even going to the mall, people would sometimes stare at me because I looked different. . . . Strangers would talk to me loudly and slowly as if I were deaf and dumb."[61] Their memories illustrate a tension concerning their ability to belong within their communities. The isolation articulated in their narrative reveals the need for honest conversations about racial difference in the adoptive family.

Addressing the impact of adoptive parents in the lives of their adopted children, Kari Ruth reveals the implications of relegating conversations of race within the family to the sidelines.[62] Writing to her friend and fellow adoptee who committed suicide, Ruth provides an emotionally raw account of adoption's multiple effects. Thinking to herself, Ruth notes, "Being adopted Korean is far more complex than choosing racial designation."[63] Her statement concerning the complexities of adoption is echoed when she writes: "The struggles of racial identity cannot be solved at culture camps, outreach events, panel discussions or trips to our birth country. They cannot be described as growing pains nor diagnosed with color-blind love."[64] Ruth highlights the disjunctures experienced between cultural tourism and ethnic commodification and the well-meaning intentions behind these acts. These attempts are mere Band-Aids deployed in a color-blind world that lacks the resources and tools to dig deeper and grapple with what it means to live in a racist world. Celebrations of multiculturalism obscure the depths of what it means to be a person of color in the United States. She further writes, "[Adoptive] parents must not understand that the price they paid for us was insignificant compared to the price we pay to fit into their world."[65] Her essay exposes how adoptees strive to protect their families from multiple losses associated with adoption and encounters with racism. In doing so, Ruth dismantles the notion that transracial adoption is a multicultural celebration.

In this making and remaking of adoptees as American, clear tensions and contradictions exist. However, I am reluctant to argue that adoptees' valorization of whiteness proves that adoptees are continually melancholic subjects in search for wholeness. Rather, their negotiation of Americanness arises within discussions of the ways Asian Americans negotiate Orientalist projections of what it means to be Asian in the United States. More importantly, their reflections illuminate how adoptees seek acceptance as an individual who belongs in a portrait of America.

THE INAUTHENTIC SUBJECT: RECONCILING ADOPTEES' KOREANNESS AND AMERICANNESS

As adoptees negotiate their legibility as Americans, for many, a trip to Korea raises the possibility of closure and a greater understanding of an individual's sense of self. This voyage reflects adoptees' engagement in acts of re/racialization. Although returning to Korea is not an essential component in the adopted Korean narrative, many adoptees correlate recovering their past with their return to the "motherland." The return is symbolic and a tangible link to his/her biological parents. Travel to Korea can occur in a myriad of ways, but some adoptees return to Korea via homecoming programs. Other adoptees return to Korea to teach English, volunteer at an orphanage, or attend university to learn Korean and perhaps pursue an advanced degree.

As returns become more commonplace and discussed in mainstream adoption conversations, adoptees recount instances of awkward questions concerning finding their "real" family and whether they will return and visit the "motherland" from family, friends, other adoptees, and strangers. These questions are predicated upon the assumption that it is natural to search for one's biological family and those individuals who do not embark on such a journey are unnatural and somehow maladjusted. This normalization of return to Korea as well as birth search may initially seem as if the adoptee is ungrateful; however, adoptees may do both without encountering charges of ingratitude. While it may seem that they are not grateful enough in that they participate in these identity exploration opportunities, I suggest that a cultural shift has

occurred. Search has become expected on an invisible checklist for those actively engaged in the adoptee community. Nevertheless, an individual's choice
does not make one *more* or *less* Korean, but reflects what it is—choice. And
the number of adoptees who do return is negligible when considering the
total number of adoptees—an estimated 200,000—sent abroad to the West.
Approximately 3,000 to 5,000 adoptees return for short-term visits, long-term
visits, or to permanently reside each year.[66]

Only upon actual return does this homeland take any tangible shape. And
when it occurs, adoptees find that the motherland is not what it seems. Adoptees arrive as foreigners in what should be their homeland and expose the
limits of what it means to "be Korean." Returnees often arrive as deficient
Koreans lacking cultural capital, even as they may be able to pass as Korean
upon landing at Incheon International Airport in Seoul. Their membership
in the Korean diaspora underscores that ethnic identity does not imbue an
automatic cultural identity. Homeland cannot be considered a place of safety
and respite for everyone. Unlike other members of the Korean diaspora, they
are unique in that, for the majority of their lives, an overwhelming number of
them lacked access to learning about Korean culture from family members.
For many adoptees, return to Korea evokes feelings of cultural inauthenticity
and questions of belonging.

Perceived as "Koreans" based on countenance, adoptees remain outsiders
within a country, where often for the first time, they "blend in" phenotypically.
Reflecting this dissonance, Wayne Berry notes that he is not a *true* Korean.
His comment captures what many adoptees discuss: the differences between
themselves and "Korean Koreans" or "Asian Asians." A *true* Korean under-
stands the cultural nuances of Korea and speaks fluent Korean in the eyes of
many adoptees. Echoing Berry's differentiation between native Koreans and
adoptees, Mark Fermi questions his ability to claim that he is Korean. Fermi
writes, "Korean people ask me if I am Korean. I said, 'Yes, I am' and question
their reaction to my answer. I know I am Korean, although some of my actions do not show it. I can only say a few words in Korean."[67] Their cultural
whiteness affirms Americanness, while simultaneously inhibiting adoptees'
ability to become *true* Koreans, which is inextricably linked to fluent language
proficiency and comprehension of Korean cultural nuances. Adoptees remain
cultural outsiders. Social death and re/birth erased an ability to claim Korean
cultural capital with ease as Korean nationals. Reflecting on her two return
visits to Korea, Jane Owen finds:

> I am also somewhat frustrated by the double standard that they hold about
> Korean-born, now American, adoptees. They want us to be "Korean" by

learning the language, eating and enjoying the food, and learning about the customs, and yet they would not keep us as their own and take us into their families to love, nurture, and raise as their own children. They seem to deny that we are Americans by culture, mind set, and family history, primarily because of their rejection of us as orphans. We are only Koreans in appearance.[68]

Her disappointment underscores the tensions produced between differentiating oneself from a "Korean Korean" or "Asian Asian." Owen's usage of the term double standard highlights how cultural authenticity and cultural capital are absent in the lives of adoptees. Their lack of cultural knowledge inhibits adoptees' ability to "be" Korean. In this regard, the legitimacy of adoptees as Korean is questioned.

Adoptees cannot seamlessly enter South Korean culture without exposing the fallacy of what it means to be Korean. Not only do adoptees kill joy in their disruption of adoption as a humanitarian, child-saving act, they also kill joy by complicating the notion of return. There is no *true* homeland, making their return incomplete. This exposes the killjoy's sense of alienation. Sara Ahmed writes, "We become alienated—out of line with an affective community—when we do not experience pleasure from proximity to objects that are attributed as being good."[69] A chasm exists between the imagined homeland—the alleged object of happiness—and what is there upon arrival. The very experience of adoption makes a *happy* return impossible.

Furthermore, the tension over legibility as "authentic, true Koreans" exists against adoptees' impersonation and desire for whiteness. Negotiating what it means to be transracially adopted, Korean, and American, I draw from Tina Chen's examination of double agency. For Chen, double agency "gestures to the multiple allegiances that impersonation makes evident; it exposes the fear of betrayal that is at the heart of charges of imposture to which Asian Americans have been subject."[70] Adoptees' negotiation of double agency remains markedly different in that their multiple allegiances are cross-racial, ethnic, and cultural identities. Their double agency becomes palpable in their intimate encounters in Korea. For example, after reunion with her birth family, Crystal Lee Hyun Joo Chappell finds, "Now I have two complete names: one Korean, one English. They encompass my two worlds, two families and two identities that sometimes clash, sometimes combine and sometimes coexist."[71] This multiple naming illustrates how identity is tied to proper names. Without a direct translation between English and Korean names, each represents a different construct—one American child, one Korean child. What is interesting in the case of Chappell is her deliberate melding of her Korean and English names, reflecting the impact of adoption on her life. Furthermore, underscoring the illusions produced by adoption is Kimberly Kyung Hee Stock's account of visiting a Korean home for unwed mothers who intended to place their unborn child for adoption.[72] Stock writes:

> I knew I was going to meet these [birth mothers], and I wanted to tell them that, because I was an adoptee, I wanted to assure them they shouldn't worry about their babies. Life in America would be good for them, and they were going to families that would love and cherish them. Their babies would grow up and understand why they were given up. I was planning to read [a birth mother] the note, but I couldn't quite double her pain by forcing her to realize that her child, like me, would never speak Korean properly.[73]

Unlike Chappell's experience of duality as a moment of double agency between birth family and adoptive family, Stock's recollection reveals how adoptees may feel like imposters through their inability to communicate outside of rudimentary Korean. The pain that she references is the pain of a birth mother perceiving adoptees as frauds, as not properly Korean. Operating within these intimate frontiers in Korea, double agency becomes even more salient. Literally able to "blend in" to the local Korean community, adoptees navigate a space whereby they appear to represent the "Koreanness" associated with cultural authenticity, even as they remain outsiders.

Distinct from other Asian Americans, adoptees' lived experiences are profoundly influenced by the primacy of their adoptee status. Concluding her narrative, Whitney Tae-Jin Ning recognizes that there is "no singular model" of identity.[74] For her, inauthenticity does not negate one's Americanness or Koreanness. Instead, inauthenticity highlights the adoptee's existence on the borderlands. The transracial composition of the adoptee's family provides the adoptee with a unique vantage point to experience the normalizing nature of whiteness as well as direct access to a culturally white identity. Adoptees remain marked for their transraciality—forever looking like "the person who does not belong" within their monoracial, white families.

The writings of adult adoptees demonstrate the limits of categorization and the need to eliminate silos separating concepts of racial and cultural belonging. Transraciality makes this apparent by providing insight into how binaries hinder the ability for adoptees to assert a positive identity as an adopted Korean American. Reflecting the anxiety produced by a need for dichotomous thinking, David Miller finds himself existing on a tightrope pulled in two directions toward Korea and the United States.[75] This metaphor provides a clear image of how straddling two worlds is untenable. Similarly, Ruth writes, "When we talk about cultural identity, we assume there is a split. And we waste our time trying to . . . [find]

balance [or create] space for two cultures or building bridges.... Their resolutions lead you to separate, pick and choose or sort and categorize. What I'd really like to do is push *puree*."[76] Adoptees lack opportunities to validate and celebrate the multiplicity of their individual experiences. Embracing the various intersections they inhabit, adoptees cast off the need to be an "authentic" subject based on the cultural scripts and norms that historically render them as outliers.

GRATEFUL FOR WHAT?

The collective subjectivity that emerges in these narratives emphasizes individuality and variety. Recognizing the heterogeneity of adoptees' experiences, adult adoptee autobiographical writings reflect how adoptees challenge the mythical adoptee that was continually spoken for by adoptive parents and professionals in the field of adoption. In the examination of the selected texts, this chapter exposes how adoptees trouble what it means to be an adopted Korean American. If we accept the premise that adoptees in general should be "grateful" for their adoption, the inclusion of their moments of alienation from language, culture, and family clearly illustrate how adoptees are more likely "dumbfounded" within those initial moments of arrival. The concept of gratefulness is further challenged through memories of overt, covert, and internalized racism. The painful recollections of the mirror serve as a reminder of their impersonation and desire to pass as *real* whites instead of only embodying cultural whiteness. Yet their dalliance with encounters of loss and ambivalence is not one that speaks to a latent melancholia nor is it indicative of a pathological search for wholeness. Instead, the tension produced by negotiating one's transraciality reveals how passing and impersonation are intertwined in the adoptee's intersectional experience.

To assume that adoptees should automatically be grateful results in their oppression. Krista Benson notes that these "hierarchies of happiness correspond to existing social hierarchies and systems of inequality."[77] Analyzing the role of norms of happy and unhappy in shaping individual subjectivity clarifies the Catch-22 that adoptees face when discussing their adoptions publicly. Sara Ahmed writes:

> To be oppressed requires you to show signs of happiness, as signs of being or having been adjusted.... If an oppressed person does not smile or show signs of being happy, then he or she is read as being negative: as angry, hostile, unhappy, and so on. Happiness becomes the expected "default position" for those who are oppressed, such that it comes to define the sphere of neutrality. You are either happy: or you are not.[78]

Adult adoptees' honest accounts of racial microaggressions in childhood and adulthood challenge this notion of "happiness." Korean adult adoptees fail to fulfill normative requirements of being "adjusted," which causes some adoptive parents to consider their writings to be "cautionary tales."[79] Narratives that diverge from the adoptive family as "the promise of happiness" results in adoptees' mischaracterization by society at large as "angry," "bitter," or "ungrateful."[80] This is why adoptees who speak out against the very thing that should result in their happiness—adoption as the best option—are rendered adoptee killjoys.[81]

This does not mean adoptees in *Seeds from a Silent Tree* or *Voices from Another Place* were prompted by anger or ungratefulness to insert their voices into mainstream adoption discourse. Their negotiations of what it means to be an adopted Korean American in the United States and Korea underscores the Korean adoptee community's heterogeneity. While each adoptee may mention a similar encounter, their reactions reflect how their various lived experiences in childhood and adolescence shape their perspectives of adoption. There is not a singular "authentic" adopted person experience. As dominant discourse's construction of the mythical adoptee becomes disrupted, adult adoptees' writings denaturalize the imagined adoptee. They provide a new perspective to a childhood and adulthood marked by transraciality. In many ways, these voices exist between and within the categories of adoptee killjoy and every adoptee. Their narratives trouble assumptions concerning what it means to be adopted—reclaiming adoptees' space in adoption discussions. Yet, these voices also complicate the dual binaries that continue to plague the adoptee community by offering multiple perspectives to consider what it means to be adopted.

Contemporary Unsettlings

Nearly twenty years after the publication of *Seeds from a Silent Tree* and *Voices from Another Place*, Dan Matthews garnered the attention of the adoption community with the release of his docu-series *akaDan* (2014). Matthews teases out the complexities of what it means to be adopted in the twenty-first century.[82] He offers a glimpse into the complexities of what it means to assert a Korean American identity even though one grew up transracially in a white family. At the same time, Matthews introduces viewers to the nuances of birth search, reunion, and engaging with the adoptee community. Regarding the latter, it is important to highlight that *akaDan* (2014) is the first production to integrate aspects of the International Korean Adoptee Association (IKAA) triennial gatherings into the cinematography. While Tammy Chu's *Resilience* (2009) and Deann Borshay Liem's *In the Matter of Cha Jung Hee* (2010) include previous IKAA Gatherings in the background, it was not until *akaDan* (2014) that viewers gain access to Gathering-related events.[83] *akaDan* (2014) launched Matthews as an adoptee voice online. As pointed out earlier, he previously was known as a hip-hop artist as a result of his appearances at Kollaboration—a platform that seeks to highlight and celebrate Asian American Pacific Islander voices—and his work for the ISAtv YouTube channel.

Matthews's web-series *asianish* highlights how adoptees complete this cultural identity work. *asianish* is structured to invite viewers to join Matthews on his journey exploring "what it means to be Korean." The visual production offers a different lens to examine adoptees' identity negotiations, unlike print media. Instead of reading about the experiences, viewers are invited to experience an adoptee's journey firsthand. Here, those unfamiliar with memoirs and essays authored by adoptees—both those adopted and non-adopted—gain insight into what it means when adoptees that lack access to Korean cultural capital actively seek out Korean culture in adulthood. His readiness to share his perceptions of Korean culture underscores how adoptees have a limited understanding of what it means to be raised in a Korean American household. As the anthologies discussed earlier reveal, many adoptees often only interact with Asian culture on the periphery, as outsiders looking in.

In the first few minutes of episode one, a strict assumption that there is a singular experience of *being* Korean in the United States is offered to the viewer. A dichotomy arises, whereby being raised with Korean parents exists in opposition to being raised by white parents because of underlying inherent perceived differences. During a voiceover in the opening credits, Matthews states:

> Do you ever feel as if you're stuck between two worlds? I do. I do all the time. As a Korean adoptee raised by a white family I've constantly found myself thinking about my transracial identity and how I never really fit in. I mean I feel like I'm Asian, but it's more like I'm Asian-ish. Growing up I never really had that traditional Asian American upbringing. Can't speak the language? Check. Never ate the food? Check.[84]

His sentiments reveal how strict notions of Asian diaspora and Asian American immigration and child-bearing patterns render adoptees outside of what is considered "Asian American." We also see how culturally relativist assumptions frame what Matthews—as well as mainstream society—sees as "being" Asian or Asian American. Being Asian was tied to "traditional" culture. Yet, Asian Americans have lived in the United States since the seventeenth century and Korean Americans arrived at the end of the nineteenth century. Nonetheless, given the restrictions on Asian immigration as discussed in chapter 2, it's not surprising that Asianness is tied to foreignness. As we saw in the anthologies, the perpetual foreigner myth oftentimes shapes how adoptees construct the mythic Asia that has been conjured in their imagination.

The overemphasis on food reveals a hyperfocus on surface notions of culture that reduces Korean culture to edible bites. This attention to food is anticipated, as many adoptees center their attention on food as a mode of consuming Koreanness. Nevertheless, even as adoptees emphasize Korean food as a marker of *being Korean*, they still may feel insecure about their knowledge of the cuisine. Addressing this unfamiliarity with Korean food, Matthews comments, "Even I feel a little weird when I go to a Korean restaurant."[85] Lack of cultural competency exposes adoptees' inadequacies as Korean subjects because, in this particular construction of Koreanness, food is a key marker of authenticity. Whether it be through the consumption of kimchi or one's first bite of gim (dried seaweed), food is the main marker in which Matthews associates one's level of Korean cultural capital.[86] Matthews notes, "I feel like food is such an easy entry way for feeling more Korean."[87] This was made explicit in *akaDan* (2014), when Matthews attends an IKAA Gathering optional event, Membership Information Training, aimed at socializing adoptees into Korean drinking and business culture. For many adoptees, food is a distinct marker of belonging.

Echoing this belief is Steve "Slim" Lim, the Korean cultural purveyor guiding Matthews in *asianish*. Lim comments, "There's nothing like food that connect the people to the land and the culture."[88] Yet this investment in food as a method of communicating with one's cultural identity and differentiating one from one's racial and ethnic identity runs the risk of reductive pathologization. There's an assumption that if one lacked access to Korean food then one somehow is *less Korean*. Such a statement negates adoptees' experiences as Korean Americans. Yet, Lim's assertion gets at the heart of what drives adoptees' search for connection with what it means to *be Korean*. Adoptees' upbringing may be vastly different than their Korean and Korean American non-adopted counterparts because of their transracial families. To this end, Matthews notes, "I feel like the food that I ate and the food that my Asian Korean friends ate was very very different. I think that's probably one of the most obvious examples of differences between growing up adopted and growing up in an Asian Korean household."[89]

Combined with an emphasis on food—not only unique dishes to Korean culture (e.g., ddukk/rice cake), but also Korean barbecue (e.g., kalbi/short ribs)—is the incorporation of Korean drinking culture. Viewers of *asianish* already familiar with Matthews from *akaDan* (2014) will know that the two-part episode five "How to Drink Like a Korean!" does not show his first time imbibing soju (Korean rice liquor).[90] Yet, Matthews and Steve Lim's interactions with *K-Town Cowboys* cast members, Danny Cho, Shane Yoon, and Angie Chung, create a sense of camaraderie whereby the adoptee is invited into a part of Korean and Korean American culture. Korean Americans are positioned as arbiters of Korean drinking truth, teaching Matthews soju and beer drinking games that many adoptees learn as they explore their Korean identities. Korean drinking games are a staple of Korean culture—so much so that celebrity chef television personality Anthony Bourdain highlighted Korean drinking culture in his Seoul episode of *Parts Unknown*.[91]

asianish exposes how an authentic Koreanness is intangible; throughout the web-series, Matthews is always engaged in performance. He is never just *being* Korean—it is always done through an interlocutor—a Korean American who is at least second generation—and involves enacting competency through the consumption of food or drink. For example, when he learns more about *dol*—the 100 days celebration for Korean infants—he performs the ceremony.[92] Given a hanbok to wear, Matthews is taught about the history of the hanbok and the traditions associated with dol. Serving as his samchon (uncle), Steve Lim, and his imos (aunts), Jen Chae and Grace Park, are positioned as gatekeepers to Korean and Korean American culture. Matthews is always in the role of the student.

Playful and fun, Matthews offers a nonthreatening perspective of adoption. He focuses on the interactions and relationships developed between adoptees and Korean Americans and questions about what it means to be Korean. This particular perspective lends itself not only to understanding the every adoptee, but also the limitations of historical conceptualizations of diaspora that assumes cultural competency is transferred between parent and child. This assumption is why knowing the norms of Korean food and drinking culture is critical for many adoptees as they assert their identity as members of the Korean diaspora. The superficial performances of cultural markers—language and food—remain at the crux of what it means to "be" a good Asian (American) subject. This may also be seen when members of ethnic minorities are all encouraged to "wear their traditional clothing" to professional events as it assumes all individuals share a particular set of cultural experiences.

Yet, truly fascinating is how *asianish* creates a new narrative to understand what it not only means to be adopted, but also to be Korean American. Matthews's identity exploration underscores how ethnic identity is not a fixed concept that is readily transferrable. Yes, one can learn more about Korean customs (e.g., *dol*), food, and drinking culture, but this does not erase adoptees' lack of

Korean cultural capital. At the same time, viewers witness how adoptees are continually working toward establishing an identity whereby it is okay to learn Korean culture.

The Adoptee as Author

Whether it is through the earliest iterations of adoptees asserting their mere existence as agents of their own experiences or in adoptees' deployment of Web 2.0 technology, Korean adoptees engage in various forms of self-definition. I suggest that these various means—print and online media—allow adoptees to create snippets of stories that are easily consumed in a single sitting. Hilde Lindemann Nelson notes, "To be optimally successful, a counterstory must be culturally digestible and widely circulated, taken up not only by those who are on the receiving end of abusive power arrangements, but also by those who have benefited from those arrangements."[93] These various autobiographical productions are just that—narratives consumed both by those touched by adoption and by individuals with no affiliation with this particular form of family making and unmaking.

Unlike the critiques lodged at adoptee print writings, Matthews's web-series *asianish* presents adoptees' identity negotiation in easy quick bites for viewers to consume. His deployment of humor offers a new perspective to understanding adoption's impact on adoptees. The medium of YouTube generates a level of perceived accessibility with Matthews, which is not offered by longer documentaries and print texts. He encourages viewers to take part in getting to know him as well as others on the episodes via additional Web 2.0, tools such as Instagram and Twitter. This level of interaction between Matthews and viewers facilitates an intimacy not offered by other platforms. He also maintains his separate YouTube channel—DANakaDAN—for viewers to interact with him outside of his work for ISAtv. Blurring the personal and professional, Matthews offers an endless array of options for his fans, including adoptees.

Autobiographical texts illustrate how adult adoptees move toward a process of self-definition, even as ambivalence in a fixed identity is apparent. In their individual and collective states, the anthologies are narrative acts of insubordination, shifting and even rejecting the master narrative of the mythical adoptee.[94] These writings may be labeled as acts of ungratefulness. Nevertheless, the fact that these works are even contested highlights adoptees' disruption of the master narrative. Their cumulative cultural productions reflect the multitude and diverse experiences of the community without running the risk of producing reductive narratives and parroting mainstream discourse's assertions of humanitarianism and child rescue. Adoptees' autonomy over their lived realities also involves resistance and an intentional construction of specific aspects of their adoption experience. Building upon this investigation of adoptees' holistic identities, the next chapter examines the everyday lives of adoptees and their perceptions of self, family, and the adoptee community.

CHAPTER 5

Adoption in Practice

Adult Adoptee Reflections

Engaging adult adoptees at the personal level and looking beyond the macro-level of the transnational adoption industrial complex (TAIC) reveals the complexities of what it means to be an adopted person. Whereas the previous chapter explored adoptees' autobiographical print writings, this chapter analyzes thirteen adult adoptee oral histories. Oral history offers a more comprehensive lens to consider how adoptees experience the world outside of narratives found in anthologies, memoirs, or documentaries. The incorporation of oral histories accounts for the voices of those who might be considered the every adoptee—the adoptee whom mainstream society wants to root for as they engage in their adoption journey—and those not involved in the adoptee community in deliberate ways. This reflects my commitment to investigating the dynamic and diverse adoptee community. If we only hear from voices garnering attention in print and online media, we risk overlooking those who may be limited to participating in nonpublic ways (e.g., local community groups). We also risk excluding those individuals who lack access to public platforms as a result of individuals' varying access to systems of power such as socioeconomic status. Their collective voices cannot be dismissed. Ignoring their perspectives means eliding the position of authority that all adoptees inhabit concerning the legacy of the TAIC on the adoptive family and the adoptee, in particular.

We must recognize the value in the every adoptee experience and incorporate their accounts in mainstream adoption conversation. The every adoptee, as a reminder, is seen as the apolitical or nonpolitical counterpart to the adoptee killjoy. Their perspectives offer an opportunity to better comprehend the significance of adoption practice in the lives of adoptees that may not be directly engaged in activist projects. In doing so, I expose the inherent messiness involved when living within the TAIC. A latent ambivalence is evident not only when the every adoptee discusses their families and the adoptee community, but also when they consider adoption in its entirety from relinquishment and social death to return to Korea and engagement with adoption in adulthood.

Oral history rescues the memories of marginalized populations from obscurity and validates their histories as significant. Gary Y. Okihiro writes, "Oral history offers an alternative way of conceptualizing history and a means by which to recover that past."[1] These oral histories situate this project within an expanding body of work advocating for the inclusion of adoptees as experts. This sample is not intended to be representative of the overall adoptee population. Instead, it is intended to address a limitation of the existing adoption studies literature, where the primary authorities on adoption are not adult adoptees themselves but, rather, adoptive parents or adoption practitioners with no experiential knowledge of adoption. Yet adoptees are the ones *living* the experience. Oral history empowers Korean adult adoptees and situates them as authoritative transnational adoption experts. This approach legitimizes adoptees' experiences unlike the ways in which their voices are routinely invalidated and rendered irrelevant to adoption discussions.

Oral histories account for how adult adoptees interact with one another. Kim Park Nelson notes, "Exchanging stories is an informal ritual of socialization among Korean adoptees."[2] These oral histories complement existing case studies of the adult adoptee community.[3] This chapter offers the opportunity to consider what it means to negotiate everyday life outside of the media gaze and positions adoptees as theorists and knowledge producers. Oral history ensures that not one voice or dominant perspective found in anthologies, memoir, or film controls the adoptee narrative. These narratives cannot be considered generalizable, as all oral histories are subjective. However, the goal of this chapter is to highlight the voices of those adoptees that may not be engaged in adoptee communities made visible in print and online texts as well as documentaries. This monograph's examination of multiple modes of expression by adoptees, including static and dynamic representations, provides opportunity for contrasting these different modes of engaging memory.

By building upon the foundations of adoptee knowledge, I suggest their expertise is a theoretical turning point to deepen our analyses of adoption. This chapter is in conversation with the works of Kristi Brian, Sara Docan-Morgan, Kim Park Nelson, and Mia Tuan and Jiannbin Lee Shiao, who examine Korean adoption from the perspective of adoptee oral testimonies.[4] I am particularly interested in Docan-Morgan and Park Nelson's examination of adult adoptee reflections on childhood and their engagement with the adult adoptee community and return to Korea. Brian also synthesizes adoptees' perspectives with those from adoptive parents and adoption practitioners, exploring the public and private spheres relationship to adoption practices. Cumulatively, this scholarship offers opportunities to consider how adoptees articulate their racial, ethnic, and cultural identities. I expand upon these investments, shining a much-needed light on the lived realities of adopted persons with its focus on the abstract concepts of family, citizenship, and national belonging. This chapter captures a critical moment in how adoptees discuss retroactive citizenship as oral histories were conducted when the issue first gained growing attention within the adoptee community.

This chapter centers thirteen oral histories (nine women and four men). Oral history participants were recruited in four main ways. First, I posted an announcement on my personal Facebook page. Second, I reached out to local and national adoptee-led organizations. Third, I posted messages on Listserves for adult adoptees and adoptive family members. Finally, snowball-sampling techniques were employed where I relied on adoptee networks to share information about the study to their friends. Interested parties reached out via email. From June 2012 to March 2013, I collected two audio-recorded oral histories with each individual via video chat or in person. In addition to transcribing the audio recordings, I took extensive field notes. I met twice with participants in order to account for any changes in their involvement in adoption-related issues. Each meeting lasted between thirty minutes to two hours due to participants' various engagements with the adoption community. Semistructured in nature, the interviews provided a framework to elicit responses exploring themes of family, community, activism, and citizenship. To protect their anonymity, all oral history participants are identified by pseudonyms.

Their testimonies elucidate the intertwined and complex relationship between the adoptive family and American citizenship. Their voices expose the tensions produced by social and legal citizenship in discussions concerning the recent cases of adult adoptee deportations. Adoptees' insights on citizenship also provide a needed perspective to how "family" is defined and the role of racial difference within adoptive families. These oral histories make evident the adoptee practices to construct kinship with birth families and the wider adult adoptee community. The discussion of kin relations outside of the adoptive family makes clear that adoptees' fluid understandings of kinship are implicated in other facets of their lives. These individuals also reveal the impact of social death—severed from their birth culture and families—and the lack of Korean cultural capital on their sense of self.

This collection of voices reflects the diversity found within the wider adult Korean adoptee community and provides an opportunity to locate the various segments of the adoptee community. Their engagement with the adoption community ranged from individuals active in adult adoptee associations and the adult adoptee counterpublic to those involved with adoptive family organizations to individuals with limited to no contact with other adoptees. Adoptees may also find their engagement evolves during their lifespan, whereby once active participation in an adoptee community may ebb and flow. Recognizing the community's nuanced nature, Robert, a fifty-two-year-old adoptee from the Midwest, reflected:

> It's funny because one thing we have in common is that we are adult adoptees. But you can meet adult adoptees and go like, "Wow. We're really totally different people." And that's great, too. And that's part of the strength. . . . But what is interesting is what people want out of their association with other adoptees is also very different. Some do want to socialize and that's great. Some want to develop deep friendships. Some want to advocate on particular causes. So I think people come into the community with very different expectations.[5]

The examination of discrete adoptee experiences reveals the limits of adoptees' deployment of what Eleana J. Kim calls contingent essentialism, whereby adoptee identity manifests itself as simultaneously a natural or biological connection and culturally or socially constructed.[6] Oral history exposes the fragmentation that exists within the adult adoptee counterpublic and wider community.[7] Their voices provide a lens to create a more holistic portrait of the adoption experience filled with nuance that cannot be reduced or generalized to a singular narrative. These adoptees may not espouse happiness and gratitude about adoption all of the time nor are they all angry and ungrateful. Instead, they exist on a continuum of adoptee affects ranging from the every adoptee to adoptee killjoy. Adoptees' self-narration functions as a mode of empowerment and site of disruption. Challenges to adoption's narrative of child rescue through competing and sometimes conflicting adoptee experiences ensures the TAIC will be held accountable for its very real and lived effects.

Being American as a Feeling of Belonging

Adoptees' awareness of anti-Asian racism was evident in their reflections on issues of citizenship and nation. At the same time, these adoptees spoke of their disillusionment with return to Korea and what it means to be "Korean." This is not to say that they disidentified as American; rather, their reflections demonstrate the tensions of transraciality, first discussed in chapter 3, and what it means to negotiate a hyperexposed body within a white family. The disjunctures produced by their multiple racial/ethnic and cultural identities are embodied by the way in which some families celebrate both the adoptees' birthday as well as their arrival day to the United States. Airplane Day or Gotcha Day is considered a cause for excitement by adoptive parents, representing the individual's entry into their American family. Yet, as we saw in the previous chapter, this cause for celebration also marks the multiple losses experienced by adoptees—the loss of birth parents, extended birth family, birth culture, and native language—and reinforces their social death. Nevertheless, I caution against discounting the positivity some adoptees associate with Airplane Day and Gotcha Day. For example, Amy, a twenty-nine-year-old from the East Coast, noted:

> When I was growing up we celebrated my birthday and the day that I was adopt [*sic*]—the day I came to this country, well came here [*sic*]. So I was born in February and I was adopted in May. So we celebrated my birthday in February and then, my parents called it Airplane Day, in May, which was the day, you know, that I arrived off the plane. So every year we'd go to a, like, very authentic Korean restaurant. Most of my immediate family would come, so it would be a really big deal, a really big celebration . . . and I would get presents and things like that. Almost a bigger deal than my birthday was, for whatever their reasonings were. So I always thought of it as very fun and very positive.[8]

While this occasion marks adoptees' entry into the nation, for Amy, it also became another yearly event to mark with one's extended family. When accounting for how Airplane Day and one's birthday are perceived as similar in importance, consider how Amy's arrival became normalized within the family. Her fond memories of Airplane Day celebrations may also be linked to her strong ties to her adoptive family. By treating it as another birthday, her family excitedly embraced their expansion and solidified their togetherness. While the consumption of Korean food may at first indicate their exacerbation of Amy's difference, I suggest that this practice was an effort of culture-keeping. Patronizing a Korean restaurant once a year to mark Airplane Day is similar to adoptees and their families making annual visits to a particular restaurant for any other holiday celebration.

The immediate dismissal of Amy's perception of Airplane Day as a sense of false consciousness undermines an adoptee's credibility as an agent of her experiences. Aware that some adoptees dismiss Gotcha Day or Airplane Day as a marker of erasing their Korean histories, I suggest that we cannot overlook the significance of these moments for some adoptees. One must account for the child's years within their adoptive family to understand the holistic experience of adoptees. These moments of arrival demarcate the beginning of their lives as Americans and the first of many instances of displacement caused by visible racial difference. The inclusion of this homecoming into their adoptive families incorporates adoptees into the U.S. nation-state. Re/birth is a tool in which these previously Korean subjects *become* Americans and the channel in which derivative citizenship is bestowed to adoptees. Airplane Day captures how adoptees became the exceptional migrant and overlooks the contradictions produced by the body of the adult adoptee of color. Their bodies remain the visible marker of difference, signifying that they do not *belong* within the normative white family.

To deepen my analysis of the disjunctures concerning adoptees' access to citizenship from childhood to adulthood, I locate these oral histories within debates concerning retroactive citizenship and undocumented adoptees, initially discussed in chapter 2. Their voices underscore how adoptees have varied understandings of why such citizenship should be bestowed on undocumented adoptees. Discussing his ambivalence, Matthew, a twenty-nine-year-old from the Mid-Atlantic region, noted: "It's not that I don't care, I do see how it is important—you know . . . especially, the retroactive citizenship. How those things are important to people. And because it is important to them, I'm not necessarily out there fighting for it, but it doesn't mean that I don't want it for them."[9] Matthew implicitly recognized how adoptees may operate under the assumption that they are citizens. While not versed in the legalities surrounding adoptees' undocumented status, he acknowledges the importance of retroactive citizenship even if it does not affect anyone he knows or himself. Adoptees' citizenship status is a consequence of what adoptive parents did or did not do for them as children. Cody, a twenty-eight-year-old from the East Coast, echoed Matthew's sentiments: "I think it's the right thing to do. It's not the adoptee's fault that they weren't able to file the paperwork."[10] Likewise, Claudia, a thirty-year-old adoptee from the Midwest, noted: "I am 150% behind it. I feel like, especially as children and one of the most vulnerable populations, you cannot retroactively hold them responsible for not jumping through those legal loopholes."[11] To contemplate reasons why adoptees' status as noncitizens should warrant removal from the United States is unfathomable. The presumption was that adoptees' parents' American citizenship outweighed the legality of one's status—undocumented or naturalized. Addressing adoptees' unique status as an isolated immigrant within their adoptive families, Kim Park Nelson notes,

> Although adoptive parents have to go through lengthy legal and immigration procedures as part of the adoption process, the procedures are different from those required of other immigrants. Adoptive families can avoid contact with immigrants (and, therefore, any association of their children with immigrants) if they wish, in their dealings with the [United States Citizenship and Immigration Services].

This perspective underscores adoptees' positioning as the exceptional exception. It is no wonder that adoptees fail to contextualize themselves and other adoptees within frameworks of migration and immigration. Their entry to the United States is facilitated by a mechanism whereby their parents never need to see their children as immigrants; instead, adoptees are seen as extensions of the *American* family in the immigration pathways offered by adoption, as discussed more in depth in chapter 2. Consequently, these adoptees' responses implicitly reflect the privilege associated with adoptees' status as derivative citizens.

When considering how many adoptees arrive as infants or toddlers, it is no surprise that Matthew, Cody, and Claudia entered the United States between five months to fourteen months old. Like many adoptees, the three of them were socialized into American culture from a young age and recognize how fortunate they were to have parents who completed naturalization for them while they were minors. They contend that it is problematic to penalize a segment of adoptees that were not fully aware of their immigration to the United States as minors or the necessary procedures to obtain citizenship. Their understanding of retroactive naturalization is tacitly linked to how re/birth signals the incorporation of the adoptee into the U.S. body politic. The possibility to be rendered outside the nation is foreclosed by embracing adoptees as *American* vis-à-vis re/birth and social death. For adoptees that agree retroactive citizenship should be bestowed to their adoptee compatriots, not providing this avenue for naturalization erases the violent histories that brought them into the United States. Further, any adoptee could be undocumented, given the arbitrary nature of adoption whereby children were considered interchangeable. There was no guarantee that the family in which an adoptee was placed would pursue all the steps to complete naturalization. Thus when we discuss notions of gratefulness, we need to reframe gratefulness as a lens to understand adoptee affect. Gratefulness and gratitude must be seen as part of a broader logic concerning care and well-being, a discourse that allows for individuals to be grateful for naturalization or entering homes where abuse was not an everyday occurrence. Blanket statements calling for all adoptees to be grateful for adoption fail to acknowledge how adoption's effects are uneven and arbitrary.

Processes of transculturalization may also directly affect adoptees' perspectives on why retroactive citizenship is an important issue. Parental racial blindness and emphasis of how racial difference was merely accidental because, according to the old colorblind adage, "underneath their skin, they were all the same," impacted adoptees' sense of self. A feeling of belonging shaped their support for retroactive citizenship. If it were not for their re/birth and integration into adoptive families, these individuals would lack ties to cultural whiteness and the white privilege that adoption bestows. Adoptive parents' investment in banal multiculturalism—the celebration of difference is limited to tokenized moments of inclusivity with little to no historicity of racial injustices—influences how adoptees consider themselves as American.[12] For example, Amy said:

> I definitely think that it is something that is very important. . . . I couldn't imagine . . . in my opinion, being American or, you know, hyphenated Asian American . . . but really being American and finding out as an adult that suddenly you're not eligible to live here and having to go to . . . not just a different country, but a completely different culture than what . . . how you've been raised with your family and the country that you've lived in your whole life . . . when in my opinion you really are American.[13]

Here, Americanness is not tied to legal citizenship. Rather, it is linked to social citizenship and cultural capital. Amy's response also may be linked to her self-identification as adopted-Korean and Jewish/Italian in adulthood. As a child, she considered herself Jewish/Italian. This strong connection to her adoptive parents' heritage speaks to her claiming strong affiliation toward the United States. Similarly, Jessica, a thirty-two-year-old from the Midwest, reflects on how the original intent of adoption practices was to secure a "forever family." She stated, "Well obviously, I'm for retroactive citizenship. I think the basis has been fascinating—that rhetoric of forever families and what it means to be in your forever family. If that's the global America or your nuclear white family."[14] Her sentiments exemplify the embedded nature of the trope of forever family in adoption discourse—it is believed as truth, reflecting adoption's perceived permanence. Invoking the notion of the adoptive family as the "forever" family,

Jessica directly speaks to rhetoric concerning how these parents were deemed "good," "fit," and "reliable" in comparison to biological parents or the Korean state. This construction of adoption as placing children into forever families is linked to the insistence of arrival day as the birth of adoptees as *American citizens*.

While adoption is constructed as one of hope and promise, the uneven ways in which adoptive parents followed through in naturalization and the limited ability agencies have in enforcing adoptive parents to naturalize the adoptee raises questions concerning the standardization of adoption practices. Ashley, a twenty-nine-year-old from the East Coast, recognized, "It's a case of broken systems on our end that kids could actually be adopted to the United States and not be naturalized properly. It's terrible that agencies don't follow through with the wherewithal, not that it's their responsibility, but that those cases happened."[15] The voices of Amy, Jessica, and Ashley reveal how conversations concerning retroactive citizenship do not affect everyone in the same way, underscoring their various levels of political engagement. However, their reflections make clear that retroactive citizenship seems almost natural and matter-of-fact.

Adult adoptees were cognizant of the retroactive citizenship campaigns' political nature. Speaking directly to the impact of retroactive citizenship within the adult adoptee community, Megan, a thirty-seven-year-old from the East Coast said, "It drives me crazy that adoptees don't consider themselves immigrants sometimes. . . . Immigration and citizenship is, of course, closely related and we're seeing it how it's been affecting adoptees more and more."[16] In linking adoptees to other immigrants, Megan compared the experiences of undocumented adoptees to those of the individuals who would be positively affected by the DREAM Act. She further commented, "I believe both groups are entitled to stay in the U.S. indefinitely as citizens." However, Megan does not place responsibility on adoptees' parents—biological or adoptive. Instead, she argued: "The people who chose that we would come to the United States are the adoption agencies . . . in the U.S. and in Korea. So this was a corporate decision. For that reason, there is even more of an obligation—moral obligation—to allow us to stay here, if that's what we want, because not all adoptees want that." Linking citizenship to a feeling of belonging rather than something bestowed by the state via naturalization, adoptees demonstrate how their families' investment in them as "future Americans" influenced their sense of self. Even as Megan expresses hesitancy to provide a blank check for adoptees' retroactive citizenship, she contends a moral obligation exists for retroactive citizenship to be extended for interested individuals.[17]

As discussed in chapter 2, we cannot assume that all children adopted within the last fifteen years will still gain U.S. citizenship, given the uneven nature of the Child Citizenship Act of 2000 on adoptive families depending on the visa issued to the child (IR-3/IH-3 versus IR-4/IH-4). We should remain skeptical similar to the unease displayed by International Social Service–American Branch officials concerning adoptive parents' ability and wherewithal to pursue naturalization for their children in the late twentieth century. The discoveries of abuse within adoptive families made by Kathryn Joyce and Megan Twohey in their investigations of evangelical Christian adoptions in the twenty-first century and rehoming—the underground practice of finding new homes for adoptees outside of the legal social welfare system—respectively, expose existing gaps in protecting adoptees from negligent adoptive parents.[18] When the United States and its forever families are touted as the best option, it's not surprising that adoptees fight for retroactive citizenship. Discussions of retroactive citizenship cannot occur without a deeper conversation concerning undocumented immigrants who arrived into the United States as minors. As noted in chapter 2, we must consider how adoption deeply shapes adoptees' sense of privilege when disidentification from broader immigration reform occurs.

While they orient themselves as American citizens, transraciality affects how adoptees discuss returning to Korea. This is not to say that all adoptees feel a sense of displacement. Rather, their individual experiences create a more comprehensive picture concerning the complexity of return, even as some adoptees feel at home in Korea. Recalling his first visit to Korea, Matthew noted: "I was curious to see whether or not when I got there if I would experience any culture shock just seeing so many Asians for the first time. Or if I would I feel different or strange in any sort of way. But when I got there, it felt pretty comfortable in that respect. I didn't feel like I stuck out."[19] Likewise, Megan recalled a similar lack of self-consciousness: "The best thing that came from that trip [in 2000 through the New York–based adult adoptee organization Also Known As, Inc.] was that I was able to really feel like I could claim Korea as my own because I actually had experienced it."[20] Their emphasis on feeling at home and an ability to claim the nation-state highlights how a return to Korea may be inextricably tied to one's negotiation of city-space and consuming Korean culture.[21] Reflecting on her first trip to Korea, Ashley echoed their sentiments: "I absolutely loved it. . . . It was definitely the first time I was exposed to an entirely different culture. I remember several times just standing on the streets of Seoul and taking it all in and feeling very whole and very impressed and kind of this is what I want to do—I want to travel and see how others are living."[22]

For these adoptees, even though their lives began in Korea, they returned to an unfamiliar place as a result of their re/birth upon adoption. Korea became Other.

Whereas some adoptees find themselves at peace or at least feeling comfortable maneuvering in Korea, not all adoptees readily found immediate solace or acceptance. For these adoptees, negotiating the land of their birth involved parsing through the entanglements caused by intersecting identities as ethnically Korean, culturally American, individuals in interracial relationships. Reflecting on her visit to Korea with her white husband, Lydia, a twenty-nine-year-old from the Midwest, noted a different type of racialized encounter in Korea. Discussing the assumption that she should "secretly know Korean" due to her ethnicity, Lydia said: "If we ever got lost, I would walk fifty feet behind my husband, so that he could walk around looking lost by himself and then people would self-select—English speakers would self-select—to go help him. So that was really frustrating as an adult."[23] She was unprepared for the cognitive dissonance her Korean body created in Korea and white privilege's significance outside of the United States. To "secretly know Korean" requires a racial performance that adoptees are unable to fulfill.

Her comments cannot be viewed as isolated. Adoptees routinely note that they are situated in a liminal space as a nonculturally Korean, non-Korean national in Korea. For example, Jane Jeong Trenka chronicles her experiences as a "functionally illiterate, deaf and mute" adoptee living in Korea in her second memoir, *Fugitive Visions: An Adoptee's Return to Korea* (2009).[24] Likewise, adult adoptee memoirist Katy Robinson recognizes how difference persists in her lack of cultural Koreanness. Discussing her struggle to re-create Korean dishes for her biological father, Robinson strains to connect with him and feels as if she's failing as a Korean, writing: "I couldn't speak Korean. I didn't look right. And I didn't know how to cook rice."[25] This alienation also impacts her interactions with other Koreans, including her biological family.[26] Lydia's frustration and dislocation in Korea must be viewed within a framework of shared experience. And yet, while adoptees may be prepared to experience this sense of loss and discomfort due to knowledge circulating within the adult adoptee community, it cannot erase the actual lived experiences of adoptees. Even as adoptees are aware of the displacement that may occur, it does not prepare them for the reality. Memoirs by Trenka and Robinson as well as the essays in the anthologies discussed in the previous chapter demonstrate how adoptees continually negotiate these complexities associated with what it means to be *authentically* Korean.

These moments of cognitive dissonance cannot be constructed solely as moments of paralysis. Susan, a thirty-six-year-old from the Midwest, mentioned a similar disjuncture to Lydia's unease. She recounts, "I think that when I first got off the plane and began interacting with other Korean nationals, their shock that I couldn't speak Korean, that I couldn't function in the same way they did as nationals just for basic things like buying a bus ticket, I think that was a direct confrontation with the loss that I had known about in the abstract, but in terms of being there physically in Korea, really grappling with it and embodying it."[27] A nine-time visitor, Susan continues to negotiate what it means to be Korean in her identity while in the nation. Participants' travel to Korea involved confronting different cultural expectations as well as adoptees' lack of social capital. Even as Susan's experiences with Korea evolved over time, for others, their initial experience shaped their understanding of the nation. Robert recalled,

> I wanted to see what it would be like. . . . It was, I have to say, extremely alienating though. . . . Well, I basically have come to realize that I would never fit in there in anywhere. So I've kind of given up a certain . . . like the first two times [I visited], I really tried to . . . everyone could tell we had Western mannerisms, but I tried to Koreanize a little bit. By the third time, I was kind of exhausted from it. . . . But, I've just come to realize that to interact with more traditional Korean Koreans is never going to be easy or comfortable to me.[28]

His candid examination of his time in Korea underscores how adoptees contradict implicit and, sometimes, explicit beliefs concerning how to behave like a Korean—whether it has to do with speech, dress, or knowledge of cultural nuances. The possibility for assimilation into Korean culture was never an option for him. As he attempted to "Koreanize" his mannerisms, he repeatedly felt as if he was not being himself. With an emphasis on "fitting in," Robert attempts to assert his authentic self, even if that means that he will disengage from striving to be "Korean." In many ways, Robert's decision is similar to Trenka's proclamation: "Because of [my adoption] *I have consciously decided not to try to assimilate; I cannot do it twice in one lifetime.* During my time on the margins of Korean society, I have lived among others who also cannot undo what has already been done to them."[29] No longer is "blending in" critical in asserting a specific national and/or cultural identity. Language is only a marker of difference, not a marker of subjectivity.

Adoptees cannot then be viewed as deficient replications seeking to mimic Koreanness, regardless of whether this is how they perceive themselves. Rather, they embody a new overseas Korean subjectivity that recognizes the legacies of adoption and its impact on shaping the Korean populace. The individual experiences highlight how return is multifaceted and that adoptees may continue to have incongruent reactions to the nation. To expect all adoptees to have identical reactions due to contingent essentialism or an alleged, innate need for acceptance marginalizes those individuals who feel disconnected with Korea or are uninterested in return.

Their discussions of retroactive citizenship and return to Korea shed light onto the role of dual citizenship and the F-4 visa on the Korean adoptee community. Formal recognition by the Korean government that confirms their status as "Korean" raises new questions concerning the validity of adoption as well as adoptees' cultural/social citizenship in Korea. Adoptees disrupt a static notion of "Koreanness" in Korea similar, yet different, ways than the burgeoning population of mixed race Koreans with Korean fathers and Southeast Asian mothers. Dual citizenship and the F-4 visa also raise questions concerning the veracity of adoption and the documents that aided adoptees' migration to the West. As noted in chapter 1, orphanages and adoption agencies were complicit in fabricating details to render children adoptable. Adoptees must utilize their orphan hojuk (family registry) even if they are reunited with their biological families to gain dual citizenship or the F-4 visa. The falsified family registry demonstrates the complicity of the state and nongovernmental organizations in adoptees' social death. Yet, rhetoric concerning adoptees' reincorporation to the nation is lauded. Focusing on adoptees' new access to a Korean identity via their legal standing erases how the state facilitates adoptions vis-à-vis fraudulent adoptions and continues to send children abroad.

Access to dual citizenship and the F-4 visa obscure the processes both internal and external to the state that facilitated the adoption. These two immigration tools reflect the Korean government's desire to erase its complicity in removing multiple generations of children from the nation. This erasure cannot compensate for adoptees' lack of cultural capital and inability to claim membership on their biological families' hojuks, if in reunion, because their adoptions were predicated on falsified orphan hojuks. If dual citizenship and the F-4 visa remain predicated upon the falsities in adoption records, what does this mean for adoptees who have reunited with their birth families? Ruminating on her Korean familial ties, Susan said:

> I'm uncomfortable with dual citizenship with regard to how the Korean government recognizes us as Korean citizens, but not necessarily as the children of our parents. . . . For instance, my mother right now is trying to

find a way to add me to her registry. She can't do that because I was illegally registered as an orphan [by the orphanage]. . . . And she can't register me as her child. If I do dual citizenship it's not a way to sponsor her or recognize her, it will be further reification of my so-called orphan status. It will be further government recognition of that orphan hojuk identity, which is a false, kidnapped identity.[30]

The adoptees' initial childhood social death cannot be overcome even as the F-4 visa and dual citizenship aim to reincorporate adoptees in the nation-state. The orphan hojuk creates a false divide between the role of the Korean government and orphanages in rendering children adoptable. Since the adoptee is created vis-à-vis their orphan status, the orphanage maintains the fiction that all of these children are unwanted while simultaneously absolving the Korean government from acknowledging the role its lack of social welfare supports have in dissolving biological families. To pick and choose when adoptees are welcome as subjects reveals the inconsistencies of whose lives hold value— children of unwed mothers or low-income families versus adults with Western cultural capital.

Adult Adoptees Reflections on Family

As adoptees negotiate the way in which citizenship—real or imagined—functions in their daily experiences in the United States and Korea, the concept of family is central to understand what it means to belong. Legitimacy and legibility remain in conversation with discussions concerning "realness" and questions of "what if." As noted in chapter 3, Korean adoption redefines what it means to be an Asian American or white family vis-à-vis the practice of transnational, transracial adoption. Yet, it is important to locate how adoptees discuss and reflect on the everyday realities of family. Oral history participants described how their perceptions of family evolved. Reflecting on their childhood understanding of family, they initially discussed how their adoptive parents and early relationships influenced their definition of "family." Megan noted, "I think as children we always consider our family as our immediate—people who live in our house with us, maybe our grandparents, cousins, all of those people with relationship names. And as you get older, you become aware—your family becomes your spouse."[31] Likewise, Tom, a fifty-two-year old from the West Coast, reflected: "I just assumed family was whoever you were living with when you grew up. . . . The factors would be whoever takes care of you when you're growing up. From a simplistic point of view, because when you're growing up, you're kind of small. You don't have that deep of thoughts and think whoever is surrounding you is family."[32] This conceptualization of family as inclusive of immediate and extended family members does not explicitly mention adoption. Rather, Tom's statement underscores the importance of socialization and the influence of how families normalize adoption. By positioning adoption—and, by extension, re/birth—as a normal method of family formation, adoptees may not question how family is shaped by genetic-relatedness.

However, adoptees are impacted by rhetoric concerning *realness*. Even as adoptive families deploy a postmodern understanding of kinship whereby adoption and biology coexist, this does not mean society at large has this progressive understanding of family. Due to the primacy placed on genetics and knowing one's roots, whether it is through the construction of family trees in elementary school or intrusive questions concerning an adoptive family's legitimacy, the language of blood lingers in the background. Discussing his own understandings of kinship, Matthew reflects:

> There was a period when I first found out I was adopted that I had to define for myself what "real" was . . . when you're young, when I found out my first thought was that my adoptive parents were not my "real" parents. And I mentioned that to my mom one time, and I really hurt her. It took me awhile to figure out who "real" parents were. So I guess I never really thought about the definition of "family" as far as parents go, I sort of took my adoptive parents as my "real" parents, birth parents as just that—they gave birth to me, and they are blood-related, but that's as far as it goes because they haven't had any hand in my development or who I am as a person.[33]

Grappling with what adoption means in his life, it is clear that the question of *real* is inextricably linked to who parented him. Nevertheless, he realizes how as a child the focus on *realness* as linked to biology deeply hurt his mother. The focus on genetic ties obscures the bonds forged vis-à-vis adoption. This binary understanding of family—adoptive versus biological—is steeped in traditional kinship beliefs of adoption mimicking the genetically related family.

The impact of the "dictionary" definition of family was evident in adoptees' discussions of families—birth, adoptive, and choice. Matthew's perspective of family is not unique as these oral histories revealed how societal perceptions of "family" directly affected adoptees. Rebecca, a forty-three-year-old from the Midwest, reflected: "You can't really get away from how family is described and conceptualized in the media, popular culture, in the books that we read."[34] Aware of how normative kinship rhetoric shapes conversations concerning adoption, Laura, a twenty-three-year-old from the Midwest, commented:

"Yeah. I mean [popular culture] doesn't change my opinion though. I have definitely gotten opinions of, 'They're not your "real" family.' I can see how society tries to influence it."[35] Popular culture's emphasis on genetics routinely undermines adoption, even as we see nonnormative families, including adoptive families, on screen in recent years. For example, in the final season of *Sex and the City*, viewers watch Charlotte York Goldenblatt (Kristin Davis) and Harry Goldenblatt (Evan Handler) struggle with infertility. While the couple eventually adopts a daughter from China, viewers witness the *biological is best* narrative in the season six premiere. Discussing their infecundity, Harry comments, "We'll adopt or something." Charlotte quickly replies, "But they wouldn't be your own."[36] Her emphasis on a child as one's own is firmly positioned as the only possibility with adoption as a second or, perhaps even avoidable, option. Even as the couple eventually adopts, it is clear that this would never occur if biological pregnancy occurred.

Adoption is also used as a comedic method for film and television to create distance between family members. This is seen in Marvel's *The Avengers* (2012) when the Black Widow (Scarlett Johansson) comments that Loki (Tom Hiddleston) killed eighty people and his brother Thor (Chris Helmsworth) replies, "He's adopted."[37] Loki's adoption is offered as an explanation for his deviancy and villainous nature, implying that if he was genetically related to Thor, he too could be an Avenger. While it may be easy to dismiss this as inconsequential, the utilization of adoption to explain away perceived difference subtly emphasizes the fact that genetics are the *real* ties that bind. In doing so, the media implicitly and explicitly shapes the public's perceptions of adoption. Adoptees find themselves and their families scrutinized as seen in Laura and Rebecca's statements. If one's exposure to adoption is only through media, a skewed and perhaps pathological understanding of the practice and adoptees may arise. In turn, adoptive families are undermined, routinely relegated as a *less than* option.

Given adoptive families' awareness of how mainstream society scrutinizes and judges adoption, it should be no surprise that re/birth has become the main method to legitimize adoption as an equal form of family formation. Re/birth muddies the waters concerning legal, biological, and social forms of parenthood. Focusing on the point of arrival to the United States, re/birth provides adoptees a similar origin story offered to biological children. Airplane Day and Gotcha Day provide adoptive families the opportunity to share the joy of their child's "birth." Considering how adoptees are routinely socialized to express gratefulness for adoption and find their histories in Korea are erased to facilitate their re/births, this should not be a surprise. To this end, Jessica said: "Yes, I think in the beginning I would have only said my adoptive family. I almost said my blood family, I meant legal family."[38] Matthew echoed such an immediate reaction to biology: "I guess blood . . . people who are blood-related to the people who have adopted me."[39] These hesitancies concerning adoption and biology as the same, if not interchangeable, expose the complications of re/birth rhetoric.

While adoption legally constructs families, it cannot be seen as a concept that yields the keys to happiness. We cannot assume all individuals maintain strong ties with their adoptive families into adulthood. Even as he is aware of how society defines family, within what he discusses as a "limited intellectual, conceptual framework," Robert stated: "It would be strange for me now to say that my cousins from my adoptive mother's side of the family are family because we have no contact. So it would be kind of odd to say that we're family."[40] Likewise, Susan noted that although legally she remains her adoptive parents' heir and linked to them in the eyes of the American and Korea governments, she "no longer consider[s] them family."[41]

Family must become disentangled from normative kinship beliefs in order to account for the ways in which not only adoption but also choice affects definitions of family from childhood to adulthood. To assume adoptees will remain tied to their adoptive families overlooks how families, in general, evolve in response to events including death, divorce, estrangement, and separation. Since the notion of gratefulness remains inextricably linked to adoption, adoptees that fail to maintain links to their adoptive families are negatively depicted and pathologized. In doing so, it becomes clear that adoptees and, by extension, their families are held to a different standard concerning the need for positive connections throughout one's lifetime compared to biological families. Like their genetically related counterparts, families linked by adoption also shift over time. And not all adoptive families are the idyllic families envisioned in child-saving adoption rhetoric. A holistic definition of kinship that recognizes how relationships ebb and flow is necessary to ensure that adoptees and families who maintain fraught and sometimes disjointed ties with one another are not marginalized as defective.

In recognizing that family is a fluid term, these adoptees possess a progressive understanding of family. A common thread in their definitions of family was a focus on individuals who stand by one's side. Amy said: "[Family] is people you love and they love you and raise you . . . you know. I guess make sacrifices for you and you for them."[42] Similarly, Cody noted: "Family, I think for me, is someone who has your back. Someone who can support you. It doesn't have to be blood. . . . It's definitely someone who is always going to be there to support you no matter what kind of decisions you make in life."[43] Claudia's definition is slightly broader incorporating those "who voluntarily stay around and help you and love you and care for you."[44] Instead of being confined to a narrow definition promulgated by normative culture, adoptees in adulthood gained access to broader notions of "family." Comprehensive definitions of family reflect how adoptees may find themselves in search of a community that recognizes their holistic experiences as adoptees, including the negotiation of their identity as Korean or identification as persons of color. Ashley echoed the theme that family is composed of individuals who remain by your side, revealing: "I think my definition of family is really my support systems. So it's, you know, my adoptive family, but it also includes a lot of my really close friends and supporters that I've had throughout my life. I would consider them family."[45] The inclusion of adoptee perspectives that explore how their definitions of family evolved provides insight into how adoptees concretely experience their transracial, transnational families. At the micro-level, family is no longer tied to conceptualizations of white or Asian American.

Defining family as connections based on origin—biological and adoptive—and choice, adoptees address the evolution of family, whereby it is no longer tied to normative, *real* kinship. Their emphasis on intimate bonds and friendships speaks to the deployment of adapted and adopted understandings of familial structure in nonnormative relations. When separating racial affiliation and identification from adoptees' conceptualizations of family, we also see the ways in which traditional understandings of kinship become absorbed in nonnormative families.

The Complexity of the Adoptee Community

To investigate where the deterritorialized adult adoptee community converges and diverges, this final section foregrounds adult adoptees' perspectives on the counterpublic, including where they locate themselves within it. These perceptions range from their superficial understanding of community based on contingent essentialism bounded by similar racial/ethnic features and a cultural white identity to a more critical viewpoint that sheds light into the community's internal dynamics. Merely being adopted does not necessarily translate into feeling a direct kinship toward other adoptees. For instance, Amy noted:

> Coming into later adulthood, [it has been] nice finding other Koreans or any other Asians who have been adopted who have a similar experience because there is a part, physically, visually and who I am is still Korean, despite how I may act, or how my family may have raised me.[46]

Her comment reflects the immediacy and familiarity other adoptees discuss concerning their initial encounters with the adoptee community. As a new-comer to the adult adoptee community, Amy emphasizes the ease in which intimate bonds can be forged with other adoptees. Contingent essentialism offers adoptees the opportunity to forge familial bonds. By focusing on com-monalities, no explanations about their families or feelings concerning iden-tity are needed.[47] This is deeply important for adoptees who may have found themselves grappling with the tensions produced by a binary identity structure that marks them either as grateful or ungrateful.

An individual's status as an adoptee provides a link that creates an invisible bond for many newcomers and individuals who actively participate in the wider adult adoptee community at local, national, and international levels. Captur-ing this instantaneous affinity between adoptees was Robert's reflection on his decades-long engagement with the adoptee community. Recalling his first adoptee event in 2000 as life-changing, he noted:

> For the first time in my life, I had a peer group. The way I describe it was, I grew up feeling like a Martian who had landed in a spaceship and when I went to my first adoptee mini-gathering it was like happening upon a convention of Martians in spaceships. And, I remember how electric it was for me. I was sitting around a table with people I had never met. I had known them for five minutes, and we were finishing each others' sentences.[48]

Contingent essentialism provides the groundwork for many adoptees, early on in their communication with the wider adoptee community, to readily share intimate details of their lives. This is one of the first times they realize there are others out there with similar experiences. Jessica captures this moment, openly noting: "As part of this community, it was the first time I didn't think of myself as having to pass. In the Korean American community, I always felt like I was passing. It was really refreshing. I could be Korean, American, and adopted. Everyone knew what that was and understood that."[49] These recollections of their "first times" with other adoptees expose how the instantaneous connec-tion among adoptees is a feeling of kinship.

Other adoptees discussed this heterogeneity differently. For instance, Re-becca deconstructed the community into age groups, noting that older adop-tees, who may be legacies of the Korean War, "seem very reluctant to criticize" adoption, while adoptees who arrived from the late 1980s or later are "still very much in the stage where they want to just explore Korean identity."[50] At the same time, Matthew distinguished activist and nonactivist adoptees from one another when he said: "It seems like the people who are most ferocious about the adoption community or about adoptees seem to be the ones with the most pain in their lives . . . but I don't think that, you know, there are divides in the adoptee community whether they think adoption is good or bad, some people can be ambivalent."[51] I include this quote not to pathologize adoptees, but rather to consider how the members of the community characterize one another. In other words, how do adoptees view individuals who are vocal in wider adoption discourse? Accounting for this varied composition of the adoptee community, Susan discussed how the heterogeneous community consists of a network of centers, such as the repatriated adoptee community in Seoul and European adoptees proactively engaging with the Korean consulate, in addition to digital networks, including Facebook and Listserves.[52] By accounting for the cleavages found within the community, these adoptees intervene in the master narrative that reifies either a monolithic adoptee community or creates an unjust binary of a community divided by happiness or anger.

As adoptees establish deeper ties to the community, their responses provide a more complex picture of the community.[53] Contingent essentialism becomes disrupted as adoptees recognize how their entrance into and maintenance of ties to the community evolves over time. Describing the adoptee community, Lydia said:

> Like a dysfunctional family. We can't help but be tied [to] one another because being a Korean adoptee is beautiful. We can't change this fact about ourselves. We can't reverse it. It's sort of like being born into a particular family. People can't help it. So we are a family. We can never escape this identity. This family is dysfunctional.[54]

While the label "family" addresses contingent essentialism, the dysfunctionality underscores how various members come to be and remain affiliated with the community for multiple reasons. Dysfunctionality calls attention to how all families, for better or worse, operate in peace and conflict with one another. To pretend families are smooth sailing overlooks how affiliations with family ebb and flow over time.

At the same time, this assessment reflects the initial reactions the majority of my participants had to the question, "how would you characterize the adoptee community?" Many of them laughed and indicated a hesitancy to openly discuss the community. Even as these adoptees presented varying views of the adoptee community, they also revealed a desire to portray adoptees positively. Their honesty and discomfort reflects a palpable fear concerning the exposure of fragmentation within the adopted community. Aware of how adoptees are routinely pathologized and negatively depicted, Jessica recalled: "I feel like as an adoptee, I felt like I had to perform Korean Americanness and portray adoptees in positive images because we're already battling against other negative images."[55] Her statement highlights how adoptees may consciously perform a specific type of outward affect to ensure an affirmative portrayal of adult adoptees. Claudia also noted a similar investment.[56] Their reflections reveal how adoptees may consciously execute a specific type of outward identity to promote an affirmative portrayal of adult adoptees. I suggest that oral history participants' apprehension to discuss the community reflects a propensity to ensure that only one type of image is put forth to mainstream society.

An emphasis on a singular, positive experience directly engages the binary framework concerning happiness and gratefulness versus anger and ungratefulness. Adoptees are tied to a respectability adoption politics that is aware of the negative portrayals of adoptees within reductive frameworks that situate adoptees that critique adoption as angry. To be vulnerable in public spaces and acknowledge the fragmentation, adoptees are cognizant that they may support pathological narratives of the overall community. Yet this self-censorship and ambivalence to disclose the cleavages within the community inadvertently allows the propagation of generalizations whereby only the loudest voices are heard. In doing so, the varied perspectives and nuances of adoptees' lived experiences and the minor affects associated with the adoptee killjoy and every adoptee may be lost.

Their collective common experiences remain useful when thinking about the wider implications of adoption in future generations of adult adoptees. As adoptees continue to create community with one another, connections are forged and renewed. For example, the once disparate deterritorialized community is finding itself becoming more organized. Ashley commented, "When you go to different [adoptee] conferences and meet folks, the adoptees that were adopted in the fifties and sixties are like, 'wow, we never had these resources.' And then when you go to different cities there are so many resources now. It's great."[57] The creation of networks allows adoptees to reexamine what it means to be an adopted person and aids their negotiation of identity. When multiple voices speak of crises occurring within identity negotiation or of the fraught nature of reconciling multiple "families," it becomes clear that it is no longer useful to dismiss certain voices because what they say is hard to hear. Instead, these similar experiences shed light onto the complex lived realities adoptees face from childhood to adulthood.

Adoptees reposition themselves in the overseas Korean diaspora as they reinsert their personal experiences into the multiple histories of Asian immigrants living in the United States. Oral histories offer an avenue to reconsider the similarities of the adopted person's experience articulated in the anthologies discussed in chapter 4. While their voices may amplify themes found in the anthologies, this collection of oral histories deepens and complicates assumptions concerning adoptees' negotiation with family and community. More importantly, their voices capture a distinct moment when retroactive citizenship entered adoptees' conversations as the issue of adoptee deportation garnered the broader adoptee community's attention. These were the early days of adoptees discussing the issue, before the coalitional politics and activism work associated with #CitizenshipForAllAdoptees discussed earlier in chapter 2. The individuals featured in this chapter provide a sample to interrogate notions of citizenship and family, as they intersect with questions of gratitude and adoption. Their oral histories provide a theoretically robust sample to address questions about Korean adult adoptees lived experiences, which cannot and should not be relegated to the sidelines.

By recognizing lived realities as knowledge, we transform who the authorities are on adoption. Ignoring their voices continues a cycle, whereby academics, adoption practitioners, and adoptive parents routinely speak on *how* adoptees feel, think, and act. These individuals' voices are powerful and the more we listen to these everyday thoughts and perspectives of adoptees, we will transform adoption discussions in mainstream media. The following chapter shifts our examination of adoptees to focus on their activism, specifically their individual and collective online efforts to enact change and advocate on behalf of a comprehensive adoption conversation that does not elide their expertise.

CHAPTER 6

Adoptees Strike Back

Who Are You Calling Angry?

The internet provides adoptees new avenues to disrupt the traditional depiction of adoptees as children, recuperate their subjecthood, and instantly engage wider debates found in the transracial, international adoption community. In November 2014, domestic and international adoptees came together on Twitter to assert their voices during National Adoption Awareness Month with the #FlipTheScript hashtag. Originating with the adoptee-centric, independent writing collaborative Lost Daughters, the hashtag launched an open-ended dialogue on Twitter for adoptees and their allies to engage in frank and honest conversation about the everlasting effects of adoption. #FlipTheScript centers adoptees' voices, as they routinely are overshadowed by adoptive parents. The momentum garnered from the campaign resulted in adult adoptees appearing on local Fox News affiliates in New York, Washington D.C., Chicago, Minneapolis, Philadelphia, and Detroit. These interviews highlighted the work of adoptees across the nation, providing a face to decades-long activism that laid the groundwork for the campaign's success. The initial momentum garnered from the hashtag resulted in *#FlipTheScript, Adult Adoptee Anthology* (2015), edited by Rosita Gonzalez, Amanda Transue-Woolston, and Diane René Christian. The hashtag's success in the creation of a sustained dialogue should not go unnoticed. Through their online activism, adoptees make clear that it is their time to be heard and they will no longer be silenced. Adoptees' online exploration of their racialized identities as part of collective activism provides a unique vantage point to the adoptee experience.[1] Here, I want to differentiate between the use of online technologies for artistic productions (e.g., Dan Matthews's *asianish*) from adoptees' engagement in activism to reframe narratives of adoption and assert adoptees' expertise on adoption.

Internet communities circumvent the physical borders produced by location in that individuals, previously alone, enter into kinship with one another across space, place, and time.[2] Cyberstudies scholarship exploring deterritorialization and reterritorialization of racialized groups aids my examination of adoptees' networked collectivized voice and engagement in broader conversations concerning the politics of transnational, transracial adoption.[3] Beginning with the popularity of Listserves in the 1990s, the last decade has seen Web 2.0 technology advancing the rate in which adoptees may engage with one another. Adult adoptees forge new friendships as a result of their online interactions. Quick media (e.g., Facebook, Twitter, Skype) facilitates spontaneous synchronous and asynchronous communications that provide an ever-present connection.[4] Yet these online articulations are fraught with tension as they disrupt mainstream adoption narratives and encounter the reductive dichotomy that positions adoptees as either grateful and happy or ungrateful and angry. The digital age is the realm in which "national, racial, and ethnic identity is articulated, reified, and re-created."[5]

In flipping the script, adoptees publicly conflict with the neoliberal proadoption regime by questioning, confronting, and dismantling the popular adoption narrative. Previous chapters exposed the messiness of living within the transnational adoption industrial complex (TAIC); this chapter elucidates what happens when adoptees fight back against the TAIC. Online communication offers adoptees immediate opportunities to critique the TAIC and its repercussions on twenty-first-century adoption practices.

By coming together online in adulthood, adoptees are no longer the voiceless and marginalized peoples of the twentieth century relegated to a state of perpetual childhood. This attention on children de-emphasizes the fact that adoption is a lifelong process and overemphasizes the plight of the most needy—infants and toddlers. By focusing on what many would describe as some of the most vulnerable populations, adoption is painted in a warm light—one that results in happy endings and good homes for at-risk children. This narrative investment overshadows their maturation into adulthood. Discussing only the most defenseless of adopted bodies—children—reifies the binary of grateful versus ungrateful, because in what world would anyone want a child to grow up in what many would consider poverty or degradation? The characterization of adoptees as children allows them to be continually *spoken for* as objects in need of rescue and saving under a rubric of Christian Americanism.

Adoptees' assertion of their adulthood dismantles what John Raible characterizes as adultism—the process that occurs "when well-meaning white adults make decisions about the fate of dependent children of color."[6] Adultism reflects how adoptive parents and practitioners fail to consult or take into account the perspectives of adoptees themselves. This perspective delegitimizes adoptees as knowledge producers and renders them perpetual children. And yet what is absurd about this labeling is the fact that many Korean adoptees (and adoptees in general) are parents and grandparents themselves. Adultism also results in adoptees' critiques of adoption becoming pathologized in mainstream discourse. Adoptive parents such as journalist John Seabrook position adoptees' lived experiences as "bittersweet," "just bitter," and "acutely painful."[7] In many instances, these adoptive parents are unable to intellectualize adult adoptee recollections outside of their personal experiences. Dismissal of adoptees' childhood and adulthood realities makes it clear that some adoptive parents lack openness to learn from adoptees. By not taking adult adoptees' experiences seriously, it becomes clear that not all perspectives on adoption are equally valued.

Disentangling childhood from adoption, adoptees assert their agency via internet activism. Unlike adoptees' print texts and oral histories, their online interactions reflect their immediate engagement with an issue in the adoption community. No longer are adoptees bounded by time. Rather, the fast-paced nature of quick media facilitates an ease in which adoptees may transmit information to one another and their allies across oceans and countries. This chapter elucidates the impact of adoptees in their deployment of online tools to shift mainstream adoption discourse. First, I investigate adult adoptee reaction to the 2007 the *New York Times'* Relative Choices blog and the posts by Korean adoptee and former Evan B. Donaldson Adoption Institute Policy Director, Hollee McGinnis. She also cofounded Also Known As, Inc.—a New York City adult Korean adoptee organization. The Relative Choices blog sought to explore the complexities of adoption but was criticized for its skewed Christian American and Orientalist perspective. The *Times'* Relative Choices blog reflects the nascent stage of adoptees deploying the Internet as an activist tool. Second, I examine the controversy surrounding a July 2012 Minnesota Public Radio (MPR) broadcast concerning the recent decline of international adoption and their failure to incorporate adoptee voices. In reaction to censure by adoptees and their allies, MPR featured two adult adoptee academics within the field of Adoption Studies and an adult adoptee memoirist four days after the original broadcast. Finally, I explore the #BuildFamiliesNotBoxes hashtag that arose to critique the utilization of baby boxes as a tool to create orphans. Baby boxes allow children to be relinquished anonymously as the child is placed in an incubator-type enclosure. This particular line of inquiry explores the ethical implications of baby boxes as a method to procure children. Cumulatively, it reflects the changing informal dissemination methods between members of the adoption community. This chapter locates adoptees' interventions in conversations concerning what it means to be an adopted person and the significance of adoptees' inclusion in mainstream media. Adoptees no longer just exist within the TAIC; rather, they have become change agents seeking to dismantle the TAIC's hold on adoption discourse.

Mainstream Inclusion, Censorship, and Questions

In fall 2007, the *Times* launched its monthlong Relative Choices: Adoption and the American Family blog, which featured posts from members of the adoption triad and adoption professionals.[8] Included in the posts were well-known voices, including Jane Aronson, an adoptive mother and founder of Worldwide Orphans Foundation, as well as journalists, such as Jeff Gammage, Gloria Hochman, and Tama Janowitz. Both Gammage and Janowitz are adoptive parents. Their narratives included themes of family legitimacy, transmitting "native" culture, the initial meeting of their child in his/her birth country or their arrival to the United States, and adoptees' medical needs. Gammage recalls multiple instances of being asked if his daughters are his "real" children and the "relative who laments that I never had 'children of my own.'"[9] Even as they discuss their families' encounter of intrusive questions due to their transracial composition or how they embrace a multicultural outlook, the narratives perpetuate dominant perceptions of adoption. For example, Dr. Aronson pathologizes orphanages, conjuring images of horrid conditions featuring the smell of feces and urine with soiled infants and toddlers existing isolated with little human contact.[10] These broad generalizations validate the dominant narrative of adoption as an act of humanitarianism with little conversation on the causal factors concerning why conditions are poor.

Domestic and international adoptees from Korea, China, and Vietnam were also featured as part of the wider blog. Their narratives explored the negotiation of racial, ethnic, and cultural identities. The authors asserted the legitimacy of their adoptive families as *real* families and explored the often intrusive questions associated with return to one's sending country if internationally adopted and birth search. These authors critiqued the reductive binary framing of adoptees' behavior and the invisible constraints that hindered open conversations between adoptees and adoptive parents concerning adoptees' origins.[11] Nevertheless, they presented a palatable experience to *Times* readers, which implicitly positions them as grateful. These posts create a false binary of "us versus them," whereby perceived outliers in the adoption triad ("angry adoptees" and "thoughtless adoptive parents") are viewed as radical and not part of the mainstream.

My interest in the blog stems from the controversy surrounding the newspaper's positioning as a "gatekeeper" for only specific types of adoptee and adoptive parent experiences to be told via its national platform. The *Times* filtered comments to the posts, resulting in the censorship of adoptee posts critical of Relative Choices content. Addressing this issue, Korean adoptee and adoptive parent blogger Paula O'Loughlin wrote, "[I]t is clear that the adoptee's point of view is seen by many as just a mere aside to the discussion about adoption."[12] O'Loughlin's criticism underscores statements discussed in the previous chapters regarding the need to ensure that adult adoptee voices are finally heard as active participants in the adoption triad—adoptive parents, birth parents, and adoptees. The *Times* contributed to a historical absence of adopted persons in mainstream conceptualizations of adoption by censoring adult adoptee critiques of portrayals of adoption.[13] To guarantee that the censored adoptee voices were heard, Jae Ran Kim, reposted adoptees' comments on her blog, Harlow's Monkey, a well-known resource for adoptees, adoptive parents, and adoption practitioners.[14] Adult adoptees proved that their speech could not be contained in the circulation of their counterpoints online.

What is most troubling is the way in which adoptees' dissent was obscured when it challenged the narratives by adoptive parents. In response to Tama Janowitz's blog post about her daughter's adoption from China, Korean adoptee blogger Sarah Kim turned to her own blog to share her comments after the *Times* censored her submission.[15] She took offense with Janowitz's flippant tone. Janowitz writes:

> A girlfriend who is now on the waiting list for a child from Ethiopia says that the talk of her adoption group is a recently published book in which many Midwestern Asian adoptees now entering their 30s and 40s complain bitterly about being treated as if they did not come from a different cultural background. They feel that this treatment was an attempt to blot out their

differences, and because of this, they resent their adoptive parents. So in a way it is kind of nice to know as a parent of a child, biological or otherwise— whatever you do is going to be wrong. Like I say to Willow: "Well, you know, if you were still in China you would be working in a factory for 14 hours a day with only limited bathroom breaks!" And she says—as has been said by children since time immemorial—"So what, I don't care. I would rather do that than be here anyway."[16]

Janowitz's deployment of the terms "bitterly" and "resent" to discuss adult adoptees' reflections on their childhood and adolescence reifies stereotypes of angry versus happy adoptees. Her language pathologizes the birth culture and places primacy upon the adoptive culture. In addition, her allegation that she saved Willow from becoming a child laborer epitomizes the type of racial microaggressions deployed by adoptive parents to remind adoptees why they should be grateful. Responding to this particular comment from Janowitz, Sarah Kim writes, "Parents who make this kind of statement do two things: 1) reinforce the 'savior' myth by showing how bad & dirty the Third World is and how lucky the adoptee is to not live there and 2) guilt the adoptee into being 'grateful' for being adopted."[17] These messages reproduce the trope of gratefulness. Constructing the adoptee (regardless of age) as a petulant child who should feel lucky about their adoption, Janowitz exhibits what transracial adoptee Lisa Marie Rollins deems as "m/paternalism" because adoptees are not grateful for living here (in the United States) versus the mythical "over there."[18] The politics of adoptive parents such as Janowitz reflect a particular investment in framing adoption as routinely a *better than* practice. In other words, adoption is better than the alternative possibilities for adoptees and, as a result, adoptees should perpetually be grateful. This type of adoption parent politics overlooks and ignores the voices of those who have lived it—adult adoptees.

Even as the *Times* suppressed adult adoptee critiques while simultaneously giving credence to adoptive parent voices, we cannot dismiss the Relative Choices blog in its entirety. Featured adoptees disrupted mainstream percep- tions of adoption, even if their conclusions presented a "resolution" to their narratives. These posts may have provided a new, adult adoptee perspective to readers. More importantly, McGinnis's posts provide a new lens to look at what types of narratives are considered "acceptable" to mainstream press. Her narrative touches upon themes in adoptee print writings that may be unknown to the broader American public.

McGinnis thrusts open the door for conversations concerning the fact that adoptees had lives prior to their adoptions. Remarking that she "seemingly dropped out of the sky on a Boeing 747, walking, talking, and potty trained," she clearly notes the re/birth and trauma of adoption.[19] Her parents recall that in her first few weeks living in the United States, McGinnis would cry and repeat the phrase, "I want to go home" in Korean. As a three-year-old arriving in the United States, McGinnis had memories of her life in Korea and her adoption was a very large adjustment in her life—uprooting her from everything she knew. This incident requires the *Times'* readers to recognize how adoptees have a past in Korea instead of solely focusing the start of the adoptee's life as when they disembark the plane from Korea. She troubles the widely held belief that adoption "rescued" children from a life to which they would never want to return. While other adoptees document these early lives in Korea in print works, McGinnis's inclusion of this experience challenges reductive notions of adoption found in mainstream popular culture that believe adoptees will immediately adjust to their new surroundings.

At the same time, McGinnis recognizes the ways adoptees are both Korean and American. She requires readers to consider the juxtaposition of inhabiting dual identities. Adoptees are all too familiar with this task. However, for many non-adoptees, including adoptive parents, this struggle is unfamiliar and quite foreign. McGinnis acknowledges a hybrid existence of both Korea and the United States. Embracing her location in the interstices, she reflects, "the reality was that I was both [Korean and American]." Yet, she also recognizes the limitations of this hybrid existence. At age twenty-four, she returned to Korea as a "foreigner again," alluding to her first entry to the United States at age three.[20] Her sense of dissonance and location as a foreigner lacking familiarity with what many call the motherland—Korea—is similar to the other adoptees in memoirs and the oral histories discussed in the previous chapters.

The complexity of adoptee identity is amplified when McGinnis openly shares her internal struggles and debates concerning pregnancy and motherhood.[21] Expecting her first child, she notes that because she and her husband are both Korean American adoptees, they will be unable to pass along their genetic history. Instead, they will provide access to the culture of adoption and the fact that the ties that bind are not based solely on blood but on relationships. The most revealing sentiment in McGinnis's post is when she writes:

> I am relieved, though, that my child will not have to answer the question "Why were you born" the way I had to answer the question, "Why were you adopted?" *I am glad that my child will not be told by well-meaning strangers he or she is "lucky" to have been born. And I certainly won't tell my child to be grateful because I brought them into the world.* And if my child feels any gratitude toward me I hope it is because I earned it (emphasis added).

This passage highlights how adoption permeates adoptees' lives, making them susceptible to intrusive comments and questions because of the salience of racial difference between parent and child. No longer considered a private affair, transracial adoption triggers public responses and inquiries. Although some individuals may be well-meaning in their comments, McGinnis's statement illustrates the negative effects such statements have in the lives of adoptees. Assumptions of automatic gratitude must be negotiated, as adoptees will always be viewed as lucky when rhetoric that adoption is the best option proliferates.

McGinnis combines her personal narrative with a critique of Korea's continued adoption participation. Her appraisal is subtle for she weaves it with a discussion of her experiences on a motherland tour. Visiting an orphanage, McGinnis remarks, "*I got out*," and notes the questions that were raised for her, including: "Why with all the wealth in Korea were these children here? What were their prospects growing up as orphans? And who were their advocates? Who could speak for their needs and best interests? Who would ensure that they would get to live to their full potentials—and not simply survive?" In raising these questions to the *Times'* readership, McGinnis opens the door for a nuanced discussion concerning international adoption. She frames adoption to include the state actors involved by naming the nation's wealth; after all, Korea is one of the top fifteen global economies. Aware of the humanitarian motivations of the early adoption of Korean children, McGinnis also provides the reader context for why Korea still participates today and discusses the stigmatized position of unwed mothers in modern Korean society. Additionally, emphasizing the importance of ethical adoptions, McGinnis writes, "Ultimately, the challenge is how to balance the need to respect a child's right to his or her ethnic identity and cultural background against the known detrimental effects caused by early deprivation of a primary caregiver." She complicates transnational adoption from merely a black-and-white argument, asking readers to consider culture-keeping and interrogate the multiple apparatuses that gird the transnational adoption industrial complex.

This post becomes political, but without the loaded baggage associated with the adoptee killjoy, for McGinnis is still seen as a model adoptee. Her status as the good, happy, grateful subject is cemented by the fact that her criticisms are not lodged loudly or angrily by refuting narratives of loving adoptive families. In fact, McGinnis carefully constructs a narrative that engages individuals who may not necessarily be open to hearing the truths fueling adoption's continuance. Her work is powerful. She subverts the censoring that other adoptees experienced in the comment section of the series. McGinnis troubles discourses of gratefulness even as her writings find acceptance for appearing nonconfrontational.

The inclusion of adult adoptee voices as series bloggers is notable because it positions adoptees as experts on the adopted experience as opposed to relying solely on narratives by adoptive parents. To be dismissive of the *Times'* foray into adoption discourse ignores these gains made by adult adopted persons. McGinnis presents the conflicts of transracial, transnational adoption in a more palatable way to adoptive parents and the wider mainstream community that characterizes adoption as an "act of love" or humanitarianism. Her critiques of international adoption as an institution do not result in her positioning as an adoptee killjoy. Her posts engage readers without the confrontational tone attached to the censored comments by non-adoptee readers. In doing so, the dichotomy of adoptee behavior is upheld, whereby the censored commenters are "angry" and McGinnis is seen as "happy" and "well-adjusted." While the comments to her posts do not laud her as "well-adjusted," this dichotomy illustrates how adoptees are rendered "exceptions" through the inclusion of their narratives within the mainstream press over other adoptee narratives. Although she received a handful of critical comments, overall the commenters lauded McGinnis for sharing her perspective and how her posts reaffirmed their thoughts and feelings. However, it would be remiss to discount McGinnis as another "happy" adoptee. Her first post demonstrates the complexities of adoption by discussing her re/birth and the ways in which an adoptee's consciousness did not emerge until adolescence. She becomes framed as a "grateful" adoptee amid other criticism of the newspaper's blog by more "angry" adoptees.

Relegated to the Sidelines

While adoptees found their voices silenced in broader discussions found on the *Times'* Relative Choices blog, they also discovered a voice in their nascent Internet activism. As the tensions between the multiple stakeholders within the adoption triad come to the fore, I turn our attention to the Minnesota Public Radio's (MPR) roundtable discussion concerning the "precipitous decline" of adoption as a result of the United States ratifying the Hague Convention on the Protection of Children and Cooperation in Respect of Inter-Country Adoption in 2008, which is intended to provide worldwide standards to safeguard transnational adoption as a practice that serves "the best interests of children."

Designed in 1993, parties of the Convention who are sending countries must first find a home for the child within their nation prior to rendering a child adoptable for international placement. All signatories must create a central authority to regulate adoptions.[22] Yet the Convention applies only to signatories, and signatories may engage in adoption practices with nonsignatory countries. The effectiveness of the Convention is further challenged when one considers the fact that Convention signatories have faced suspension (e.g., Guatemala and Vietnam), while other countries (e.g., China, Russia, and Ethiopia) have found their adoption practices critiqued for not adequately securing the rights of the children involved.[23] Receiving countries, including the United States, still maintain ties to "sending" countries that have yet to sign the Convention. In the case of Korea, the government did not sign the Hague Convention until May 2013, but "there is no set date when South Korea will deliver its instrument of ratification or when the Convention will enter into force with respect to South Korea."[24]

Posing the question, "what does the future hold for international adoption?" the Minneapolis Public Radio host Tom Weber emphasized that this decline victimized children because it meant languishing in orphanages. Guests included Dr. Dana Johnson, cofounder of the International Adoption Clinic at the University of Minnesota; Maureen Warren, president of Children's Home Society; and Jodi Harpstead, chief executive officer of Lutheran Social Service of Minnesota. Both agencies featured on the panel facilitated many of Minnesota's intercountry adoptions from Korea. The panelists noted that while the movement of international adoption is declining, the number of children available for adoption worldwide is actually growing. Yet, Warren noted the need for caution as agencies "realign or reset" their international adoption programs. Rather than focusing on the "volume of placement," Warren finds that agencies and practitioners must be focused on ensuring children's safety.

Joining the panelists at the end of the segment was David McKoskey, an adoptive father and an adjunct professor of computer science at St. Catherine University. McKoskey focused on the increase in waiting times for adoptive parents. He echoed themes mentioned by Warren regarding how legislative changes resulted in a more unpredictable process: waits for children are extended and agencies are seeing greater numbers of older children (over the age of two years old), children with medical conditions, and sibling groups as available for transnational adoption. McKoskey was included to discuss his personal experiences as an adoptive father with waiting times, even though he lacks formal expertise on international adoption.[25] On a superficial level, it appeared as if his status as an adoptive father trumped any knowledge of an expert studying adoption in academia.

As Warren discussed "how much [agencies] are learning from adult adoptees," it was notable that only adoptive parents and practitioners were featured on the broadcast.[26] MPR faced criticism for overlooking adult adoptees in favor of adoption practitioners because the Twin Cities boasts an active adoptee scholar and activist community. Directly addressing this remarkable absence, Kevin Vollmers phoned the show and inquired about why MPR did not invite local adoptees to participate, given the high numbers of adoptee researchers and activists in the local area. Vollmers also asked the agencies to discuss their postadoption services, as many of the transracial adoptee placements enter predominately white communities. Weber noted that because the show focused on the legislative changes, MPR wanted to speak with the local agencies, and the question-and-answer period with phone-in participants was meant for other voices to be included. Addressing the second question, Warren discussed how agencies are preparing parents to discuss and recognize racism and how their children will have a different experience than the adoptive parents.

In response to Vollmers's question as well as criticism from adoptees and their allies, Minnesota Public Radio's Korean adoptee assistant producer, Meggan Ellingboe, posted a short piece entitled "What are your experiences as an adoptee?" on July 10, 2012.[27] Relying on first person anecdotes, Ellingboe provided sample questions and answers she and her family encounter due to their family's transracial composition. Her post received over fifty comments, many of which were from adult adoptees critiquing the negligence of MPR in their exclusion of adoptee voices. Their remarks echoed themes mentioned by Jane Jeong Trenka, who asked: "If adoption is really all about the best interests of the child (the adoptee, even if that child has grown into an adult adoptee), then why completely sideline the population that is at the heart of the practice you want to report on?"[28] Adoptees and their allies encouraged Ellingboe and Minnesota Public Radio to host a follow-up segment that included the expertise of adult adoptees. Their criticism resulted in a July 13, 2012, adult adoptee roundtable discussion featuring Adoption Studies scholars Kim Park Nelson and JaeRan Kim as well as Kelly Fern, adult adoptee memoirist of *Songs of My Families* (2011).[29]

Instead of continuing the conversation from the earlier panel concerning the decline of international adoption, the follow-up roundtable focused on how adoptive parents and adoptees negotiate race and culture difference. Panelists discussed the importance of socializing the child into communities of color and the adoptee community. Park Nelson noted that while the cultural aspects of culture camp may be superficial, the camps provide adoptees an opportunity to meet other adoptees and aid the formation of a network. At the same time, Kim warned that while it is important to allow adoptees to explore their birth culture, adoptive parents should be wary of cultural tourism (i.e., language lessons, consumption of Chinese food, trips to China) because such activities do not teach the child how to be Chinese American or Asian American. Both Park Nelson and Kim provided their professional expertise and discussed the need for adoptive parents' cultural competency and ability to understand how racism will affect their children. They focused on the fact that many adoptees are raised in predominately white communities and their ability to develop language and skills for coping with racism do not come until much later in life. Fern also recalled that as a child she avoided discussing issues of racism with her parents because of their lack of response and inability to relate to such incidents.

Many listeners were unsatisfied by the segment's focus on identity, rather than a more nuanced discussion of adoption policy. This frustration stems from the fact that the majority of the time when adoptees are included on adoption panels, they are asked only to speak to their experiences of negotiating identity and not asked to speak as experts. Using the platform of Land of Gazillion Adoptees, the precursor to Gazillion Strong, Vollmers held a follow-up podcast conversation with Park Nelson and Kim.[30] This conversation centered on questions submitted to the Land of Gazillion Adoptees blog by readers. Dividing the interview in five parts, Park Nelson and Kim were asked to discuss the following topics: the decline of adoption and the conflation of the Hague; the financial underbelly of adoption; adoption-based trauma, relevant issues for adoptees, and the adoptee community; and accountability legislation and representation of adoptees in literature, popular culture, and film. By facilitating questions to Park Nelson and Kim, Vollmers achieved something unaccomplished by others, including Weber. Namely, Vollmers reframed conversations of transnational adoption by positioning adoptees as experts and recognizing that adult adoptees are involved in a professional capacity in the field of Adoption Studies.

Redefining Family: Rethinking Adoption Practices

While adoptees' engagement with the *Times* and Minnesota Public Radio reflect their participation in disrupting mainstream portrayals of adoption, their use of Twitter—among other quick media tools—underscores their investment in directly shaping adoption conversations. Hashtags offer adoptees a distinct mode of intervention, one that can create a deterritorialized activist community linking individuals across the globe. One of the earliest deployments of a hashtag to unify the adoption community occurred in January 2014. Adoptees and their allies launched a protest against Korean Pastor Lee Jong-rak's baby box at the Jusarang Community Church in a working-class Seoul neighborhood.

Depicted in the documentary *The Drop Box* (2014), the baby box serves a site for anonymous abandonment of children. Nearly 400 children have been abandoned via the baby box since its establishment in 2009.[31] Pastor Lee and the box are praised in Christian media to "save" children.[32]

Responding to the pro-abandonment rhetoric promoted by the baby box, adult adoptee activist Laura Klunder developed the social media hashtag #BuildFamiliesNotBoxes to problematize the baby box during her tenure with KoRoot, an organization for returning Korean adoptees that promotes adoptees' human rights. In an open letter concerning the campaign, KoRoot writes:

> We believe that every person has the right to family, and that we have a responsibility to help preserve families that are targeted by economic and social injustices. Moreover, we are distraught by the media's celebration of the Baby Box as a humanitarian effort, while the fight for family preservation led by unwed mothers and adult adoptees has been overlooked.[33]

The social media hashtag aimed to raise increased awareness regarding how the baby box contributes to the breakdown of families. Adoptee activists in Korea locate these newly abandoned children within the larger historical narrative of adoption and the lack of supports for unwed mothers and low-income families. KoRoot also developed a black-and-white image that circulated across social media networks, such as Twitter and Facebook. The image depicts multiple types of families—single mother and child, single father and child, same-sex parents and child, and heterosexual parents and child. The simple and yet poignant tagline "How do you define family?" raises the question of whether two individuals simply make a family or if something more is needed. In response to this question, many adoptees and allies took to Twitter to discuss their definitions of family, using the hashtag to create an ongoing conversation of what kinship truly means. Complicating the narrative promulgated by Pastor Lee and the documentary, KoRoot and adoptee activists dismantled the inaccurate information concerning the need for a baby box. The #BuildFamiliesNotBoxes campaign moves the notion of family preservation to the forefront of adoption conversation and aligns with social justice advocacy work completed by Adoptee Solidarity Korea and TRACK concerning the rights of unwed mothers.

The campaign garnered intense support from the wider adoptee counterpublic. Adoptees located the baby box within a longer history of denied reproductive justice for Korean women and the erasure of children's rights to know their origins.[34] Korean adoptee and adoption activist Shannon Bae writes, "While I'm sure the intent is good, in the end, it does more to exacerbate the social problems that essentially force single moms in Korea to give up their

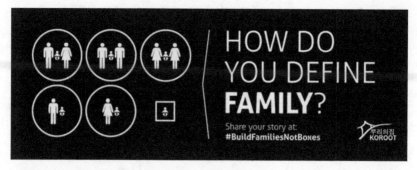

Figure 2: "How Do You Define Family?" This image arose as part of activism concerning the #BuildFamiliesNotBoxes campaign, which was in response to pro-abandonment rhetoric promoted by Korean Pastor Lee Jong-rak's baby box. Created by Tiemen Hilbers.

children. The answer is NOT to make it 'easier' for women to abandon their children, but to give them a TRUE choice to raise them."[35] The baby box serves as an emerging apparatus whereby the Korean state is absolved from helping parents, grandparents, or extended kin to raise the child. Since they are not formally relinquished, the children are ineligible for adoption. These particular children will remain in an orphanage until they age out.[36]

Children relinquished via the baby box are undocumented due to the absence of birth registration. Jane Jeong Trenka notes, "If you do not have birth registration, you do not legally exist. If you do not legally exist, it means that people can do whatever they want to do [with you]. You can be trafficked and you can be sold illegally for adoption."[37] Given these children's undocumented status, it is clear that they inhabit a similar position of those adoptees sent from Korea twenty to thirty years prior. In order for these children to gain legitimacy and state recognition, they—like adult adoptees—require registration with orphan hojuks. Moreover, there is a latent assumption that their biological parents willingly relinquished these newly abandoned children, like their adult adoptee counterparts, when there is no evidence that this is true.

Adoptees and adoptive parents in North America and Europe came together to raise the awareness of family preservation and challenge outdated assumptions of adoption offered in *The Drop Box*. They worked in conjunction with activists in Korea, disseminating information concerning the #BuildFamiliesNotBoxes campaign across social media (e.g., Twitter, Facebook) and online writings. Adoptees like SuLyn Weaver orient this debate within their own adoption histories:

They will likely never know their birth families or be adopted due to the absence of birth registration information required to legally relinquish a child. I am an adoptee in search of my past and my birth family. I seek answers to the questions I have regarding my abandonment, my life before, and from whom I inherited many aspects of my personality. As an adoptee searching, I cannot view the pastor's work as admirable but a theft of a child's family, history, and hope.[38]

Positioning the futures of these children within her history creates an accessible narrative for individuals who may initially believe the baby box solves a growing issue concerning the abandonment of unwanted children. Acknowledging the losses experienced by adoption and fictitious or poorly kept records, Weaver deftly challenges the notion that baby boxes are humanitarian. She raises the question of whether the deployment of baby boxes will launch a new generation in search of answers decades later.

This activism is not limited to the adoptee community. Addressing the rights of adoptees to this information, adoptive parent and activist Maureen Mc-Cauley Evans writes, "The goal of family preservation has to be the priority. Children should stay with their mothers and fathers, if it is safe for them. Also, children grow up. They should have the right to know who they are, the truth of their stories, even if they are adopted—maybe especially if they are adopted."[39] Echoing McCauley Evans's assertions, adoptive parent Margie Perscheid situates the rights of birth mothers alongside the rights of adoptees:

Suggesting that this [the baby box] is the only alternative a Korean woman will take to abandoning her child anonymously is a real affront to all Korean women. Loss of identity is not minor collateral damage, as baby box proponents suggest. Adoptees, who are the top experts on adoption, tell us very clearly that birth identity is critical to well-being. Adoptees are fighting for access to birth identity wherever it is denied them, including Korea, where baby boxes would take the fight back centuries. We should be fighting *with*, not *against*, them.[40]

Perscheid underscores the gravity of denying women the right to parent and children the right to know their parents. These two issues must be considered part and parcel with one another. For adoption to be a celebration of family formation, it also must be considered within the larger picture that results in the loss of family. The overarching themes emerging from adoptees and adoptive parents are the need to recognize the rights of individuals to know their truths and the detrimental effects of adultism and not listening to adoptees' voices on this issue. A holistic perspective that accounts for the voices of adult adoptees and those individuals who work with unwed mothers reveals why the baby box is a problematic solution for an ongoing systemic issue in Korea.

The need for these voices was further made evident in the film's U.S. debut, which was sponsored by Focus on the Family—a designated anti-Lesbian, Gay, Bisexual, Transgender hate group by the Southern Poverty Law Center. At the Los Angeles screening in 2015, Adoptee Solidarity Korea–Los Angeles (ASK-LA) held a teach-in outside of the theater aimed at raising awareness about the circumstances of unwed mothers. In raising awareness about the baby box, KoRoot, Adoptee Solidarity Korea, and their allies seek to dismantle a larger assemblage that routinely obscures birth families' and adoptees' rights. As part of their teach-in, ASK-LA revived the hashtag #BuildBabiesNotBoxes; developed a new hashtag, #ThinkOutsidetheBabyBox; and created handouts for passersby to deepen their understanding of contemporary Korean adoption. Generated by ASK-LA, these flyers prompt individuals to contextualize the phenomenon of the baby box within broader histories of women's inequality and lack of rights to parent in Korea, as well as Korea's international adoption participation. Directly commenting on the notion that faith, hope, and love fuels the baby box as a method to secure happy lives for these abandoned children, Figure 3 rhetorically asks individuals to contemplate the belief that "every mother has the right to raise her child with dignity." By deploying rhetoric used by pro-adoption individuals, ASK-LA creates a new narrative whereby compassion is placed on birth families, situating family preservation at the center of adoption narratives.

When contextualizing the #BuildFamiliesNotBoxes campaign against a worldwide understanding of baby boxes, it becomes clear that KoRoot, ASK-LA, adoptee activists, and allies are not outliers. In response to the rise of baby boxes across Europe, the United Nation Committee on the Rights of the Child argues such hatches "violate key parts of the Convention on the Rights of the Child (UNCRC) which says children must be able to identify their parents and even if separated from them the state has a 'duty to respect the child's right to maintain personal relations with his or her parent.'"[41] Reporting on the baby box phenomenon in Europe, Kevin Browne of the Centre for Forensic and Family Psychology at The University of Nottingham notes:

> There is growing evidence that it is frequently men or relatives abandoning the child, raising questions about the mother's whereabouts and whether she has consented to giving up her baby. You also have to ask whether an anonymous drop allows the authorities to check whether there's a chance for the baby to remain with its family in the care of other relatives.[42]

THE BABY BOX IS NOT THE ONLY OPTION

**Every mother has the right
to raise her child with dignity**

Faith
+Hope
+Love
=

**Having compassion
and supporting
unwed mothers
and their children**

#BUILDFAMILIESNOTBOXES #THINKOUTSIDETHEBABYBOX!

© 2015 MAGNA CITIZEN STUDIO

Figure 3: "Faith, Hope, Love." Stemming from the 2015 teach-in led by Adoptee Solidarity Korea—Los Angeles (ASK-LA) outside a screening of the film *The Drop Box* (2014) in Los Angeles, this poster requires viewers to consider what it means to promote adoption over a compassionate understanding of birth mothers' rights. Created by HyunJu Chappell/Magna Citizen Studio for Adoptee Solidarity Korea—Los Angeles (ASK-LA).

These comments echo the birth parents' rights discourse discussed earlier. Browne clearly underscores how a lack of accountability exists to ensure that these children were relinquished with the consent of the biological parents. Utilizing the baby box to mask the true causes for abandonment pardons the nation-state from helping its most vulnerable population. To accept baby boxes at face value overlooks human rights violations as delineated by the UNCRC. *The Drop Box* and the accolades given to Pastor Lee reflect an overwhelming desire to continue Korea's troubled history of abandonment and adoption with little attention given to adoptee voices.

Social media greatly impacts and amplifies adoptees' calls to action. Given their ability to rapidly share information from Korea with their adoptee peers elsewhere and allies, adoptees challenge the notion that they will be silent. Adoptees disrupt legacies that equate adoption with gratitude by questioning the logics and motivations behind adoption. No longer are adoptees voiceless. The deployment of #BuildFamiliesNotBoxes and #ThinkOutsidetheBabyBox by adoptees and their allies reveals the evolution in how adoption is understood. Instead, these individuals are in continuous dialogue with one another to create a more comprehensive and ethical understanding of adoption even if that means they are still subject to reductive characterizations of anger.

Adoptees Assert Their Adulthood

Adoptees' location as experts of their own experiences is fraught with tension. Individuals who challenge the elision of adoptee voices in mainstream conversations are seen as defective or unhappy about their adoption experience. Positioned as angry, these adoptees sit in direct opposition to individuals such as McGinnis or other adoptees whose voices are considered "acceptable" or "happy." And yet, McGinnis is not a passive participant blindly promoting adoption. I suggest that she, too, is an adoptee killjoy, but because her anger is not read as similar to other adoptees, she is positioned as happy. McGinnis is not taking an explicit activist stance in her critiques in comparison to individuals such as Jane Jeong Trenka or adoptees advocating for birth mother rights. Nevertheless, it is this lack of nuance in understanding how adoptees can criticize adoption in a myriad of ways that inhibits a deeper discussion of the manner in which anger manifests itself.

To be angry means that adoptees actively critique the chronic pathologization that renders them perpetual children. These adoptee killjoys also challenge their elision from history as legitimate knowledge producers regarding transnational, transracial adoption. Based on this understanding of "anger," I locate McGinnis as part of this broader community who actively reclaim their subjectivity. Challenging normative binary categories that frame the depiction of the adult adopted person, adoptees demonstrate the limitation of labels and need for a more expansive and nuanced understanding of the term adoptee.

Due to their assertion of agency and adulthood, adoptees find themselves finally being heard in ways previously unknown to them. Even as memoirs and anthologies proliferate, adoptees find their narratives being analyzed around issues of identity negotiation and not necessarily based on their critiques of the practice of international adoption. The online interventions discussed in this chapter reflect the multiple ways adoptees deploy the internet to their benefit. Whether utilizing the blogosphere to critique mainstream news sites, facilitating podcast conversations among adult adoptee scholars and memoirists, or implementing hashtag activism to raise awareness of an issue, adoptees are proving that they will not be silent. Digital media and artistic productions strengthen how adoptees and their allies communicate and critique the transnational adoption industrial complex.

Adoptees continually deploy online tools to intervene in mainstream narratives. The relevance of digital communication becomes particularly acute when considering adoptee activists' utilization of memes. For individuals, adoptees and non-adoptees alike, user-generated sites such as reddit, Facebook, and YouTube facilitated the increased popularity, creation, and distribution of internet memes. While memes gained popularity for their inane depictions of cats (i.e., lolcats) and use of the 1987 Rick Astley song, "Never Gonna Give You Up," for the means of "rickrolling," memes have also become a tool for activism. Limor Shifman writes: "Memes shape the mindsets, forms of behavior, and actions of social groups."[43] In the context of the adult adoptee counterpublic, the use of images shared between social networks is a new avenue for adoptees and allies to interact with one another.

As static art forms, memes capture a particular moment within international adoption discourse and history. Provocative in tone, memes challenge widely held beliefs or raise sensitive subjects concerning adoption. Their creators incorporate their knowledge of the transnational adoption industrial complex for satire. Memes reflect the twenty-first-century political cartoon. While they may be considered a lowbrow form of culture, memes are expressive and are not merely for comic effect. Rather, memes may also be a form of intellectual, cultural critique. Adoptees are able to summarize and capture information in smaller snapshots than blogs and even tweets via Twitter. Even as these memes may have a low rate of circulation vis-à-vis the number of Facebook "friends" linked to the disseminator, memes demonstrate the new possibilities for adult adoptees to engage the wider adoption community.

Figure 4: "Y U No Tell Me Black Kids Are Cheaper than Asian Babies?!" Meme. Deploying the sarcastic "Y U No Guy" meme, this image caustically critiques the adoption marketplace, whereby prices are attached to children's bodies based on race or national origin. Created by Anonymous and Kevin Vollmers.

Through politicized language associated with the meme, these individuals aim at the heart of discourse that centers adoption as an act of humanitarianism and child rescue. Memes dispel any fantasy of the adult adoptee as completely supportive of the practice of adoption. The creators reclaim the label "angry" through their criticism. For example, on January 14, 2013, an adoptee shared the following meme (Figure 4) that she developed with Kevin Vollmers.

The choice of utilizing the "Y U No Guy" meme speaks to the deliberate use of sarcasm to directly address the financial realities and inequities of adoption.[44] Viewers must reflect on their own prejudices and the legacies of racism that permeate adoption practices and policies. The meme capitalizes on the racial hierarchies found in both domestic and international adoption and the discomfort that results when such monetary values are placed on children's bodies.

Yet the use of memes is not limited to commenting on abstract concepts shaping the adoption industry. Engaging the American adoption industry's response to Russia's announcement of their international ban in December 2012, Vollmers released a meme (Figure 5) on January 14, 2013, in direct response to comments made by the Joint Council on International Children's Services.[45] Tom DiFilipo asserts: "It's been a cataclysmic implosion of intercountry adoption. It's truly the children who are suffering."[46]

Utilizing DiFilipo's own language regarding the "cataclysmic implosion" of adoption, Vollmers challenges the notion that the decline of international adoption is an issue for concern. After all, transnational adoptions continue globally even if the numbers are lessening, which is what Minnesota Public Radio discussed in the case study cited earlier in this chapter. Through the use of the rhetorical, DiFilipo's motives are questioned when considering whether the "best interests of the child" are in mind. Are members of the adoption industry more interested in keeping their consumers—adoptive parents—happy over ensuring the safety of the children involved? This broader question is critical to consider as many viewed the Russian ban as a death knell signaling

Figure 5: Tom DiFilipo/Tom Cruise Meme. The image engages the accusation that international adoption rates are decreasing through sarcasm. In doing so, the image challenges whether this decline should be of concern, implicitly raising the question of how the best interests of the child are served in adoption practices. Created by Kevin Vollmers.

the overall shift in adoption, where available children would decrease even as demand remained the same.

Within this particular meme, Vollmers capitalizes on implicit knowledge of Tom Cruise as an adoptive parent of two transracially adopted children (Connor and Isabella) with his former wife Nicole Kidman after the couple married in 1990. As an individual who has fallen from his status as a Hollywood legend due to his various media mishaps, Cruise also raises questions concerning parental fitness. His on-air television attacks against Brooke Shields on *Access Hollywood* and *The Today Show* and his emphatic declaration of love to Katie Holmes on *Oprah* in May 2005 raised questions concerning his stability.[47] Yet, there was little questioning within the media over his ability to parent and set a good example for his children. The utilization of Tom Cruise as the meme background calls all adoptive parents into question with the subtext that financial success does not translate directly into good parenting skills.

The two memes illustrate how social media continually facilitates new methods to intervene in adoption discourse. In the creation and distribution of memes, adoptees effectively garner attention to issues immediately affecting the adoption community. These memes are a twenty-first-century iteration of the political cartoon in that both lambast individuals, organizations, and governments, while also providing social commentary.

When considering the cumulative body of online adoptee activism, it becomes clear that the counterpublic and wider community will no longer be contained. The messages promulgated to sustain the TAIC are now questioned with vigor, openly and honestly online. Adoptive parents and practitioners can no longer overlook the expertise adult adoptees have as scholars and as laypersons on issues of transnational, transracial adoption. If the experiences of adoptive parents are validated, their counterparts in the adoption triad must also be viewed as legitimate. The adoptive community can no longer be viewed as a static concept that situates adoptive parents against birth parents or adult adoptees and divides adoptees into two groups of "grateful and happy" and "ungrateful and angry." Rather than castigating adoptee killjoys, I urge a closer reading of why this "anger" occurs and what triggers adoptees' responses.

Even as adultism persists, it is slowly dissipating as the tides of adoption discourse shift to one that recognizes the value of adoptees' lived experiences. Reflecting this change in mainstream media's acceptance of adoptees, Maggie Jones profiled adult adoptees living in Korea as part of the *New York Times Magazine's* cover story on January 18, 2015.[48] Jones complicates mainstream understandings of adoption, recognizing the value in learning from and listening to adoptees. Aware that while she is part "of a generation that is supposedly savvier and better educated about raising adopted children," Jones implicitly acknowledges that adoptive parents need to accept when and if their children question international adoption, and its failures, and whether they as adoptive parents worked to create a more ethical system.[49] Jones complicates the existing dichotomy that historically bound mainstream understanding of adoptees in her examination of the lives of adoptees living in Korea. Existing in the messiness of identity, Jones provides an avenue to hear multiple perspectives without pathologizing members of the adoptee community.

Conclusion

Considering the Future
of International Adoption

The long-standing relationship between the United States and Korea elucidates how a single program laid the groundwork for international adoption programs across the globe. The various actors—governments, adoption agencies, and orphanages—involved in adoption's rise never imagined the rate at which adoptees would return to their birth countries. While not all of these returned adoptees search for their families or return to live permanently, the influx of these migrants reshapes our understanding of adoption. There is no worldwide estimate for the numbers of adoptees who travel back and forth from their adopted and birth countries, yet it is clear by advertisements for homeland tours, adoptee-authored blogs, and Facebook groups that adoptees embark on these types of journeys. In the case of Korean adoption, adoption agencies and adoptee-run organizations facilitate homeland tours; adoptees are encouraged to study in Korea (e.g., the Inje Institute for International Human Resources International Korean Adoptee Program), and the triennial International Korean Adoptee Association Gathering draws hundreds of adoptees back to Seoul. Korean adoptees also may return under their own accord without program affiliation to live and work or volunteer in Korea.

As adoptees return to Korea, it is clear that they are being reincorporated into the neoliberal nation-state (e.g., access to the F-4 visa and dual citizenship). Korean nationalism is strongly encouraged and seen as a marker of pride for some adoptees. Examples of this patriotism include supporting Team Korea in soccer (football), purchasing LG and Samsung products, and embracing Korean food. In fact, often one's knowledge of Korean food and ability to eat a variety of dishes solidifies one's status as a "Korean" in the eyes of adoptees. Adoptees also arrive to the land of their birth as consumers ready to purchase their Korean heritage. From buying pottery in Insadong and clothes in Myeongdong to drinking in Hongdae and wandering around Namdaemun and Dongdaemun markets, adoptees consume Korea while exploring Seoul. This consumption renders the adoptee as a neoliberal figure in twenty-first-century Korea. The majority of adoptees are fluent in English and even if they are not, they still hold Western cultural capital by virtue of being raised in European countries, the United States, or Australia.

In considering the impact of adoptees' return, we need to account for the amount of money injected into the sending countries' economies. From flying Korean airlines such as Korean Air or Asiana Airlines to staying in Korean owned and operated hotels (e.g., Lotte Hotel and Resorts), as well as their consumption of products and food once in the nation, adoptees are a new type of consumer.[1] Not only were adoptees a boom to the economy upon their adoption, but also in adulthood, or even as youth, because if they return alone or with their adoptive families, they inject additional monies into the local economy.

This discussion has yet to mention the exchange of money and gifts between those adoptees in reunion with their birth families. Korea is known to have an exquisite gift-giving culture and, for adoptees in reunion, this often translates into purchasing American (for those adopted to the United States) gifts for their birth families. Adoptees routinely solicit their friends online and off for ideas of what to bring. At the same time, birth families may also save money to spend on the adoptee once they return. By taking their returned child to dinner or to travel around Korea, the family infuses new money that may otherwise be saved.

More importantly, reunion exposes the lasting impact adoption had on birth families.[2] Adoption is not the neatly tied bow on a child arriving in the West. Rather, adoption's real and imagined consequences become quite evident when recognizing the losses of birth families. From biological mothers who have held on to the secret knowledge of their child's adoption to birth siblings wondering what happened to their brother or sister, adoption leaves holes in families. To underestimate how adoption shapes and reshapes families in sending countries overlooks the psychological and social impact of giving up a child.

Recently, I personally witnessed the real and psychic legacies of adoption on birth families. Reunited in 2013 with omma (Korean mother) and appa (Korean father), the next few years involved meeting appa's wife, the offspring from both families, and extended family members. The melancholia associated with Korean *han* is palpable as no amount of words will bridge the chasms between us. Adoption left a permanent mark on our interactions—mediated through the use of my siblings' English language proficiency and Google and Naver dictionaries to translate. The intricacies of language cannot be overlooked, as moments are literally lost in translation between my biological parents and me. To pretend that language deficiencies do not affect reunion ignores the ways in which transnational adoption fundamentally disciplines adoptees bodies to gain new mother tongues.

Mapping the intimacies associated with reunion also is complex as it involves situating birth and adoptive families in conversation and constellation with one another. And yet, I recognize how I fulfill the normative requirements of the good, neoliberal adoptee subject. From flying Korean Air or Asiana Airlines and purchasing gifts for my biological family to the presents entrusted in my care to bring back to the United States for my American family, the commodities associated with adoption continue to grow. Love becomes commercialized. Gifts are the only visible way to attempt to mitigate the losses adoption causes between adoptee and birth family. This results in the most banal items carrying the weight of decades of uncertainty—uncertainty of reunion and what might be. Such products may range from eyeglasses and pajamas to undergarments and blankets. Perhaps the monetization of adoption will never end, at least not until the last of adoption constellations cease and adoptees' desire to consume their cultural identities are no longer. The adoption economy cannot be seen only as the funds transacted during the initial adoption.

Disrupting Kinship traces the multifaceted nature of adoption that not only affects institutions and governments but also families and individuals. The connections between the macro- and micro-level politics of the transnational adoption industrial complex (TAIC) cannot be overlooked. The TAIC is a lens to understand the rise of adoption and explore how kinship and citizenship are inextricably linked. The macro-level of adoption produces circumstances that facilitate the dissolving of biological ties in favor of adoptive ones under the rubric of "saving" children. Through complicating adoptees' citizenship, the adoptive family must account for its location as both a white and Asian American unit. The persistence of adoption as a method of family unmaking and remaking will no longer be viewed within a singular lens. The activism of the adoptee, birth parents, and their allies expose the inherent messiness of adoption and reveal that adoption cannot be discussed in black-and-white terms.

At the same time, the TAIC serves as a framework to examine what it means to be an adoptee because the TAIC always disciplines adoptee bodies even as adoptees challenge its norms and continued existence. Adoption's routine positioning as *better than* remaining in the country of origin regardless of treatment within the adoptive family or adoptive parents' completion of citizenship reinforces expectations of gratefulness. To be a filial adopted child, a presumption of automatic gratitude persists and shapes adoptees' experiences. The adoptee killjoy and every adoptee exist on a continuum of minor affects that arise in adoptees' critiques of adoption practices. Adoptees also continue to connect with mechanisms of the TAIC as they negotiate their identities and their relationship with the wider adoption community.

While the TAIC is not disappearing overnight, we are seeing what happens when its various tentacles are challenged and exposed for the falsehoods promulgated by adoption as humanitarian rescue narrative. Denmark halted international adoptions from Ethiopia in March 2013 due to concerns over the ethical practices of orphanage workers and orphanage conditions.[3] In February 2014, the United States Department of Justice charged four current and former employees of International Adoption Guides, Inc., an adoption services provider, with crimes including violating the rights of adoptive parents and children affiliated with their Ethiopian adoption program.[4] Acting Assistant Attorney General of the Justice Department's Criminal Division Mythili Raman notes, "The defendants are accused of obtaining adoption decrees and U.S. visas by submitting fraudulent adoption contracts signed by orphanages that never cared for or housed the children, thus undermining the very laws that are designed to protect the children and families involved."[5] As the twenty-first century progresses, it becomes evident that rhetoric of the best interests of the child can no longer be solely linked to having the child enter a home with "good" parents.

Attention to the corruption practices of the adoption market also exposes how this previously touted narrative is not a guarantee of a forever family. At the end of 2012, the American media became aware of abuses to Russian children and concerns of adoptees' safety. Headlines such as "Why Are Other Countries Wary of American Adoptions?" "Ukraine to Probe Foreign Adoptions," "Red Flags Wave over Uganda's Adoption Boom," and "Russia Seeks Interpol Investigation of Deaths in Adoptive U.S. Families" reflect heightened scrutiny over the alleged nefarious practices of orphanages, adoption agencies, and families who adopt across national borders.[6] Two months after a suspension in adoptions had been declared, a toddler adopted from Russia died in Texas in February 2013. Although his adoptive parents were eventually cleared of his death, initial reports alleged their culpability.[7] Russian unease was fueled following accounts of a seventeen-year-old adoptee that returned to Russia to live with his grandmother following a failed adoption. Russian news agencies report that the child was forced to steal to survive on the streets of Philadelphia due to maltreatment by his adoptive parents.[8] Concerned by the news regarding the welfare of Russian children in the United States, Yuriy Pavlenko, Children's Ombudsman under the president of Ukraine, visited Ukranian adoptees and their families on a four-day trip across the United States in the beginning of April 2013.[9]

The adoptive parents of Eastern European children are not the only ones facing scrutiny. Madoc Hyeonsu O'Callaghan, a three-year-old Korean adoptee, was murdered in his Maryland home in February 2014 at the hands of his adoptive father, Brian Patrick O'Callaghan, a top official at the National Security Agency. O'Callaghan was charged with first-degree murder and child abuse.[10] He was sentenced to twelve years in prison in July 2016.[11] Earlier in March 2008, Steven Sueppel murdered his four Korean adopted children and his wife in their Iowa City, Iowa, home.[12] These seemingly isolated incidents of abuse are part of a broader picture concerning inadequate post-adoption services and the safety of adoptees. The inadequacies of the American social welfare system for adoptees were made particularly evident by the exposés on adoption fraud conducted by Kathryn Joyce and Megan Twohey.[13] But for the young lives lost too soon and adult adoptees, including Adam Crapser, this particular attention to the systemic abuse within international adoptive families is too late.

Murders and abuse of adopted children as well as disrupted adoptions are not inventions of the late-twentieth and twenty-first centuries. For example, in 1959, *Coronet* magazine published an article highlighting the 1957 murder of a twenty-two-month-old Korean orphan adopted by proxy.[14] This death is not an anomaly for the decade. Studying proxy adoptions on behalf of Child Welfare League of American and International Social Service–American Branch, Laurin Hyde and Virginia P. Hyde, in their 1958 report, highlighted cases of children who experienced physical neglect or abuse or were placed in families with "persons grossly inadequate to provide care for them."[15] Hyde and Hyde discovered children beaten by adoptive parents and experiencing severe neglect as well as instances of rehoming. These early years of Korean adoption also included the disrupted adoption of a Korean child placed by Holt Adoption Program, whose adoptive parents were unstable and raised the child in unsuitable and unsanitary living conditions. The adoption was disrupted on behalf of the child's adoptive extended family that reported the abuse.[16] And yet, these known instances were not harbingers for stricter regulations or post-adoption services as the narratives of adoption as *only* child rescuing proliferated.

The best intentions cannot account for unseen abuses and legal oversights. Cases of abuse document how the TAIC aided the standardization of adoption practices, offering a unique lens for other countries to model monetary success and a how-to formula regarding adoption as a de facto social welfare option.[17] Korea's approach typified a successful international adoption program. Adoption became a rote process whereby government and nongovernmental organizations and actors easily facilitated the exchange of children and enabled Korea to maintain a weak welfare state. Yet even as adoption continues, this decade marks a shift in how the public consumes narratives of adoption. To ensure the safety for adoptees—minors and adults—their voices must be validated and recognized as truths and given equal weight in mainstream adoption discourse. No one will have a better sense of what it means to be adopted and live as an adopted person than another adoptee. The adoptee renaissance has arrived as the TAIC finds itself openly challenged. No longer is rhetoric of child rescue accepted without question; rather, adoption has become more nuanced to account for the rights of birth parents and adoptees.

Notes

Introduction

1. I utilize the term *Korea* instead of *South Korea* in accordance with how adoptees discuss where they are from in daily conversations.

2. See Marcas and Saka, "Assemblage"; DeLanda, *A New Philosophy of Society*; and Yu, "The Use of Deleauze's Theory."

3. See Tracy and Guidroz, *The Intersectional Approach*.

4. DeLanda, *A New Philosophy of Society*, 28.

5. Korean American adoptees address themselves as both Korean American and Asian American. The terms will be used interchangeably in this work because, when speaking about their location as Koreans and/or Asians in the United States, adoptees invoke both terms. Moreover, due to the racialization process of nonwhite ethnic minorities in the United States, "many ethnic minority people are often attributed not only ethnic, but also racial, labels and images by others—whether or not these labels and images accord with their own ethnic and racial identities"; Song, *Choosing Ethnic Identity*, 9. As ethnic Koreans, adoptees are subsumed under the racial label of Asian Americans. See also McGinnis et al., *Beyond Culture Camp*.

6. Briggs, *Somebody's Children*; Yngvesson, *Belonging in an Adopted World*. For a critique of the American domestic adoption market, see Riben, *The Stork Market*.

7. Marre and Briggs, *International Adoption*, 2.

8. Ibid., 17; Colen, "With Respect and Feelings"; Colen, "Like a Mother to Them."

9. Briggs, *Somebody's Children*.

10. See Dorow, *Transnational Adoption*.

11. Davidson, "These 7 Household Names"; Davis, *Are Prisons Obsolete?*; Schlosser, "The Prison-Industrial Complex."

12. Roberts, *Shattered Bonds.*

13. Staff, "The Wedding Industrial Complex"; Blakely, "Busy Brides and the Business of Family Life."

14. Pate, *From Orphan to Adoptee*; Oh, *To Save the Children of Korea.*

15. Box 35, Folder "Korea—General, 1961." In accordance to regulations by International Social Service–American Branch, please note that points of view in this monograph are mine and do not necessarily represent the official position or policies of International Social Service, United States of America Branch, Inc. Holt International Children's Services is one of the four practicing South Korean government-sanctioned adoption agencies. The other sanctioned agencies include: Eastern Social Welfare Society, Inc.; Korea Social Service; and Social Welfare Society, Inc. See Altstein and Simon, *Intercountry Adoption*; and Simon and Altstein, *Adoption across Borders.*

16. For a discussion of Korea's continued participation in conversation with the emergent and existing global markets of adoption, see Condit-Shrestha, "South Korea and Adoption's Ends."

17. See Hübinette, *The Korean Adoption Issue between Modernity and Coloniality*; Kim, "Wedding Citizenship and Culture"; and Park Nelson, "Shopping for Children."

18. Hübinette, *Comforting an Orphaned Nation.*

19. Park Nelson, *Invisible Asians.*

20. Kim, *Adopted Territory*, 8–9. For more information about publics and counterpublics, see Warner, *Publics and Counterpublics.*

21. See Bergquist et al., *International Korean Adoption*; Dubinsky, "The Fantasy of the Global Cabbage Patch"; Hübinette, *Comforting an Orphaned Nation*; Hübinette, *The Korean Adoption Issue*; Kim, *Ends of Empire*; Kim, *Adopted Territory*; Park Nelson, "Shopping for Children"; Park Nelson, "Loss Is More Than Sadness"; Sarri et al., "Goal Displacement and Dependency"; and Song and Lee, "The Past and Present Cultural Experiences."

22. Cho, *Haunting the Korean Diaspora*, 74.

23. Mayo (1954, May), "Korea, Key to the Orient."

24. Eisenhower, "President Dwight D. Eisenhower's Farewell Address."

25. See Enloe, *Maneuvers.*

26. Kim, "The Ending Is Not an Ending At All," 809.

27. Mu Films, "Geographies of Kinship—The Korean Adoption Story."

28. Mayo (1954, May), "Korea, Key to the Orient."

29. Kim, "A Country Divided," 5.

30. Emphasis mine; Smolin, "Of Orphans and Adoption, Parents and the Poor, Exploitation and Rescue."

31. McKee, "Controlling Our Reproductive Destiny"; McKee, "Adoption as Reproductive Justice."

32. Myers, "'Real' Families."

33. Ninh, *Ingratitude*, 16.

34. Ibid., 36.
35. Ahmed, *The Promise of Happiness*, 68.
36. Ibid., 76.
37. Ibid., 13.
38. Ibid., 65.
39. Ibid., 67.
40. Ibid., 66.
41. See hooks, *Black Looks*.
42. Ngai, *Ugly Feelings*.
43. Ahmed, *The Promise of Happiness*, 106.
44. Ibid.
45. Bruining, "A Few Words, 64.
46. See Pate, *From Orphan to Adoptee*; and Oh, *To Save the Children of Korea*.
47. Given that adopted people's access to their case histories is fraught with tension and the veracity of information presented to adoptees is questioned, I was privileged in my ability to access the ISS–American Branch sealed case records. Adoptees in the United States and abroad often find their access to case records denied or mediated by adoption agencies and orphanages. Adult adoptees from Korea continue to seek access to their records in their entirety. Many adoptees say that they are told multiple stories concerning their records and discover new information each time they contact the agencies that facilitated their adoption. Adoptees also encourage one another to use a trusted translator when visiting their respective Korean agencies to ensure that information is not literally lost in translation. The concern over the veracity of information is rooted in how adoptees remain located as perpetual children, presumed unable to process their own histories or those of their birth families.
48. See O'Brien, *The Racial Middle*; Kim, *Imperial Citizens*; and Tuan, *Forever Foreigners or Honorary Whites?*
49. See Kim, *Ends of Empire*; Klein, *Cold War Orientalism*; and Pate, "Genealogies of Korean Adoption. Notably, Kim Park Nelson seeks to capture the experiences of the first generation of adoptees in *Invisible Asians*.
50. McKee, "Real versus Fictive Kinship," 221–336. See Butler, "Is Kinship Always Heterosexual?"; and Sedgwick, *Tendencies*.
51. The term *Korean adoptive family* is used to discuss families who adopt children from South Korea. Please note that when discussing adoptees' biological families, the terms *Korean biological family* or *biological family* will be deployed.
52. Bishoff and Rankin, eds., *Seeds from a Silent Tree*; and Cox, *Voices from Another Place*.
53. Park Nelson, *Invisible Asians*, 20.
54. Ortner, "Resistance and the Problem of Ethnographic Refusal."
55. Simpson. "On Ethnographic Refusal."
56. Zahara, "Refusal as Research Method in Discard Studies"; See also Smith, *Decolonizing Methodologies*.
57. For an example of an adoptee, Adoption Studies scholar who inserts her personal narrative into her scholarship, see Prébin's *Meeting Once More*.

Chapter 1. Generating a Market in Children

1. Oh, "A New Kind of Missionary Work, 167."

2. See Yoshihara, *Embracing the East.*

3. This distinction arose because Korean mothers of mixed race children suffered condemnation and were labeled "U.N. madams," "comforters," or "Western queens"; Kim, "Contextualizing Adoption from a Korean Perspective," 10.

4. See Box 247, Folder 52, Sealed Case Records; and Box 255, Folder 8, Sealed Case Records.

5. Box 360, Folder 24, Sealed Case Records.

6. Box 252, Folder 78, Sealed Case Records.

7. "Letter from Assistant Director Susan T. Pettis," Box 10, Folder 12.

8. Mixed-race children served as reminders of war as well as the joint legacies of colonialism and imperialism imposed on Korea. Report of the Rusk Mission to Korea, March 11–18, 1953, Box 3, Folder American Korean Foundation; Mayo, "Children of a New World"; Valk, "Korean-American Children in American Adoptive Homes"; Hyde and Hyde, *A Study of Proxy Adoptions*; Report of Visit to Korea, June 18 to July 13, 1962; Field Trip to Korea, Department of Health, Education and Welfare; and Report on 1965 Korea Visit to Paul R. Cherney. See also Howell, *Kinning of Foreigners*; Kim, "Contextualizing Adoption from a Korean Perspective"; Kim and Carroll, "Intercountry Adoption of South Korean Orphans,"223–253; Sarri, "Goal Displacement and Dependency."

9. Do-hyun Kim, "Overseas Adoption."

10. O'Brien, *The Racial Middle.*

11. Green, *Black Yanks in the Pacific,* 89.

12. See Box 332, "October 1972 Sealed Case Record" Sealed Case Records; and Box 360, Folder 5, Sealed Case Records.

13. Green, *Black Yanks in the Pacific,* 90. Unlike the American policy, in her examination of European colonies in Southeast Asia, Ann Stoler found the mixed race progeny of Dutch male settlers and their Asian concubines were not necessarily recognized by their fathers, even as "native women had responsibility for but attenuated rights over their own offspring"; Stoler, *Carnal Knowledge and Imperial Power,* 68.

14. Box 87, Folder 14, Sealed Case Records.

15. United States Department of Justice Immigration and Naturalization Service, *Public Law 97-359.*

16. Ibid., 9.

17. Condit-Shrestha, "South Korea and Adoption's Ends."

18. Dubinsky, *Babies without Borders*; Briggs, *Somebody's Children*; Choy, *Global Families.*

19. DeLanda, *A New Philosophy of Society,* 44.

20. Since Japanese occupation (1910–1945), Korean women have organized around numerous issues including capitalism, worker exploitation, legislation, sexual violence, and sexual enslavement of Korean women during World War II. Working in coalitions, the Korean women's movement has engendered change, including the establishment of the

Korean Women's Development Institute in 1983; Gelb and Palley, *Women of Japan and Korea*. In 1984, Korea entered the United Nations Convention on the Elimination of All Forms of Discrimination. Four years later, President Roh Tae Woo (1988–1993) provided formal recognition to gender policy in the establishment of the Second Ministry of Political Affairs to concentrate on women's issues, which was previously covered under the Ministry of Health and Welfare. The Presidential Commission on Women's Affairs was launched in 1998 by President Kim Dae Jung (1998–2003). In 2001, the Ministry of Gender Equality was established. See Chung, "Together and Separately"; Davis, "Korean Women's Groups Organize for Change"; Jones, "Mainstreaming Gender South Korean Women's Civic Alliances; Kim, "Feminist Philosophy in Korea"; and Palley, "Feminism in a Confucian Society."

21. Choe, "National Identity and Citizenship."

22. Ibid., 106.

23. It was not until 2005 that Korea's judicial system deemed the family registry incommensurable with the nation's Constitution. The government officially abolished the registry in 2008; Moon, "Begetting the Nation," 53; Gelb and Palley, *Women of Japan and Korea*; Moon, *Militarized Modernity and Gendered Citizenship*; and Palley, "Feminism in a Confucian Society." Though a milestone, the simple act of a legal change—allowing children to inherit the family name of their mothers, in addition to their fathers—does not necessarily entail a shift in societal mores or increased economic support for single mothers or low-income families; Koh, "Gender Issues and Confucian Scriptures." .

24. Kim, *Birth Mothers and Transnational Adoption Practice in South Korea*, 29.

25. Koh, "Gender Issues and Confucian Scriptures."

26. Gelb and Palley, *Women of Japan and Korea*; and Palley, "Feminism in a Confucian Society."

27. Moon, *Militarized Modernity and Gendered Citizenship*, 134.

28. Sarri et al., "Goal Displacement and Dependency," 99.

29. Ibid.

30. Kim, *Birth Mothers and Transnational Adoption Practice in South Korea*, 50.

31. Höhn and Moon, *Over There*; Lee, *Service Economies*. Discussing the state's erasure of birth mothers' labor, Hosu Kim asserts these efforts contribute to the state's interest in "obscur[ing] the multitudes of interpersonal and institutionalized gendered violence that occur in the state's promotion of transnational adoption as the best, even natural, solution for dealing with excess children from single, working-class, poor mothers in crisis; thereby, it obviates any need to allocate national expenditures toward children or families that exist beyond the patriarchal national family framework"; Kim, *Birth Mothers and Transnational Adoption Practice in South Korea*, 10.

32. Lee, "Single Moms' Day Shifts."

33. Pearson, "Towards the Re-politicization of Feminist Analysis," 609.

34. Over time, Confucian beliefs in conjunction with volunteer organizations' support limited the growth of state social welfare provisions. Confucian emphasis on filial piety has been the basis for the Korean state's expectation that "individual families [should] be primarily responsible for health care, housing, education, child care, and care of the

elderly"; Moon, *Militarized Modernity and Gendered Citizenship*, 118. See also Aspalter, "The East Asian Welfare Model"; Cho et al., "Korea's Miracle and Crisis"; Gough, "Globalization and Regional Welfare Regimes"; Kwon, "Beyond European Welfare Regimes"; and Kwon and Holliday, "The Korean Welfare State."

35. Woo, *The Politics of Social Welfare Policy*, 1–2.

36. Jung, "Korea's Welfare Expenditures Lag at 1/10 of GDP."

37. See Cho et al., "Korea's Miracle and Crisis"; Choi, "Status of the Family and Motherhood for Korean Women"; and Elson, "From Survival Strategies to Transformation Strategies."

38. In 1991, four accidental infant deaths occurred as a direct result of parents having to leave their children at home unattended in order to go to work; Roh, "Women Workers in a Changing Korean Society."

39. Davis, "Korean Women's Groups Organize for Change," 232.

40. Na and Moon, *Early Childhood Education and Care Policies*.

41. Chosun Ilbo, "Childcare Remains Obstacle to Women's Careers."

42. Kim, "After 6 Months, a U-turn on Costly Free Day Care"; and Shin and Jang, "Parents Take Full Advantage of Day Care."

43. Selman, "Intercountry Adoption in the New Millennium."

44. Social Welfare Society, Inc., "Support for Families of Single Parents."

45. "Korean Intercountry Adoptees Support."

46. Korean Unwed Mothers Support Network, "New Study Makes Recommendations."

47. Choe, "Group Resists Korean Stigma for Unwed Mothers." A report by the Korean Unwed Mothers Support Network and Korean Women's Development Institute notes that the rate of mothers choosing unwed motherhood "has increased from 5.8 percent in 1984 to 31.7 percent in 2005"; Korean Unwed Mothers Support Network, *Reviewing Issues on Wed Mothers' Welfare in Korea*.

48. Korean Unwed Mothers Support Network, *All Mothers Have the Right*; Ramstad, "Organization Helps Korea's Single Moms"; Jones, "Why a Generation of Adoptees Is Returning."

49. Lee, "Single Moms Denied Parental Allowance."

50. Lee, "Single Mom's Day Shifts."

51. See Pate, *From Orphan to Adoptee*, 77.

52. I draw from Orlando Patterson's discussion of social death in the context of slavery. This process renders the slave to exist as a social nonperson; Patterson, *Slavery and Social Death*, 5. Deploying the term *social death* does not mean that I draw a direct comparison between slaves and adoptees. Rather, similar to Jodi Kim, I am invested in how social death and natal alienation provide an avenue to better comprehend the loss in sovereignty experienced by adoptees; Kim, *Ends of Empire*, 281 (note 56).

53. Kim, *Birth Mothers and Transnational Adoption*, 9.

54. Ibid.

55. Schwekendiek, "Happy Birthday?"

56. Jones, "Portland's Korean Adoptees Help Others."

57. Stock, "The Note," 10.

58. Sieck, "A True Daughter," 87.

59. Hawley Fogg-Davis, *The Ethics of Transracial Adoption*. This allusion between Cabbage Patch dolls and adoptees was taken up directly by Karen Dubinksy in her *Feminist Theory* article (2008) titled: "The Fantasy of the Global Cabbage Patch: Making Sense of Transnational Adoption."

60. Neff, "The Rose," 60.

61. *In the Matter of Cha Jung Hee.*

62. *First Person Plural.*

63. Sun-ah Shim documents this practice, which is described as "child laundering"; Shim, "Dark Side of Inter-racial Adoption Surfaces."

64. McKee, "Rewriting History."

65. Box 129, Folder 10, Sealed Case Records.

66. See Box 255, Folder 75, Sealed Case Records; Box 322, Folder 61, Sealed Case Records; Box 328, Folder 2, Sealed Case Records; Box 328, Folder 66, Sealed Case Records; Box 328, "Spence Chapin Adoption," Sealed Case Records; Box 331, "Spence Chapin Adoption," Sealed Case Records; Box 332, "October 1972 Sealed Case Record," Sealed Case Records; Box 332, "Family and Children Services of Albany Adoption," Sealed Case Records; Box 332, "Department of Children and Family Services, Chicago Adoption," Sealed Case Records; Box 358, Folder 2, Sealed Case Records; Box 358, Folder 17, Sealed Case Records; Box 358, Folder 22, Sealed Case Records; Box 358, Folder 38, Sealed Case Records; Box 360, Folder 14, Sealed Case Records; Box 360, Folder 11; and Box 360, Folder 5, Sealed Case Records.

67. See Box 318, Folder 87, Sealed Case Records; Box 322, Folder 79, Sealed Case Records; Box 322, Folder 61, Sealed Case Records; Box 328, "Department of Children and Family Services, Chicago Adoption 1972," Sealed Case Records; Box 328, Folder 2, Sealed Case Records; Box 331, "Spence Chapin Adoption," Sealed Case Records; Box 332, "Department of Children and Family Services, Chicago Adoption," Sealed Case Records; Box 332, "Family and Children Services of Albany Adoption," Sealed Case Records; Box 332, "October 1972 Sealed Case Record," Sealed Case Records; Box 358, Folder 2, Sealed Case Records; Box 358, Folder 17, Sealed Case Records; Box 359, Folder 8, Sealed Case Records; Box 360, Folder 5, Sealed Case Records; Box 360, Folder 7, Sealed Case Records; Box 360, Folder 14, Sealed Case Records; and Box 360, Folder 21, Sealed Case Records.

68. The individual country prices for children are not unique to the twenty-first century. In 1972, International Social Service–American Branch noted additional country fees existed for prospective adoptive parents. To adopt from Korea, parents paid an additional $780 fee, while the Hong Kong and Jamaica program fees amounted to $400 and $190, respectively; Cost of Intercountry Adoption Program, Box 11, Folder 1.

69. Holt International, "Adoption Fees."

70. Holt International, "Adoption Fees Overview."

71. Ibid.

72. United States Census Bureau, *Income and Poverty in the United States: 2016.*

73. United States Census Bureau, *Income, Poverty, and Health Insurance Coverage in the United States 2010, 6.*

74. Addressing this unease, Elizabeth Raleigh notes: "For adoption stakeholders, the very idea of combining the terms 'market' and 'baby' is rife with controversy because the idea of commodifying children threatens the underlying foundation of the adoptive family"; Raleigh, *Selling Transracial Adoption*, 9. See also D'Arcy, "If Adoptees Are Gifts"; Prébin, "Gifts and Money between Adoptees and Birth Families"; Prébin, *Meeting Once More*; Triseliotis, "Intercountry Adoption; and Yngvesson, "Placing the 'Gift Child' in Transnational Adoption."

75. Holt International, "Financial Assistance."

76. The IRS defines foreign adoptions as "the adoption of an eligible child who isn't yet a citizen or resident of the United States or its possessions before the adoption effort begins"; Internal Revenue Service, "Topic Number 607."

77. For information concerning the high cost of adoption, please see Kevin Haebeom Vollmers's critique of adoption fund-raisers, "Top Seven Reasons."

78. Cost of Intercountry Adoption Program, Box 11, Folder 1.

79. Cost of WAIF Intercountry Adoption Program, Box 11, Folder 2.

80. Cartwright, "Photographs of 'Waiting Children,'" 83.

81. Klein, *Cold War Orientalism*, 153. See also Burditt, "Seeing Is Believing"; and Cartwright, "Photographs of 'Waiting Children.'"

82. Oh, "A New Kind of Missionary Work," 170.

83. Park Nelson, *Invisible Asians*, 13.

84. McKee, Kimberly. "From Adoptee to Trespasser: The Female Asian Adoptee as Oriental Fantasy." In *Adoption & Discourses of Multiculturalism: Europe, the Americas and the Pacific*, edited by Tobias Hübinette, Indigo Willing, and Jenny Wills (Under Review).

85. Box 318, Folder 87, Sealed Case Records.

86. Correspondence, Box 10, Folder 14.

87. See Box 332, "October 1972 Sealed Case Record," Sealed Case Records; Box 358, Folder 17, Sealed Case Records; and Box 360, Folder 5, Sealed Case Records.

88. Box 358, Folder 38, Sealed Case Records.

89. Box 359, Folder 8, Sealed Case Records.

90. Kim, "Overseas Adoption: Child Welfare for Abuse?"

91. Kim, "International Adoption," 143.

92. Sarri et al., "Goal Displacement and Dependency," 95.

93. Sarri et al., "Goal Displacement and Dependency," 95.

94. Chira, "Babies for Export."

95. Alstein and Simon, *Intercountry Adoption*, 5.

96. Maggi, *Ours*.

97. Sarri et al., "Goal Displacement and Dependency," 96. The Korean government's desire to place only mixed race or disabled children for adoption reveals how national belonging, race, and ability status are intertwined. Given the fact that full Korean children were considered ineligible for adoption under this plan, the implicit anti-Blackness associated with mixed race Korean children in the post–Korean War period cannot go uninterrogated. The initial Korean-Black children eligible for adoption were considered hard to place. Such children also sometimes find themselves labeled "special needs" along-

side older children or sibling groups in adoption. Designations of special needs are determined based on country of origin. More broadly, antimiscegenation rhetoric often made comparisons to mixed race status as linked to disability; O'Dell et al., "Supporting Families Throughout." Korean-Black children found their intellectual capabilities tested as well, given the eugenic assumptions concerning the IQ of children born as a result of interracial sexual relationships. For example, a March 1970 Child Placement Service, Inc., report by Youn-Taek Tahk, general director, reveals that "mixed blood children's IQs are quite similar to pure Korean children, and their mean IQ is normal although there are some with low IQ"; Box 35, Folder 7. This attention to intelligence arose again the following year in a June 1971 Report on ECLAIR (Eurasian Children Living as Indigenous Residents) Program, Child Placement Service, Inc. The report notes, "IQ of 80–90 is most common among mix-blooded children and some are above 100. Some exception is granted but most of the children with IQ above 100 enjoy normal school life"; Box 35, Folder 5. Further analyses concerning mixed race children and disabled children in the context of international adoption from Korea is needed to deepen understandings of how rhetoric concerning hard-to-place children included both mixed Korean-Black children and those children with intellectual or physical disabilities.

98. Sarri et al., "Goal Displacement and Dependency," 96.

99. Selman, "Intercountry Adoption in the New Millennium," 222.

100. Selman, "The Demographic History of Intercountry Adoption," 23, 34.

101. Chosun Ilbo, "Gov't in Bid to Encourage Adoption in Korea."

102. Kim, "Adoption Quota Causes Backlash."

103. Onishi, "Korea Aims to End Stigma."

104. Bureau of Consular Affairs, U.S. Department of State, "Statistics."

105. Yim, "Korea Passes Law to Change Adoption Policy." The legislation's language was crafted not only by policy makers, but also included a coalition of single mothers and adult adoptees.

106. Embassy of the Republic of Korea in the USA, "Visa Issuance." Kim notes that the F-4 visa "allows adoptees, as overseas Koreans, to stay in Korea for up to two years with rights to work, make financial investments, buy real estate, and obtain medical insurance and pensions."; Kim, "Wedding Citizenship and Culture," 59. The visa exempts male adoptees from compulsory military service and disallows voting in elections; Hübinette, *The Korean Adoption Issue*, 166. Lee, "Dual Citizenship to Be Allowed." In April 2011, the first thirteen Korean adoptees obtained their dual citizenship; *Yonhap News*, "13 Korean Adoptees Obtain Dual Citizenship."

Chapter 2. (Un)documented Citizens, (Un)naturalized Americans

1. An example of anti-Asian racism linked to the bombing of the Korean peninsula occurred in Southern California; Phil Yu, "God Bless Trump."

2. Mira Rapp-Hooper, "The Cataclysm that Would Follow"; Victor Cha, "Giving North Korea a 'Bloody Nose'"; Beauchamp, "This Was the Scariest Part."

3. Dawsey, "Trump Derides Protections for Immigration"; Gambino, "Trump Pans Immigration Proposal."

4. I draw upon Martha Gardner's concept, *derivative citizenship*, which accounts for how female European immigrants gained naturalized citizenship upon marriage to American citizens; Gardner, *The Qualities of a Citizen*, 24.

5. See Gotanda, "Exclusion and Inclusion"; and Zhou and Gatewood, eds., *Contemporary Asian America*.

6. Kim, "Adoptees Struggle with Uncertain Nationalities."

7. Chan, *Asian Americans*. See also Hing, *Making and Remaking Asian America*; and Takaki, *Strangers from a Different Shore*. Between 1790 and 1870, naturalization practices differed at the state level. For example, "California could rigidly refuse naturalization to Chinese residents while Massachusetts routinely granted citizenship to Chinese from the 1850s onwards"; Lee, *Orientals*, 60. Nevertheless, beginning on the West Coast, a series of discriminatory state laws were enacted to limit the numbers of Chinese and Asian Indians, for example, in cities and communities. Such xenophobia impacted Asians, more generally, via the denial of naturalized citizenship and pathologization as "alien" residents of the United States.

8. See Lee and Yung, *Angel Island*; and Okihiro, *Margins and Mainstreams*.

9. Even as this restrictive legislation became enacted, the Supreme Court upheld birthright citizenship of persons of Chinese descent in 1898; Kanstroom, *Deportation Nation*, 128.

10. Gotanda, "Exclusion and Inclusion," 137; Ong and Liu, "U.S. Immigration Policies and Asian Migration."

11. Gotanda, "Exclusion and Inclusion," 137.

12. Kanstroom, *Deportation Nation*, 132. This law effectively curtailed Asian migration given the 1790 Naturalization Law. These various legal provisions promoted the long-standing belief that persons of Asian descent are, in fact, foreigners. In many ways, the 1924 Immigration Act is neatly paired with enacted Alien Land Laws in California and other states in the 1910s and 1920s, which limited landholding to American citizens, prohibiting alien residents (i.e., individuals ineligible for citizenship) from landowning rights.

13. Chan, *Asian Americans*, 106.

14. Ibid.

15. Gardner, *The Qualities of a Citizen*, 122.

16. Palumbo-Liu, *Asian/American*, 33.

17. Ibid.

18. Ibid.

19. Ibid.

20. Chan, *Asian Americans*, 146. At the same time these low quotas operated, the War Brides Act of 1947 aided female Asian migration to the United States; Lim, *A Feeling of Belonging*. However, only Chinese women were included in the War Brides Act, while war brides from Japan and Korea entered through "special acts of Congress that established temporary windows of opportunity through which American soldiers could bring home their Asian wives"; *Beyond the Shadow of Camptown*, 2. Additionally, Filipino nurses en-

tered and sometimes settled in the United States as a result of their ability to enter the United States as skilled migrants through the U.S. Exchange Visitor Program prior to 1965; Choy, *Empires of Care.*

21. Following the 1965 Immigration Act, the United States saw the first influx of Asian refugees from Southeast Asia as a result of the Vietnam War. Additionally, the Indochina Migration and Refugee Assistance Act of 1975 and the Refugee Assistance Act of 1980 aided migration from Southeast Asia; Zia, *Asian American Dreams,* 51.

22. Choy, *Global Families.* For a discussion of adoptees' reflections on the individual laws that facilitated their entry to the United States, see Park Nelson, *Invisible Asians.*

23. Kim, *The Origins of Korean Adoption,* 9. "Children adopted before 1924 were expressly excluded from the definition of 'child' outlined under the 1924 Quota Act"; Gardner, *The Qualities of a Citizen,* 231.

24. Oh, "From War Waif to Ideal Immigrant," 38.

25. Appendix I: Refugee Relief Bill of 1953.

26. Ibid.

27. Kim, "Scattered Seeds," 154.

28. Park, "Forced Child Migration," 45. For a discussion of these individual pieces of legislation, see Oh, "From War Waif to Ideal Immigrant."

29. Park, "Forced Child Migration," 45–46; and Oh, "From War Waif to Ideal Immigrant," 38.

30. Park, "Forced Child Migration," 50.

31. The Amerasian Immigration Act 1962 and Amerasian Homecoming Act 1987 stand alone because their passage remains inextricably linked to United States paternalism in Vietnam and the criticism against Operation Babylift as the majority of the "orphans" airlifted were not, in fact, orphans but had living family members in Vietnam.

32. Oh, "A New Kind of Missionary Work."

33. Correspondence from Associate Director, Susan T. Pettiss, to Ann Davison.

34. Box 34, Folder 24.

35. Procedures Affecting Foreign-Born Children Adopted in the United States.

36. New U.S. Immigration and Nationality Provisions. .

37. Communication to Senator Kennedy.

38. Ibid.

39. The IR-3 and IR-4 visas are for children whose birth countries are not signatories of the Hague Convention, while the IH-3 and IH-4 visas are for children whose birth countries are party to the Convention; Department of Homeland Security, "Your New Child's Immigrant Visa." United States Citizenship and Immigration Services, May 17, 2011.

40. Department of Homeland Security, "Your New Child's Immigrant Visa," U.S. Citizenship and Immigration Services, March 17, 2015, accessed February 2, 2018, https://www.uscis.gov/adoption/bringing-your-internationally-adopted-child-united-states/your-new-childs-immigrant-visa.

41. Department of Homeland Security, "Before Your Child Immigrates." U.S. Citizenship and Immigration Services notes, "The U.S. Embassy or consulate will issue an IR-4/

IH-4 visa to your child if he or she is an orphan coming to the United States to be adopted by you, or (if you already adopted your child overseas in an [IR-3] non-Hague adoption) you and/or your spouse (if you are married) did not see your child before or during the adoption proceeding"; Department of Homeland Security, "Your New Child's Immigrant Visa," U.S. Citizenship and Immigration Services, March 17, 2015, accessed February 2, 2018, https://www.uscis.gov/adoption/bringing-your-internationally-adopted-child-united -states/your-new-childs-immigrant-visa.

42. Bureau of Consular Affairs, U.S. Department of State, "India." When considering children whose adoptions were finalized abroad, the United States State Department notes: "The Child Citizenship Act of 2000 allows your child to acquire American citizenship when he or she enters the United States as lawful permanent residents"; Bureau of Consular Affairs, U.S. Department of State, "Thailand."

43. Trenka, "No Rubber-stamp Court for Int'l Adoptions."

44. AdopSource, "Stop the Deportation of Russell Green."

45. Vollmers, Interview with Adam Crapser.

46. Hewitt, "International Adoptee Faces Deportation."

47. Wang, "A Push to Protect Adult Adoptees."

48. Jones, "Adam Crapser's Bizarre Deportation Odyssey."

49. Disaggregated data concerning whether deportees are adopted persons, refugees, or immigrants who entered the United States unlawfully is unavailable.

50. Jones, "Adam Crapser's Bizarre Deportation Odyssey"; see also Chishti and Mittelstadt, "Unauthorizing Immigrants with Criminal Convictions."

51. Singh, "ICE Confirms Kairi Shepherd Deportation."

52. Frailey, "Citizenship for ALL Adoptees."

53. Pertman, "An Unnerving Reality"; Pound Pup Legacy, "Deportation Cases"; and Riben, "Help Is Needed."

54. Yoo Soo-Sun, "A Sad Ending for Deported Adoptee"; Fuchs, "Deported Adoptee's Death Heightens Calls"; Choe, "Deportation a 'Death Sentence' to Adoptees." .

55. See Kwon Dobbs et al., "Deporting Adult Adoptees."

56. Trenka, "No Rubber-Stamp Court." The plight of noncitizen Korean adoptees has garnered the attention of Korean media. However, no formal overtures to address the issue on an international level have occurred; Shin, "Korean Woman, Adopted as Infant"; Sung-soo Kim, "Adoptees Deported by US." The Adoptee Rights Campaign reports that an estimated 35,000 international adoptees lack citizenship; Adoptee Rights Campaign, "Progress Updates #CitizenshipForAllAdoptees." Korean adoptee activist A. K. Salling from the Adoption Finalization Naturalization and Citizenship Deportation Project suggested that there are roughly 15,000 Korean adoptees worldwide—including in the United States—with unconfirmed citizenship status; Salling, "Adoption Finalization Naturalization and Citizenship Deportation."

57. Ewing, "She'll Get US Citizenship."

58. Goetz, "They Came to America as Adoptees."

59. Korean Focus Metro DC, "Citizenship for All US Intercountry Adoptees." For more information regarding adoption deportation cases, visit Pound Pup Legacy, "Deportation Cases."

60. Ibid.

61. Concern over the ways in which false binaries of undocumented persons are generated through the use of different labels for subcategories of persons without citizenship has led some to advocate for no longer using the term DREAMer, a category that emerged in the wake of the failed Development, Relief, and Education for Alien Minors (DREAM) Act; Perez, "Challenging the 'DREAMer' Narrative"; Rivas, "Why You Should Stop."

62. Citizenship for All Adoptees, "Can I Just Get a Passport Please?"

63. Ibid.

64. Janine, "Janine's Story."

65. Adoptee Rights Campaign, "Summary of the Family Is More."

66. Holt Alumni Blog, "Senator Landrieu Passes Amendment."

67. Ibid.

68. Park Nelson, *Invisible Asians*, 169.

69. Jones, "Adam Crasper's Bizarre Deportation Odyssey."

70. Ibid.

71. Adoptee Citizenship Act of 2015, S.2275, 114th Congress, 2015.

72. Wang, " Bill Would Provide Retroactive Citizenship."

73. Ibid.

74. Kessel, "Over 70 Community Members Join."

75. Tooley, "South Korean Adoptee Deportation."

76. Office of U.S. Senator Amy Klobuchar, "Klobuchar Calls On Colleagues."

77. Kessel, "Over 70 Community Members."

78. NAKASEC, "Release."

79. Tooley, "South Korean Adoptee Deportation."

80. Seattle Human Rights Commission Letter.

81. Shoichet, "Americans Adopted Him." *CNN.com*, November 7, 2016. http://www .cnn.com/2016/11/04/us/adam-crapser-deportation/.

82. Choe, "Korean Mother Awaits a Son's Deportation."

83. It is important to note that as of May 2018, the DREAM Act remains unsuccessful in finding support in either the House of Representatives or the Senate and there are continued overtures to end DACA by the Trump administration. For more information concerning DACA, visit National Immigration Law Center, "DACA Renewal FAQ"; Official Website of the Department of Homeland Security, "Consideration of Deferred Action"; American Immigration Council, "The DREAM Act."

84. National Immigration Law Center, "DACA Renewal FAQ"; Official Website of the Department of Homeland Security, "Consideration of Deferred Action."

85. Bosniak, *The Citizen and the Alien*, 66.

86. Maira, "Radical Deportation," 298.

87. Perry, "Korean Adoptee in Immigration Battle." .

88. Lee and Baldoz, "Donald Trump Fails History"; Vivian Shaw et al., "Collective Statement by Asian American Studies Scholars"; and Marcotte, "With El Salvador Decision, Trump's Immigration Policy."

89. Adoptee Citizenship Act of 2018, S. 2522, 115th Cong. (2018); Adoptee Citizenship Act of 2018, H.R. 5233, 115th Cong. (2018).

90. Ibid.

Chapter 3. The (Re)production of Family

1. Due to this construction of fictive kinship, since the first modern adoption statute passed in Massachusetts in 1851, adoption practices in the United States became clouded in secrecy, leading to the normalization of closed adoptions. See Terrell and Modell, "Anthropology and Adoption"; Carp, *Family Matters*; Berebitsky, *Like Our Very Own*; and Modell, *A Sealed and Secret Kinship*.

2. My deployment of the term *heteronormative* is rooted in the work of Stevi Jackson, who notes: "Heteronormativity defines not only a normative sexual practice but also a normative way of life"; Jackson, "Interchanges," 107.

3. To shield their perceived abnormality, adoptive families were originally formed via race-matching as any visible difference would mark the family as deviant. Race-matching remained so stringent that families and babies would be matched not only based on race and phenotype, but also matched via the religion of both the adoptive and biological parents; Herman, *Kinship by Design*. For information concerning Black and Native American domestic adoptions, see Jacobs, *White Mother to a Dark Race*; Solinger, *Beggars and Choosers*; Turner Strong, "To Forget Their Tongue" ; and Roberts, *Shattered Bonds*. Addressing the binary of fictive versus real kinship, Shelley M. Park notes: "Adoptive relationships . . . until recently, were governed by the principle that such relationships should mimic . . . the relationships of the biological kinship unit"; Park, "Real (M)othering," 176. This assertion acknowledges the historical marginalization of families who differ from the traditional "natural" family narrative.

4. Eng and Hom, *Q & A*, 1. See also Halberstam, *In a Queer Time and Place*.

5. Eng, *The Feeling of Kinship*; and Park, *Mothering Queerly*.

6. Butler, *Gender Trouble*.

7. Butler, *Bodies that Matter,"* 22. See also Halberstam, *Female Masculinity*.

8. Muñoz, "Feeling Brown, Feeling Down.

9. Ibid., 678–679.

10. Ibid., 679.

11. McKee (2015, June 16), "An Open Letter."

12. McClain DaCosta, "All in the Family," 65.

13. Eng, *The Feeling of Kinship*.

14. Ibid., 10.

15. Obasogie, *Blinded by Sight*, 44.

16. Trepagnier, *Silent Racism*, 15.

17. Obasogie, *Blinded by Sight*, 37.

18. Trepagnier, *Silent Racism, Expanded Edition*, 57.

19. Obasogie, *Blinded by Sight*, 115.

20. Bonilla-Silva, *Racism without Racists*, 104.

21. Judith Butler asserted queer theory's fluidity: "If the term 'queer' is to be a site of collective contestation . . . it will have to remain that which is, in the present, never fully owned . . . redeployed, twisted, queered from a prior usage"; Butler, *Bodies that Matter*, 228; see also Edelman, "Queer Theory"; Sullivan, *A Critical Introduction to Queer Theory*; and Giffney, "Denormatizing Queer Theory."

22. Edelman notes that the child "embodies the citizen as an ideal"; Edelman, *No Future*, 11, 17.

23. This is not to say that single individuals and same-sex couples do not adopt transracially or internationally; however, given this inquiry's interest in the Korean adoptive family, I limit my discussion to nonnormative heterosexual relationships and their perceived deviance in their failure to reproduce some, if not all, of their children gestationally.

24. Butler, *Bodies that Matter*, 228.

25. Edelman, *No Future*.

26. Ibid., 11.

27. Winnubst, "Review Essay. No Future, 182."

28. Muñoz, *Cruising Utopia*, 95.

29. Butler, "Is Kinship Always Heterosexual?" 126.

30. Warner, "Introduction: Fear of a Queer Planet," 7.

31. Ibid., 9.

32. Ting, "Bachelor Society," 277.

33. *Adoptees Have Answers*.

34. Park, *Mothering Queerly, Queering Motherhood*.

35. Bureau of Consular Affairs, U.S. Department of State, "South Korea." Please note that "prospective adoptive parents must be between 25 and 44 years old"; Bureau of Consular Affairs, U.S. Department of State, "South Korea."

36. For example, the ABC primetime sitcom *Modern Family* follows a "traditional" nuclear family, one marked by divorce and interracial marriage, and a gay couple with an adopted daughter from Asia.

37. See Cahn, *The New Kinship*.

38. To this end, Judith Stacey writes: "White, middle-class families . . . are less the innovators than the propagandists and principal beneficiaries of contemporary family change. African-American women and white, working-class women have been the genuine postmodern family pioneers, even though they also suffer from its most negative effects"; Stacey, *Brave New Families*, 252.

39. Lee et al., "The Coming of Age of Korean Adoptees," 205.

40. Awkward, *Negotiating Difference*, 19, 180.

41. Hallowell, "American Indians, White and Black," 523.

42. Box 360, Folder 3, Sealed Case Records, International Social Service, American Branch Records, SWHA, University of Minnesota.

43. Box 360, Folder 14, Sealed Case Records.

44. Box 255, Folder 75 Sealed Case Records.

45. Box 360, Folder 21, Sealed Case Records.

46. Box 360, Folder 11, Sealed Case Records.

47. Box 328, Folder 2, Sealed Case Records.

48. Higgins Swick, "Becca," 76.

49. See Omi and Winant, *Racial Formation in the United States*; Obasogie, *Blinded by Sight*.

50. See Lo, "Korean Psych 101."

51. Unlike mixed race families, who at the outset recognize their transracial or multiracial composition, the transracial, transnational adoptive family desires to gain legitimacy within *real* kinship structures based on genetic and racial connectedness.

52. Bishoff and Rankin, *Seeds from a Silent Tree*; Cox, *Voices from Another Place*; Wilkinson and Fox, *After the Morning Calm*; and Lee et al., *Once They Hear My Name*.

53. K. Bhabha, *The Location of Culture*.

54. McKee, "Scenes of Misrecognition"; Newton, "I Am Not My Dad's Girlfriend."

55. Gates, "I Was Taking Pictures of My Daughters"; Dokoupil, "What Adopting a White Girl Taught."

56. Jacobson, *Culture Keeping*, 2.

57. Delale-O'Connor, "Learning to Be Me, 204."

58. hooks, *Black Looks*.

59. Katz Rothman, *Weaving a Family*, 167.

60. Evans, *The Lost Daughters of China*, 187.

61. See Fanon, *Black Skin, White Masks*.

62. Ibid. See also Wright, *Becoming Black*, 113.

63. Wright, *Becoming Black*, 122.

64. Butler, *Gender Trouble*, 139.

65. Eng, *The Feeling of Kinship*,151. Tobias Hübinette contends that adoptees' pastiche of whiteness is similar to the performances of "ethnic drags and cross-dressers, transvestites or even transsexuals or the transgendered who are troubling, mocking and parodying supposedly fixed racial, ethnic, and national identities and belongings"; Hübinette, "Disembedded and Free-floating Bodies, 143.

66. Discussing her personal experiences with domestic, transracial adoption, Barbara Katz Rothman writes, "As long as there is a color line in America, we'll be straddling those worlds, and white families will have to raise their black children for worlds their mothers and fathers can never fully enter"; Katz Rothman, *Weaving a Family*, 22. While Katz Rothman believes that she and her partner are unable to fully enter this world, I argue that transracial adoptive families require expanding what it means to be members of these communities to fully account for how not all persons of color grow up in families that reflect their racial or ethnic identities.

67. McKee, "An Open Letter."

68. See Spickard, *Mixed Blood*.

69. While this inquiry centers on the estimated 75 percent of adoptees who entered white families, I recognize a deeper exploration of adoptees that entered Black and Asian families is necessary and will produce new insights into how processes of racialization occur in the United States. For example, Korean adoptee firefighter, Emile Mack, was profiled by *KoreAM* magazine about his experiences growing up in a transracial, African American home; Eun, "Where I Came From." Mack recalls: "There were people who didn't know me or my family, and they didn't tease me because I had black parents, but they teased me because I looked Asian. So it was the typical thing, 'Hey Chinese, hey this, hey that.' And then my friends would respond, 'He's black!! His parents are black, leave him alone!!'" Exploring the Korean-Black experience for adoptees will add depth to existing studies engaging Korean-Black relations following the 1992 Los Angeles riots. In addition, discussing Korean adoptees' entrance into Asian American families will add new insights into how these families may be similar to same-race domestic adoptive families predicated upon race matching. The performative nature of these families may be more complex because they are not transracial adoptions; rather, these adoptions are intraracial adoptions. Consequently, unlike their counterparts in transracial families, adoptees may lack knowledge of their adoption or feel more Chinese American, for example, than Korean American. Reaching out to this community of adoptees and their families in the future will also serve as a comparison to the experiences of intraethnic and interracial families outside of the dominant norm pervading Asian American interracial marriages.

Chapter 4. Rewriting the Adoptee Experience

1. Bishoff and Rankin, *Seeds from a Silent Tree*; and Cox, *Voices from Another Place*.

2. Of these narratives, twenty-nine are authored by Korean American adoptees, with one narrative by a Belgian-Korean adoptee. Of the Korean American adoptees, seven narratives are written by men and twenty-two are authored by women.

3. The First Gathering was a seminal moment in adult adoptee history, whereby adoptees who previously may have engaged one another via Listserves, came together and shared their experiences growing up in North America and Europe. The second Gathering was held in Stockholm, Sweden, in 2001. The subsequent Gatherings were held in Seoul, South Korea, beginning in 2004 and occur every three years. Since the second one, the Gatherings have been organized by the International Korea Adoptee Association planning committee, which includes representatives from worldwide adult Korean adoptee organizations.

4. Gruber, "New Documentary Film, Twinsters, Shines a Light on Twins Separated at Birth"; Luhar, "Twin Adoptees Reunite in 'Twinsters' Documentary'"; Navales, "More On the 'Separated @ Birth' Twins."

5. Kollaboration, "Empowerment through Entertainment."

6. McKee, "Gendered Adoptee Identities."

7. Hao, "YouTube Has Made Asian-Americans Impossible."

8. See Friedman, "Women's Autobiographical Selves"; Gilmore, *Autobiographics*; Smith, *Subjectivity, Identity, and the Body*; and Stanley, "Feminist Auto/Biography and Feminist Epistemology."

9. Gilmore, *Autobiographies*, 42.

10. For example, due to racially discriminatory immigration legislation, many early writers viewed themselves as sojourners and exiles, working to change Orientalist perceptions of Asians; Kim, "Defining Asian American Realities through Literature"; and Wong, "Immigrant Autobiography." Additionally, in her examination of second-generation writers, Elaine H. Kim (1982) notes: "These writers, when confronted with racial barriers, could not easily identify with Asia, since they had been born, raised, and educated in the United States. Their autobiographical writings reflect the conflicts caused in their personal lives by race discrimination and popular misconceptions about the relationships between race and culture"; Kim, *Asian American Literature*, 58.

11. Cheung, *An Interethnic Companion to Asian American Literature*, 9–10, 26; Geok-Lim and Ling, *Reading the Literatures of Asian America*.

12. Grice, *Negotiating Identities*, 29.

13. See Fenkl, "The Future of Korean American Literature"; and Kim, "Roots and Wings."

14. Jerng, *Claiming Others*; Park Nelson, "Loss Is More Than Sadness," 101–128.

15. See Nelson, *Damaged Identities, Narrative Repair*.

16. Ibid.S, 18.

17. Ibid., 151.

18. Ibid., 106. Emphasis original.

19. Ibid., 133–134.

20. hooks, *Talking Back*.

21. For a deeper examination of how Korean adoptees deploy documentaries as a method of talking back, see McKee, "Rewriting History."

22. Kim, *Ends of Empire*, 5, emphasis original.

23. Much of the Korean Adoption Studies literature uses ethnic and racial identity measures, with many relying on Jean S. Phinney's (1990) Multigroup Ethnic Identity Measure (MEIM) and open-ended survey questions; Phinney, "Ethnic Identity in Adolescents and Adults." The two largest quantitative studies to date were commissioned by the Evan B. Donaldson Adoption Institute and represent 167 and 179 Korean American adoptees, respectively; Freundlich and Lieberthal, *Survey of Adult Korean Adoptees*; McGinnis et al., *Beyond Culture Camp*. Smaller studies include Song and Lee, "The Past and Present Cultural Experiences."

24. See Baden and Steward, "A Framework for Use."

25. Studies that explore the initial moment of racial salience in adoptees' lives in the shift from childhood to adulthood may overlook whether these moments reoccur in other scenarios (e.g., invitations to join Asian American student organizations in college; questions concerning "where they're really from" by coworkers); see Lieberman, "The Process of Racial and Ethnic Identity Development." Further, studies that explore the initial moment of racial

salience in adoptees' shift between childhood to adulthood lack a sufficient exploration of whether racial salience in adulthood is context-specific outside of this initial moment of salience. Additionally, Dani Meier found adoptees first experienced a heightened level of racial diversity only after they entered university or the workforce because their childhood was marked predominately by whiteness; Meier, "Cultural Identity and Place." For more information concerning Meier's study, see Meier, "Loss and Reclaimed Lives."

26. See Palmer, *The Dance of Identities*; Shiao and Tuan, "Korean Adoptees and the Social Context"; and Tuan and Shiao, *Choosing Ethnicity, Negotiating Race.*

27. Chen, *Double Agency*, 17.

28. Kwapisz, "Perception vs. I Am," 51.

29. Tuan, *Forever Foreigners or Honorary Whites?*

30. Wells, "Native 'Korean' American," 120.

31. Kauffman, "Bulgogi," 46.

32. Vance, "Who Do I Resemble?" 114.

33. Box 360, Folder 24, Sealed Case Records.

34. Chappell, "Now I'm Found," 124.

35. Dorin Kobus, "Hello Good-bye Hello," 42.

36. Ibid., 43.

37. Clement, "School Daze," 7.

38. Sherilyn Cockroft, "New Beginnings."

39. See Box 332, "Family and Children Services of Albany Adoption," Sealed Case Records. For example, a social study concerning a child adopted to California reports, "He arrives a sheet of paper [*sic*] which showed his date of birth, when he was found abandoned. His name was given by our agency"; Box 359, Folder 8, Sealed Case Records. Another second child's social study noted the child's date of birth was provided among the abandoned child's belongings, but her name was provided by the hospital; Box 322, Folder 61, Sealed Case Records.

40. Chappell, "Now I'm Found," 126.

41. Dorin Kobus, "Hello Good-bye Hello."

42. Caraway, *Segregated Sisterhood*, 95.

43. See Kaw, "Medicalization of Racial Features"; Hall, "Asian Eyes"; Chung, "Finding My Eye-dentity"; and Kwak, "Asian Cosmetic Facial Surgery."

44. Teresa A. Mok notes, "Asian Americans are the most likely ethnic minority group to pursue cosmetic surgery" (6); Mok, "Asian Americans and Standards of Attractiveness." For a more in-depth examination of Asian American women's body image, see Yokoyama, "The Double Binds of Our Bodies." In recent years, there has also been an increase in articles documenting Asian Americans utilization of cosmetic surgery practices to give them a more Western appearance. See O'Connor, "Is Race Plastic?"; and Chow, "The Many Stories behind Double-Eyelid Surgery."

45. CBS News Staff, "Julie Chen Reveals She Had Plastic Surgery"; O'Connor, "Julie Chen Says Eyelid Surgery." .

46. Mok, "Asian Americans and Standards of Attractiveness."

47. Lau et al., "Asian American College Women's Body Image," 262.
48. Palmer, "Korean Adopted Young Women."
49. Lau et al., "Asian American College Women's Body Image," 263–264.
50. Chen, *Double Agency*, 5.
51. YoungHee, "Laurel," 86, emphasis added.
52. Ibid.
53. Turner, "Planted in the West: The Story of an American Girl," 137.
54. Ibid.
55. Clement, "The Unforgotten War."
56. Espiritu, *Asian American Women and Men*; Lee, *Orientals*; Ma, *The Deathly Embrace*; Okihiro, *Margins and Mainstreams*; Lau, "Exploring the Lives of Asian American Men"; Mok "Asian Americans and Standards of Attractiveness."
57. Kwapisz, "Perception vs. I Am," 50.
58. Jim Milroy, "The Stone Parable," 58.
59. Berry, "Completing My Puzzle. . . ."
60. Cockroft, "New Beginnings," 16.
61. Ibid.
62. Ruth, "Dear Luuk," 143.
63. Ibid.
64. Ibid.
65. Ibid., 144.
66. Kim-Cavicchi, "Power, Resistance and Subjectivity."
67. Fermi, "A Sense of Loss," 20.
68. Owen, "It's a Wonderful Life!" 68.
69. Ahmed, *The Promise of Happiness*, 41.
70. Chen, *Double Agency*, xix.
71. Chappell, "Now I'm Found," 135.
72. Stock, "My Han."
73. Ibid., 101–102.
74. Ning, "Returning . . .," 130.
75. Miller, "Tightrope," 107.
76. Ruth, "Kimchee on White Bread," 80.
77. Benson, "Tensions of Subjectivity," 24–40.
78. Ahmed, *The Promise of Happiness*, 66.
79. Jacobson, *Culture Keeping*.
80. See Seabrook, "The Last Babylifti"; and Bae, "John Seabrook NPR Segment."
81. Ahmed, *The Promise of Happiness*.
82. McKee, "Gendered Adoptee Identities."
83. Although *Twinsters* (2015) also included portions of the 2013 IKAA Gathering, the film did not become widely distributed on Netflix until July 17, 2015.
84. ASIAN-ISH Ep. 1 W/ DANakaDAN—Korean Adoptee vs Korean Food."

85. "Korean Adoptees Talk Korean Food!"

86. In the second episode, viewers witness him discuss eating Korean food for the first time and what foods adoptees and non-Koreans are most likely to be introduced to in a conversation with Lim, Sam Futerman, and Jenna Ushkowitz; "Growing Up on Asian Food vs American Food!?

87. "Korean Adoptees Talk Korean Food!"

88. Ibid.

89. Ibid.

90. "ASIAN*ISH—How to Drink like a Korean!

91. Bourdain. *Anthony Bourdain: Parts Unknown.* "Korea."

92. "My 1st Korean Birthday "DOL."

93. Nelson, *Damaged Identities, Narrative Repair,* 151.

94. Ibid., 8.

Chapter 5. Adoption in Practice

1. Okihiro, "Oral History and the Writing of Ethnic History," 211. See also Barnett and Noriega, *Oral History and Communities of Color.*

2. Park Nelson, "Korean Looks, American Eyes," 24–25.

3. Baden and Steward, "A Framework for Use"; Brian, *Reframing Transracial Adoption*; Freundlich and Lieberthal, *Survey of Adult Korean Adoptees*; Hatchard, "Racial Experiences of Korean Adoptees?"; Lieberman, "The Process of Racial and Ethnic Identity Development"; Meier, "Cultural Identity and Place"; Palmer, *The Dance of Identities*; Shiao and Tuan, "Korean Adoptees and the Social Context"; Tuan and Shiao, *Choosing Ethnicity, Negotiating Race*; Wesolowski Kim, "Ethnic Identity Development"; Wickes and Slate, "Transracial Adoption of Koreans."

4. Brian, *Reframing Transracial Adoption*; Docan-Morgan, "They Were Strangers Who Loved Me"; Docan-Morgan, "Cultural Differences and Perceived Belonging"; Park Nelson, *Invisible Asians*; and Tuan and Shiao, *Choosing Ethnicity, Negotiating Race.*

5. Oral History 13. Oral histories are coded by chronological order in which the adoptee's story was collected.

6. Kim, *Adopted Territory,* 86, 97. Elizabeth Kopacz examines the advent of adoptees' employment of familiar terms to describe their relationships with one another and the rise of Korean adoptee cousins with the increase in use of DNA at-home test kits; Kopacz, "From Contingent Beginnings to Multiple Ends."

7. See Larsen, "Organizing without an Anchor."

8. Oral History 1.

9. Oral History 5.

10. Oral History 10.

11. Oral History 7.

12. Tobias Hübinette, Indigo Willing, and Jenny Wills, eds., *Adoption & Discourses of Multiculturalism: Europe, the Americas and the Pacific* (Under Review). For a discussion of

banal multiculturalism, see Thomas, *Multicultural Girlhood*; and Derickson, "The Racial Politics of Neoliberal Regulation."

13. Oral History 1.

14. Oral History 6.

15. Oral History 12.

16. Oral History 2.

17. Ibid.

18. Twohey et al., "Reuters Investigates,"; and Joyce, *The Child Catchers.*

19. Oral History 5.

20. Oral History 2.

21. Kim, *Adopted Territory*; Docan-Morgan, "Cultural Differences and Perceived Belonging."

22. Oral History 12.

23. Oral History 8.

24. Trenka, *Fugitive Visions*, 14.

25. Robinson, *A Single Square Picture*, 148.

26. Ibid., 149.

27. Oral History 9.

28. Oral History 13.

29. Trenka, *Fugitive Visions*, 174 (emphasis added).

30. Oral History 9.

31. Oral History 2.

32. Oral History 4.

33. Oral History 5.

34. Oral History 3.

35. Oral History 11.

36. "To Market, to Market."

37. Mashable, "'Avengers' Joke Ignites Online Protest."

38. Oral History 6.

39. Oral History 5.

40. Oral History 13.

41. Oral History 9.

42. Oral History 1.

43. Oral History 10.

44. Oral History 7.

45. Oral History 12.

46. Oral History 1.

47. See also Kim, *Adopted Territory*, 86.

48. Oral History 13.

49. Oral History 6.

50. Oral History 3.

51. Oral History 5.

52. Oral History 9.

53. These connections include individual friendships, participation in local adult adoptee organizations, utilization of Facebook or Listserves, and/or attending International Korean Adoptee Association gatherings/minigatherings. However, it is important to note that connections with the adult adoptee community varied for each oral history participant.

54. Oral History 8.

55. Oral History 6.

56. Oral History 7.

57. Oral History 12.

Chapter 6. Adoptees Strike Back

1. Jones, "Information, Internet, and Community"; Mark Poster, "Virtual Ethnicity"; Turkle, *Life on the Screen*; and Wilson and Peterson, "The Anthropology of Online Communities."

2. Baym, "The Emergence of On-Line Community." I draw upon Gloria Anzaldúa's work concerning living on the psychological, spiritual, sexual, and physical borders; Anzaldúa, *Borderlands, La Frontera*.

3. Baym, "The Emergence of On-Line Community"; Baym, *Personal Connections in the Digital Age*; Ignacio, *Building Diaspora*; Nakamura, *Cybertypes*; Nakamura, *Digitizing Race*. Eleana J. Kim notes reterritorialization reframes and remaps adoptees' lived experiences from the private sphere into what she defines as multiple national and transnational public spheres—in Korea, Europe, and the United States; Kim, *Adopted Territory*, 8, 15.

4. May Friedman and Silvia Schultermandl discuss how multimedia facilitates transnational connections and how kinship and community ties evolve and transform in response to these hybridized connections; Friedman and Schultermandl, *Click and Kin: Transnational Identity and Quick Media*.

5. Ignacio, *Building Diaspora*, 4.

6. Raible, "Ally Parenting for Social Justice," 90; see also Raible, "TRA Oppression."

7. Seabrook, "The Last Babylift."

8. One birth mother, Lynn Lauber, participated in the blog.

9. Gammage, "A 'Normal' Family."

10. Aronson, "Betrayal of Body and Soul."

11. Anonymous, "Well-Adjusted"; Robinson, "Helping the Next Generation"; and Robinson, "Tracing My Roots Back to Korea." See Nissl, "Return to the Homeland."

12. O'Loughlin, "A Comment about the Comments."

13. For example, in the wake of the April 2010 scandal involving an American couple returning their child to Russia, many news outlets featured stories of struggle and joy written by adoptive parents, while ignoring the voices of the adult, transnational adoptee community; Kim, "I'm Tired of Adoptive Parent Confessionals"; Raible, "Learning from Artyom's Plight"; and Raible, "Sticking with a Wounded Child."

14. Note that, in 2015, Jae Ran Kim completed her PhD in Social Work from the University of Minnesota. At the time of the incidents discussed in this chapter, she was a doctoral student; Kim, "We Will Not Be Silenced"; and Kim, "*New York Times* aka 'the Adoption

Police'?" *Harlow's Monkey* served as a platform for Kim to weave her experiences as an adult adoptee and licensed social worker. She garnered attention for her insightful posts, and found her work cross-posted on *Racialicious,* "a blog at the intersection of race and pop culture"; Kim, "Is the Food Network?"; Kim, "Freaking Out over Freakonomics"; and Kim, "Adopted Chinese Daughters Seek Their Roots." Kim was also an advisor to Adoptees Have Answers, a program funded by the Minnesota Department of Human Services, and cofounder of the Adoption Policy and Reform Collaborative.

15. Janowitz, "The Real Thing"; and Kim, "To Willow Janowitz."

16. Janowitz, "The Real Thing."

17. Kim, "To Willow Janowitz."

18. Rollins, "Racist M/Paternalism at Its Best."

19. McGinnis, "Who Are You Also Known As?"

20. McGinnis, "South Korea and Its Children."

21. McGinnis, "Blood Ties and Acts of Love."

22. Bureau of Consular Affairs, U.S. Department of State, "Understanding the Hague Convention."

23. Bureau of Consular Affairs, U.S. Department of State, "Convention Countries."

24. Bureau of Consular Affairs, U.S. Department of State, "Adoption Notice."

25. A week previously, on July 2, 2012, he participated in a Minnesota Public Radio feature entitled "Tighter Regulations Prompt Drop in International Adoptions"; Baran, "Tighter Regulations Prompt Drop."

26. Johnson et al., "Daily Circuit: International Adoption." .

27. Ellingboe, "What Are Your Experiences as an Adoptee?" See also Park Dahlen, Comment on "MPR, International Adoption."

28. Ellingboe, "What Are Your Experiences as an Adoptee?"

29. Park Nelson et al., "Roundtable."

30. Park Nelson and Kim, "Special Edition." .

31. McDonald, "Opinion Divided on the Merits."

32. Brumfield, "Korean Pastor Fighting Epidemic"; "See That Box?"; and Lam On, "The 'Drop Box' for Unwanted Babies."

33. KoRoot, "Build Families Not Boxes."

34. McKee, "Why I #ThinkOutsidetheBabyBox."

35. Heit, "BUILD FAMILIES NOT BOXES!!

36. McDonald, "Opinion Divided on the Merits."

37. Ibid.

38. Weaver, "An Adoptee at the Baby Box."

39. McCauley Evans, "Build Families, Not Boxes."

40. Perscheid, "#BuildFamiliesNotBoxes."

41. Ramesh, "Spread of 'Baby Boxes' in Europe"; and Evans, "The 'Baby Box' Returns to Europe."

42. Ramesh, "Spread of 'Baby Boxes' in Europe."

43. Shifman, *Memes in Digital Culture,* 18.

44. The origins of the meme trace to the use of SMS shorthands and carefree grammar as a way to bring someone's attention on a particular subject or issue; For more information concerning this meme, see "'Y U NO' Guy." For a discussion of this price differential attached to the bodies of Black children in domestic and international adoption and its introduction to American popular culture as part of NPR programming in 2013, see Raleigh, *Selling Transracial Adoption.*

45. Belogolova, "Russian Adoption Ban Is Personal." On June 30, 2015, the Joint Council on International Children's Services closed permanently.

46. Koch, "Adoption Options Plummet as Russia Closes Its Doors."

47. Newcomb, "Tom Cruise at 50"; and World Entertainment News Network, "Tom Cruise Slams."

48. Jones, "Why a Generation of Adoptees Is Returning."

49. Ibid.

Conclusion

1. This is not the first time that airlines have garnered adoptee business. From the inception of Korean international adoption as well as other transnational adoption programs, airlines operated by both Korea and receiving countries of adoptees have been instrumental in the exchange of children. Airlines benefited from travel arrangements for orphan escorts and the group bookings of flights made on behalf of adoption agencies. Outlining the travel arrangements with Canadian Pacific Airlines, Mrs. Fran Buchholtz, travel officer from International Social Service–American Branch, wrote to Mr. J. J. Trainor, general agent at Canadian Pacific Airlines on August 18. 1966, noting: "Each child will be ticketed as appropriate to his/her age with the exception that at least one child per group will pay a full, adult fare to the final destination"; Box 16, Folder 11, "Orphan travel," International Social Service, American Branch Records, SWHA, University of Minnesota. Buchholtz also confirmed that escorts would receive a "round-trip pass written by [Canadian Pacific Airlines], or obtained by CPAL from connecting carriers, to cover all travel from Seoul." Based on documents from other agencies, it is evident that the complimentary escort fare is calculated into the travel costs adoptive parents cover for their children. For example, an April 1975 Travelers Aid International Social Service of America/WAIF document, "Travel Arrangements for Children Coming from Eastern Asia," notes that travel costs are "based on jet economy fares [and] include escort service, airport and meeting assistance in route, and other out-of-pocket expenses to TAISSA directly connected with the child's travel"; "Travel Arrangements for Children Coming from Eastern Asia," Box 11, Folder 2, International Social Service, American Branch Records, SWHA, University of Minnesota. Travel costs ranged based on age of the child—over or under the age of twelve years old—and destination from Seoul (e.g., Seattle, Chicago, New York). Nevertheless, this complimentary escort fare seems short-lived. Northwest Orient Airlines (Northwest Airlines) ended the practice on February 14, 1977, and required escorts to fly with a full-fare ticket. Notifying the director of Travelers' Aid International Social Service

of America, Wayne E. Hinrichs, on February 22, 1977, Myung Woo Kim, field director of the Child Welfare Department at Social Welfare Society, Inc., also disclosed, "If we do not select competent escorts and possibly give less financial burden to the Airlines, Pan Am will also have the above-mentioned same attitude like NWA and also cease issuing the free escort passes"; Box 34, Folder 19, "SWS Correspondence Re: Flights/Escorts," International Social Service, American Branch Records, SWHA, University of Minnesota. Even as Pan Am was willing to support travel, they did not fly to Korea, which meant that Social Welfare Society, Inc., embarked on a relationship with Korean Airlines to fly orphans and escorts between Seoul and Tokyo. Myung Woo Kim noted, "Korean Airlines will charge one escort for every five children (regardless of age) a 50% reduced-fare ticket. . . . If the number of escorts exceeds this limit (i.e., many infants and subsequently more than one escort to five children) Korean Airlines will charge each additional escort a full-fare ticket." Three days later, Myung Woo Kim wrote again to Hinrichs clarifying that "[Social Welfare Society, Inc. didn't] want both adoptive parents [to] use free ticket as an escort . . ., so in the case that adoptive parents pick up their children, it is desirable that parents buy their tickets with ordinary fare"; Box 34, Folder 19, "SWS Correspondence Re: Flights/Escorts," International Social Service, American Branch Records, SWHA, University of Minnesota. Even as airlines shifted to requiring escorts to purchase airfares, we cannot overlook how, by providing their airlines to orphan groups, airlines garnered positive news coverage and good publicity. Examples of this include newsreel footage of Harry Holt arriving in the United States with children in the late 1950s as well as newspaper articles of local adoptees; Park Nelson, *Invisible Asians*. Whether or not a child was eligible for publicity was even documented in travel arrangement documents from Travelers Aid Society International Social Services of America. After providing each orphans name, sex, age, and adoptive parents' information, whether or not publicity was okay or if there should be no publicity was indicated; Box 16, Folder 12, "Travel Confirmation 1974–75," International Social Service, American Branch Records, SWHA, University of Minnesota. In addition, travel agencies working on behalf of adoption agencies made commissions on flights. Darien, Connecticut–based agency Friends of Children, Inc. notified Youn Teak Tahk, director of Social Welfare Society in Korea, that their preferred agency, Bellinger Davis Travel Agency, charges an 8 percent commission over working directly with Pan Am Airlines in 1977; "Friends of Children correspondence dated April 5, 1977," Box 34, Folder 19, International Social Service, American Branch Records, SWHA, University of Minnesota.

2. For a discussion of adoptees' reflections on reunion with their Korean biological families, see Docan-Morgan, "They Were Strangers Who Loved Me"; Docan-Morgan, "Cultural Differences and Perceived Belonging."

3. Weaver, "Social Minister Stops Adoptions."

4. Department of Justice, "Four Employees of Adoption Services Provider Charged."

5. Ibid.

6. Indo Asian News Service, "Ukraine to Probe Foreign Adoptions"; Khazan, "Why Are Other Countries Wary?"; RT, "Russia Seeks Interpol Investigation of Deaths"; Schwarzschild, "Red Flags Wave."

7. BBC News, "Russia 'Concerned'"; Gerber, "Adopted Russian Toddler's Death"; Lally and Bahrampour, "Death of Adopted Russian Child"; and Weir, "Adopted Toddler's Alleged Death-by-Abuse."

8. Vasilyeva, "Russian Boy Adopted by Americans." Adoption maintained a central role in its relationship with the United States even after the 2016 election; Joyce, "Why Adoption Plays."

9. World Wide News Ukraine, "Ukraine Tracks the Fate."

10. Wright, "Md. Father Charged."

11. Forzato and Moore, "Md. Dad Who Killed Adopted." Given a twenty-year sentence by Judge John Debelius, O'Callaghan's sentence was reduced when Judge Debelius suspended eight years from the sentence and allowed for credit for time served to be applied.

12. "Four Korean Adoptees Murdered in U.S."

13. Twohey et. al., "Reuters Investigates"; and Joyce, *The Child Catchers*.

14. Skalarewitz, "The Shocking 'Babies-by-Mail' Scandal."

15. "A Study of Proxy Adoptions," Box 1, Folder 1, "Adoption: Proxy Adoption, 1957–59," Child Welfare League of America Records, SWHA, University of Minnesota.

16. "Letter Miss Lucille DeVoe, Director of Children's Division of State Department of Public Welfare Indiana."

17. See Dunn, "Standards and Person-making."

References

Primary Sources

Anne M. Davison to International Social Service Korea, May 23, 1960, Box 34, Folder 26, International Social Service, American Branch Records, Social Welfare History Archives, University of Minnesota.

Appendix I: Refugee Relief Bill of 1953 As Passed by Congress and Sent to the President, Box 14, Folder 8, Refugee Relief Act 1945–1958, International Social Service, American Branch Records, Social Welfare History Archives, University of Minnesota.

A Study of Proxy Adoptions, Box 1, Folder 1, "Adoption: Proxy Adoption, 1957–59," Child Welfare League of America Records, SWHA, University of Minnesota.

Box 11, Folder 2, International Social Service, American Branch Records, SWHA, University of Minnesota.

Box 16, Folder 11, "Orphan Travel," International Social Service, American Branch Records, SWHA, University of Minnesota.

Box 16, Folder 12, "Travel Confirmation 1974–75," International Social Service, American Branch Records, SWHA, University of Minnesota.

Box 34, Folder 19, "SWS Correspondence Re: Flights/Escorts," International Social Service, American Branch Records, SWHA, University of Minnesota.

Box 34, Folder 24, International Social Service, American Branch Records, SWHA, University of Minnesota.

Box 35, Folder 5, International Social Service, American Branch Records, SWHA, University of Minnesota.

Box 35, Folder 7, International Social Service, American Branch Records, SWHA, University of Minnesota.

Box 35, Folder "Korea—General, 1961," International Social Service, American Branch Records, Social Welfare History Archives (SWHA), University of Minnesota.

Box 87, Folder 14, Sealed Case Records, International Social Service, American Branch Records, SWHA, University of Minnesota.

Box 129, Folder 10, Sealed Case Records, International Social Service, American Branch Records, SWHA, University of Minnesota.

Box 247, Folder 52, Sealed Case Records, International Social Service, American Branch Records, Social Welfare History Archives, University of Minnesota.

Box 252, Folder 78, Sealed Case Records, International Social Service, American Branch Records, Social Welfare History Archives, University of Minnesota.

Box 255, Folder 8, Sealed Case Records, International Social Service, American Branch Records, Social Welfare History Archives, University of Minnesota.

Box 255, Folder 75, Sealed Case Records, International Social Service, American Branch Records, Social Welfare History Archives, University of Minnesota.

Box 318, Folder 87, Sealed Case Records, International Social Service, American Branch Records, Social Welfare History Archives, University of Minnesota.

Box 322, Folder 61, Sealed Case Records, International Social Service, American Branch Records, Social Welfare History Archives, University of Minnesota.

Box 322, Folder 79, Sealed Case Records, International Social Service, American Branch Records, Social Welfare History Archives, University of Minnesota.

Box 328, "Department of Children and Family Services, Chicago Adoption 1972," Sealed Case Records, International Social Service, American Branch Records, Social Welfare History Archives, University of Minnesota.

Box 328, Folder 2, Sealed Case Records, International Social Service, American Branch Records, Social Welfare History Archives, University of Minnesota.

Box 328, Folder 66, Sealed Case Records, International Social Service, American Branch Records, Social Welfare History Archives, University of Minnesota.

Box 328, "Spence Chapin Adoption," Sealed Case Records, International Social Service, American Branch Records, Social Welfare History Archives, University of Minnesota.

Box 331, "Spence Chapin Adoption," Sealed Case Records, International Social Service, American Branch Records, Social Welfare History Archives, University of Minnesota.

Box 332, "Department of Children and Family Services, Chicago Adoption," Sealed Case Records, International Social Service, American Branch Records, Social Welfare History Archives, University of Minnesota.

Box 332, "Family and Children Services of Albany Adoption," Sealed Case Records, International Social Service, American Branch Records, Social Welfare History Archives, University of Minnesota.

Box 332, Folder 46, Sealed Case Records, International Social Service, American Branch Records, Social Welfare History Archives, University of Minnesota.

Box 332, "October 1972 Sealed Case Record," Sealed Case Records, International Social

Service, American Branch Records, Social Welfare History Archives, University of Minnesota.

Box 358, Folder 2, Sealed Case Records, International Social Service, American Branch Records, Social Welfare History Archives, University of Minnesota.

Box 358, Folder 17, Sealed Case Records, International Social Service, American Branch Records, Social Welfare History Archives, University of Minnesota.

Box 358, Folder 22, Sealed Case Records, International Social Service, American Branch Records, Social Welfare History Archives, University of Minnesota.

Box 358, Folder 38, Sealed Case Records, International Social Service, American Branch Records, Social Welfare History Archives, University of Minnesota.

Box 359, Folder 8, Sealed Case Records, International Social Service, American Branch Records, Social Welfare History Archives, University of Minnesota.

Box 360, Folder 3, Sealed Case Records, International Social Service, American Branch Records, Social Welfare History Archives, University of Minnesota.

Box 360, Folder 5, Sealed Case Records, International Social Service, American Branch Records, Social Welfare History Archives, University of Minnesota.

Box 360, Folder 7, Sealed Case Records, International Social Service, American Branch Records, Social Welfare History Archives, University of Minnesota.

Box 360, Folder 11, Sealed Case Records, International Social Service, American Branch Records, Social Welfare History Archives, University of Minnesota.

Box 360, Folder 14, Sealed Case Records, International Social Service, American Branch Records, Social Welfare History Archives, University of Minnesota.

Box 360, Folder 21, Sealed Case Records, International Social Service, American Branch Records, Social Welfare History Archives, University of Minnesota.

Box 360, Folder 24, Sealed Case Records, International Social Service, American Branch Records, Social Welfare History Archives, University of Minnesota.

Case Records, 1929–1995, International Social Service, American Branch Records, Social Welfare History Archives, University of Minnesota.

Communication to Senator Kennedy, Box 16, Folder 4, Naturalization of Adopted Child 1971, International Social Service, American Branch Records, Social Welfare History Archives, University of Minnesota.

Correspondence, Box 10, Folder 14, International Social Service, American Branch Records, Social Welfare History Archives, University of Minnesota.

Correspondence from Associate Director, Susan T. Pettiss to Ann Davison, International Social Service—Korea, Box 34, Folder 23, General 1957–1974, International Social Service, American Branch Records, Social Welfare History Archives, University of Minnesota.

Cost of Intercountry Adoption Program, Box 11, Folder 1, International Social Service, American Branch Records, Social Welfare History Archives, University of Minnesota.

Cost of WAIF Intercountry Adoption Program, Box 11, Folder 2, International Social Service, American Branch Records, Social Welfare History Archives, University of Minnesota.

Field Trip to Korea, Department of Health, Education and Welfare, Box 35, Folder 2, International Social Service, American Branch Records, Social Welfare History Archives, University of Minnesota.

Friends of Children correspondence dated April 5, 1977, Box 34, Folder 19, International Social Service, American Branch Records, SWHA, University of Minnesota.

Hyde, Laurin, and Virginia P. Hyde. *A Study of Proxy Adoptions*. New York: Child Welfare League of American and International Social Service, American Branch, 1958, Box 17, Folder 1, Child Welfare League of America Records, Social Welfare History Archives, University of Minnesota.

Letter from Assistant Director Susan T. Pettis, Box 10, Folder 12, International Social Service, American Branch Records, Social Welfare History Archives, University of Minnesota.

Letter from Miss Lucille DeVoe, Director of Children's Division of State Department of Public Welfare Indiana, Box 10, Folder 31, International Social Service, American Branch Records, SWHA, University of Minnesota.

Mayo, Leonard W. (1954, May), "Korea, Key to the Orient." *Junior League Journal*, "The Observer," Box 1, Folder "Korea, Key to the Orient," Leonard Mayo Papers, Social Welfare History Archives, University of Minnesota.

Mayo, Leonard W. "Children of a New World." *New York Times*, March 1953, Box 1, Folder "2,000 Reasons to Help South Korea," Leonard Mayo Papers, Social Welfare History Archive, University of Minnesota.

New U.S. Immigration and Nationality Provisions, Box 17, Folder 7, INS Revisions, International Social Service, American Branch Records, SWHA, University of Minnesota.

Procedures Affecting Foreign-Born Children Adopted in the United States, Box 11, Folder 3, Forms for Adoption Procedures, International Social Service, American Branch Records, Social Welfare History Archives, University of Minnesota.

Report of the Rusk Mission to Korea, March 11–18, 1953, Box 3, Folder American Korean Foundation, Leonard Mayo Papers, Social Welfare History Archives, University of Minnesota.

Report of Visit to Korea, June 18 to July 13, 1962, by the Director of ISS, American Branch, Box 35, Folder "Korea—Reports and Visits," International Social Service, American Branch Records, Social Welfare History Archives, University of Minnesota.

Report on 1965 Korea Visit to Paul R. Cherney, ISS American Branch, Box 35, Folder 2, International Social Service, American Branch Records, Social Welfare History Archives, University of Minnesota.

Report on Eclair Program June 1971, Box 35, Folder 5, Child Placement Service, Inc. Records, Social Welfare History Archives, University of Minnesota.

Skalarewitz, Norman. "The Shocking 'Babies-by-Mail' Scandal," Box 4, Folder "ISS-General Administrative, 1964–66," International Social Service, American Branch Records, SWHA, University of Minnesota.

Sponsor Advertisement. "Help Heal a Child's Broken Heart," Box 10, Folder 28, International Social Service, American Branch Records, Social Welfare History Archives, University of Minnesota.

Travel Arrangements for Children Coming from Eastern Asia, Box 11, Folder 2, International Social Service, American Branch Records, SWHA, University of Minnesota.

United States Department of Justice Immigration and Naturalization Service, *Public Law 97–359: Amerasian Processing Manual*, Box 46, Folder 5, International Social Service, American Branch Records, Social Welfare History Archives, University of Minnesota.

Valk, Margaret A. "Korean-American Children in American Adoptive Homes," National Conference on Social Welfare, 1957, Box 34, Folder 19, International Social Service, American Branch Records, Social Welfare History Archives, University of Minnesota.

Secondary Sources

AdopSource. "Stop the Deportation of Russell Green." AdopSource, 2013. http://www.adopsource.org/deportation_russell.html.

Adoptee Citizenship Act of 2018, H.R. 5233, 115th Cong. (2018).

Adoptee Citizenship Act of 2018, S. 2522, 115th Cong. (2018).

Adoptee Rights Campaign. "Progress Updates #CitizenshipForAllAdoptees," Adoptee Rights Campaign. http://adopteerightscampaign.org/progress/.

Adoptee Rights Campaign. "Summary of the Family Is More Than DNA Postcard Campaign," Adoptee Rights Campaign, 2016. http://adopteerightscampaign.org/wp-content/uploads/sites/23/2016/09/Summary-of-the-Postcard-campaign_English.pdf.

Adoptees Have Answers: Sandy White Hawk. Produced by Adoptees Have Answers. Performed by Sandy White Hawk. YouTube, April 7, 2010. http://www.youtube.com/watch?v=ZH-BHvACYiw.

Adoptive Families. "Latest Adoption Cost and Wait Time Data." Adoptive Families, 2013. http://www.adoptivefamilies.com/articles.php?aid=2161.

Ahmed, Sara. *The Promise of Happiness*. Durham: Duke University Press, 2010.

Altstein, Howard, and Rita J. Simon. *Intercountry Adoption: A Multinational Perspective*. New York: Praeger, 1991.

American Immigration Council. "The DREAM Act." Last modified June 16, 2014. http://www.immigrationpolicy.org/issues/DREAM-Act.

Anchisi, Lidia. "One, No One, and a Hundred Thousand: On Being a Korean Woman Adopted by European Parents." In *The Intersectional Approach: Transforming the Academy through Race, Class, and Gender*, edited by Michele Tracy Berger and Kathleen Guidroz, 290–299. Chapel Hill: University of North Carolina Press, 2009.

Anonymous. "Well-Adjusted." *New York Times* (web log), December 1, 2007. http://relativechoices.blogs.nytimes.com/2007/12/01/well-adjusted/.

Anzaldúa, Gloria. *Borderlands, La Frontera: The New Mestiza*. San Francisco: Aunt Lute, 1987.

Arce, Rose, and Soledad O'Brien. "Most Have Homes, but Some Haitian Orphans Still in Shelters." CNN, January 13, 2011. http://edition.cnn.com/2011/US/01/11/haiti.us.orphans/index.html.

Arnold, D. "The Adoption Custom." *Sunday Oregonian* (Portland), January 15, 1989.

Aronson, Jane. "Betrayal of Body and Soul: A Tribute to Ben." *New York Times* (web log), November 28, 2007. http://relativechoices.blogs.nytimes.com/2007/11/28/betrayal -of-body-and-soul-a-tribute-to-ben/.

"ASIAN-ISH Ep. 1 W/ DANakaDAN—Korean Adoptee vs Korean Food," YouTube Video, 7:14, posted by "ISAtv," August 25, 2015. https://www.youtube.com/watch?v =eQnHOIKJQEI.

"ASIAN*ISH—How to Drink like a Korean!—EP 5 PART 1." YouTube Video, 6:14. posted by "ISAtv," March 15, 2015. https://www.youtube.com/watch?v=NVy-c-FI5ik.

Aspalter, Christian. "The East Asian Welfare Model." *International Journal of Social Welfare* 15, no. 4 (2006): 290–301. doi:10.1111/j.1468–2397.2006.00413.x.

Associated Press. "Boy Sent Back to Russia; Adoption Ban Urged." MSNBC, April 9, 2010. http://www.nbcnews.com/id/36322282/ns/world_news-europe/t/boy-sent-back -russia-adoption-ban-urged/#.UWLhEBk8z6Z.

Australian Government. "Past Adoption Practices." Australian Government Department Families, Housing, Community Services and Indigenous Affairs, January 25, 2013. http:// www.fahcsia.gov.au/our-responsibilities/families-and-children/programs-services/ past-adoption-practices.

Awkward, Michael. *Negotiating Difference: Race, Gender, and the Politics of Positionality.* Chicago: University of Chicago Press, 1995.

Baden, Amanda L., and Robbie J. Steward. "A Framework for Use with Racially and Culturally Integrated Families: The Cultural-Racial Identity Model as Applied to Transracial Adoption." *Journal of Social Distress and the Homeless* 9, no. 4 (2000): 309–337.

Bae, Gang Shik. "John Seabrook NPR Segment." *The Transracial Korean Adoptee Nexus* (web log), May 17, 2010. http://kadnexus.wordpress.com/2010/05/17/john-seabrook -npr-segment.

Bagley, Christopher, Loretta Young, and Anne Scully. *International and Transracial Adoptions: A Mental Health Perspective.* Aldershot: Avebury, 1993.

Balcom, Karen. "Back Door In: Private Immigration Bills and Transnational Adoption in the US in the 1940s and 1950s." Lecture, Alliance for the Study of Adoption and Culture Conference, Scripps College, Claremont, March 22, 2012.

Banda, P. Solomon. "Utah Woman Adopted as Baby Faces Deportation to India, despite No Connections There." *Deseret News*, May 28, 2012. http://www.deseretnews.com/ article/865556540/Utah-woman-adopted-as-baby-faces-deportation-to-India-despite -no-connections-there.html?pg=1.

Baran, Madeleine. "Tighter Regulations Prompt Drop in International Adoptions." *Minnesota Public Radio*, July 2, 2012. http://minnesota.publicradio.org/display/web/2012/ 07/02/social-issue-international-adoption.

Barnett, Teresa, and Chon A. Noriega, eds. *Oral History and Communities of Color.* Los Angeles: UCLA Chicano Studies Research Center Press, 2013.

Baym, Nancy K. *Personal Connections in the Digital Age.* Cambridge: Polity Press, 2010.

———. "The Emergence of On-Line Community." In *CyberSociety 2.0: Revisiting Computer-mediated Communication and Community,* edited by Steven G. Jones, 35–68. Thousand Oaks: Sage Publications, 1998.

BBC News. "Russia 'Concerned' over Max Shatto Texas Death Ruling." *BBC News*, March 2, 2013. http://www.bbc.co.uk/news/world-europe-21640246.

Beauchamp, Zack. "This Was the Scariest Part of Trump's State of the Union," Vox, January 30, 2018. https://www.vox.com/world/2018/1/30/16953558/state-of-the-union-trump -north-korea.

Belogolova, Olga. "Russian Adoption Ban Is Personal for Some U.S. Lawmakers." *National Journal*, January 29, 2013. http://www.nationaljournal.com/congress/russian-adoption -ban-is-personal-for-some-u-s-lawmakers-20130129.

Benson, Krista. "Tensions of Subjectivity: The Instability of Queer Polyamorous Identity and Community." *Sexualities* 20, no. 1–2 (2017): 24–40.

Berebitsky, Julie. *Like Our Very Own: Adoption and the Changing Culture of Motherhood, 1851–1950*. Lawrence: University Press of Kansas, 2000.

Bergquist, Kathleen Ja Sook, M. Elizabeth Vonk, Dong Soo Kim, and Marvin D. Feit, eds. *International Korean Adoption: A Fifty-year History of Policy and Practice*. New York: Haworth Press, 2007.

Berry, Wayne A. "Completing My Puzzle. . . ." In *Seeds from a Silent Tree: An Anthology by Korean Adoptees*, edited by Tonya Bishoff and Jo Rankin, 121–123. San Diego: Pandal Press, 1997.

Bhabha, Homi K. *The Location of Culture*. London: Routledge, 1994.

Bishoff, Tonya, and Jo Rankin, eds. *Seeds from a Silent Tree: An Anthology by Korean Adoptees*. San Diego: Pandal Press, 1997.

Blakely, Kristin. "Busy Brides and the Business of Family Life: The Wedding-Planning Industry and the Commodity Frontier." *Journal of Family Issues* 29, no. 5 (2007): 639–662.

Bonilla-Silva, Eduardo. *Racism without Racists: Color-blind Racism and the Persistence of Racial Inequality in America*. Lanham: Rowman and Littlefield, 2013.

Bosniak, Linda. *The Citizen and the Alien: Dilemmas of Contemporary Membership*. Princeton: Princeton University Press, 2006.

Bourdain, Anthony. *Anthony Bourdain: Parts Unknown*. "Korea." CNN, April 26, 2015.

Brennan, Chris. "Gov. Rendell aboard Haitian Orphan-rescue Flight." *Philadelphia Inquirer*, January 19, 2010. http://articles.philly.com/2010–01–19/news/24956212_1 _rendell-orphanage-medical-supplies.

Brian, Kristi. *Reframing Transracial Adoption: Adopted Koreans, White Parents, and the Politics of Kinship*. Philadelphia: Temple University Press, 2012.

Briggs, Laura. *Somebody's Children: The Politics of Transracial and Transnational Adoption*. Durham: Duke University Press, 2012.

Bruining, Mi Oak Song. "A Few Words from Another Left-Handed Adopted Korean Lesbian." In *Seeds from a Silent Tree: An Anthology by Korean Adoptees*, edited by Tonya Bishoff and Jo Rankin, 64–72. San Diego: Pandal Press, 1997.

Brumfield, Natalie M. "Korean Pastor Fighting Epidemic of Abandoned Babies with Anonymous 'Baby Box.'" LifeSiteNews, May 28, 2013. http://www.lifesitenews.com/ news/korean-pastor.

Burditt, Rebecca. "Seeing Is Believing: 1950s Popular Media Representations of Korean Adoption in the United States." In *Proceedings of the First International Korean Adoption*

Studies Research Symposium, edited by Kim Park Nelson, Eleana Kim, and Lena Myong Petersen, 107–123. Seoul: Dongguk University, 2007.

Bureau of Consular Affairs, U.S. Department of State. "Adoption Notice: The Republic of Korea Signs the Hague Adoption Convention." http://travel.state.gov/content/ adoptionsabroad/en/country-information/alerts-andnotices/south-korea-2.html.

———. "Convention Countries." http://travel.state.gov/content/adoptionsabroad/en/ hague-convention/convention-countries.html.

———. "India." Intercountry Adoption, November 2013. http://adoption.state.gov/ country_information/country_specific_info.php?country-select=india.

———. "Non-Hague Adoption Process," Intercountry Adoption, 2013. http://adoption .state.gov/adoption_process/how_to_adopt/nonhague.php.

———. "South Korea," Intercountry Adoption, 2013. http://adoption.state.gov/country _information/country_specific_info.php?country-select=south_korea.

———. "Statistics," Intercountry Adoption, 2010. http://adoption.state.gov/about_us/ statistics.php.

———. "Thailand," Intercountry Adoption, February 2014. http://adoption.state.gov/ country_information/country_specific_info.php?countryselect=thailand.

———. "Understanding the Hague Convention," Intercountry Adoption, 2013. http:// adoption.state.gov/hague_convention/overview.php.

Butler, Judith. *Bodies that Matter: On the Discursive Limits of "Sex."* New York: Routledge, 1993.

———. *Gender Trouble: Feminism and the Subversion of Identity.* New York: Routledge, 1990.

———. "Is Kinship Always Heterosexual?" In *Going Public: Feminism and the Shifting Boundaries of the Private Sphere,* edited by Joan Wallach Scott and Debra Keates, 123–150. Urbana: University of Illinois Press, 2004.

Cahn, Naomi R. *The New Kinship: Constructing Donor-conceived Families.* New York: NewYork University Press, 2013.

Caraway, Nancie. *Segregated Sisterhood: Racism and the Politics of American Feminism.* Knoxville: University of Tennessee Press, 1991.

Carp, E. Wayne. *Family Matters: Secrecy and Disclosure in the History of Adoption.* Cambridge: Harvard University Press, 1998.

Carsten, Janet. *After Kinship.* Cambridge: Cambridge University Press, 2004.

Cartwright, Lisa. "Photographs of 'Waiting Children'": The Transnational Adoption Market." *Social Text* 21, no. 1 (2003): 83–109.

CBS News Staff. "Julie Chen Reveals She Had Plastic Surgery to Make Her Eyes Look Bigger." CBSNews, September 12, 2013. http://www.cbsnews.com/news/julie-chen -reveals-she-had-plastic-surgery-to-make-eyes-look-bigger.

Cha, Victor. "Giving North Korea a 'Bloody Nose' Carries a Huge Risk to Americans." *Washington Post,* January 30, 2018. https://www.washingtonpost.com/opinions/victor -cha-giving-north-korea-a-bloody-nose-carries-a-huge-risk-to-americans/2018/01/30/ 43981c94–05f7–11e8–8777–2a059f168dd2_story.html.

Chan, Sucheng. *Asian Americans: An Interpretive History.* Boston: Twayne, 1991.

Chappell, Crystal Lee Hyun Joo. "Now I'm Found." In *Seeds from a Silent Tree: An Anthology by Korean Adoptees*, edited by Tonya Bishoff and Jo Rankin, 124–135. San Diego: Pandal Press, 1997.

Chen, Tina. *Double Agency: Acts of Impersonation in Asian American Literature and Culture.* Stanford: Stanford University Press, 2005.

Cheung, King-Kok, ed. *An Interethnic Companion to Asian American Literature.* Cambridge: Cambridge University Press, 1997.

Chira, Susan. "Babies for Export: And Now the Painful Questions." *New York Times*, April 21, 1988. http://www.nytimes.com/1988/04/21/world/seoul-journal-babies -for-export-and-now-the-painful-questions.html?pagewanted=all.

Chishti, Muzaffar, and Michelle Mittelstadt. "Unauthorizing Immigrants with Criminal Convictions: Who Might Be a Priority for Removal?" Migration Policy Institute, November 2016. https://www.migrationpolicy.org/news/unauthorized-immigrants-criminal-convictions-who-might-be-priority-removal.

Cho, Grace M. *Haunting the Korean Diaspora: Shame, Secrecy, and the Forgotten War.* Minneapolis: University of Minnesota Press, 2008.

Cho, Hyoung, Ann Zammit, Jinjoo Chung, and In-Soon Kang. "Korea's Miracle and Crisis: What Was in It for Women." In *Globalization, Export-oriented Employment, and Social Policy: Gendered Connections*, edited by Shahra Razavi, Ruth Pearson, and Caroline Danloy, 30–66. New York: Palgrave Macmillan, 2004.

Choe, Hyun. "National Identity and Citizenship in the People's Republic of China and the Republic of Korea." *Journal of Historical Sociology* 19, no. 1 (2006): 84–118. doi:10.1111/j.1467–6443.2006.00270.x.

Choe, Sang-Hun. "Deportation a 'Death Sentence' to Adoptees after a Lifetime in the U.S." *New York Times*, July 2, 2017. https://www.nytimes.com/2017/07/02/world/asia/south-korea-adoptions-phillip-clay-adam-crapser.html.

———. "Group Resists Korean Stigma for Unwed Mothers." *New York Times*, October 8, 2009. http://www.nytimes.com/2009/10/08/world/asia/08mothers.html.

———. "Korean Mother Awaits a Son's Deportation to Confess Her 'Unforgivable Sin.'" *New York Times*, November 16, 2016. http://www.nytimes.com/2016/11/17/world/asia/korea-adoption-adam-crapser.html?_r=0.

Choi, Elizabeth. "Status of the Family and Motherhood for Korean Women." In *Women of Japan and Korea: Continuity and Change*, edited by Joyce Gelb and Marian L. Palley, 189–205. Philadelphia: Temple University Press, 1994.

Chosun Ilbo. "Childcare Remains Obstacle to Women's Careers." *Chosun Ilbo*, July 18, 2011. http://english.chosun.com/site/data/html_dir/2011/07/18/2011071800349.html.

———. "Gov't in Bid to Encourage Adoption in Korea." *Chosun Ilbo*, July 18, 2006. http://english.chosun.com/site/data/html_dir/2006/07/18/2006071861031.html.

Chow, Kat. *Global Families: A History of Asian International Adoption in America.* New York: New York University Press, 2013.

———. "Institutionalizing International Adoption: The Historical Origins of Korean Adoption in the United States." In *International Korean Adoption: A Fifty-year History of Policy and Practice*, edited by Kathleen Ja Sook Bergquist, M. Elizabeth Vonk, Dong Soo Kim, and Marvin D. Feit, 25–42. New York: Haworth Press, 2007.

———. "The Many Stories behind Double-Eyelid Surgery." NPR. November 18, 2014. http://www.npr.org/blogs/codeswitch/2014/11/18/364670361/the-many-stories -behindthe-double-eyelid-surgery.

Choy, Catherine Ceniza. *Empires of Care: Nursing and Migration in Filipino American History*. Durham: Duke University Press, 2003.

Choy, Catherine Ceniza, and Gregory Paul Choy. "Transformative Terrains: Korean American Adoptees and the Social Constructions of an American Childhood." In *The American Child: A Cultural Studies Reader*, edited by Caroline Field Levander and Carol J. Singley, 262–279. New Brunswick, N.J.: Rutgers University Press, 2003.

Chuh, Kandice. *Imagine Otherwise: On Asian Americanist Critique*. Durham: Duke University Press, 2003.

Chung, Hyun-back. "Together and Separately: 'The New Women's Movement' after the 1980s in South Korea." *Asian Women* 5 (Fall 1997): 19–38.

Chung, Olivia. "Finding My Eye-dentity." In *Yell-oh Girls! Emerging Voices Explore Culture, Identity, and Growing Up Asian American*, edited by Vickie Nam, 137–139. New York: Quill, 2001.

Citizenship for All Adoptees, "Can I Just Get a Passport Please?" Citizenship for All Adoptees, 2013. http://citizenshipfor alladoptees.tumblr.com.

Clement, Thomas Park. "School Daze." In *Voices from Another Place: A Collection of Works from a Generation Born in Korea and Adopted to Other Countries*, edited by Susan Soon-Keum Cox, 6–9. St. Paul: Yeong and Yeong Book, 1999.

———. "The Unforgotten War." In *Seeds from a Silent Tree: An Anthology by Korean Adoptees*, edited by Tonya Bishoff and Jo Rankin, 21–30. San Diego: Pandal Press, 1997.

Cockroft, Sherilyn. "New Beginnings." In *Seeds from a Silent Tree: An Anthology by Korean Adoptees*, edited by Tonya Bishoff and Jo Rankin, 10–17. San Diego: Pandal Press, 1997.

Cole, Barbara Ann. "Gender, Narratives and Intersectionality: Can Personal Experience Approaches to Research Contribute to 'Undoing Gender'?" *International Review of Education* 55 (2009): 561–578.

Colen, Shellee. "'Like a Mother to Them': Stratified Reproduction and West Indian Childcare Workers and Employers in New York." In *Conceiving the New World Order: The Global Politics of Reproduction*, edited by Faye D. Ginsberg and Rayna Rapp, 78–102. Berkeley: University of California Press, 1995.

———. "With Respect and Feelings: Voices of West Indian Child Care and Domestic Workers in New York City." In *All American Women: Lines that Divide, Ties that Bind*, edited by Johnetta B. Cole, 36–70. New York: Free Press, 1986.

Collier, Stephen J., and Aihwa Ong, eds. *Global Assemblages: Technology, Politics, and Ethics as Anthropological Problems*. Malden, Mass.: Blackwell Publishing, 2005.

Condit-Shrestha, Kelly. "South Korea and Adoption's Ends: Reexamining the Numbers and Historicizing Market Economies." *Adoption & Culture* 6, no. 2 (Forthcoming, 2018).

Constable, Pamela. "Russian Orphan Reaches D.C. Home Just as Moscow Bans Further U.S. Adoptions." *Washington Post,* January 7, 2013. http://www.washingtonpost.com/local/russian-orphan-reaches-dc-home-just-as-moscow-bans-further-us-adoptions/2013/01/07/7ed81d3c-5688–11e2–8b9e-dd8773594efc_story.html.

Cornell, Stephen E., and Douglas Hartmann. *Ethnicity and Race: Making Identities in a Changing World.* Thousand Oaks: Pine Forge Press, 1998.

Cosslett, Tess, Celia Lury, and Penny Summerfield, eds. *Feminism and Autobiography: Texts, Theories, Methods.* London: Routledge, 2000.

Cox, Susan Soon-Keum. *Voices from Another Place: A Collection of Works from a Generation Born in Korea and Adopted to Other Countries.* St. Paul: Yeong and Yeong Book, 1999.

D'Arcy, Claudia Corrigan. "If Adoptees Are Gifts Then Adoption Is Regifting God's Presents." *Musings of the Lame,* December 9, 2014. http://www.adoptionbirthmothers.com/adoption-is-regifting-from-god/.

Davidson, Kelley. "These 7 Household Names Make a Killing Off of the Prison-Industrial Complex." *U.S. Uncut,* August 30, 2015. http://usuncut.com/class-war/these-7-household-names-make-a-killing-off-of-the-prison-industrial-complex/.

Davis, Angela Y. *Are Prisons Obsolete?* New York City: Seven Stories Press, 2003.

Davis, Lisa Kim. "Korean Women's Groups Organize for Change." In *Women of Japan and Korea: Continuity and Change,* edited by Joyce Gelb and Marian L. Palley, 223–239. Philadelphia: Temple University Press, 1994.

Dawsey, Josh. "Trump Derides Protections for Immigration from 'Shithole' Countries," *Washington Post,* January 12, 2018. https://www.washingtonpost.com/politics/trump-attacks-protections-for-immigrants-from-shithole-countries-in-oval-office-meeting/2018/01/11/bfc0725c-f711–11e7–91af-31ac729add94_story.html.

Delale-O'Connor, Lori. "Learning to Be Me: The Role of Adoptee Culture Camps in Teaching Adopted Children Their Birth Culture." *Adoption & Culture* 2, no. 1 (2009): 203–226.

DeLanda, Manuel. *A New Philosophy of Society: Assemblage Theory and Social Complexity.* London: Continuum, 2009.

Department of Homeland Security. "Before Your Child Immigrates to the United States," U.S. Citizenship and Immigration Services, March 28, 2017. https://www.uscis.gov/adoption/bringing-your-internationally-adopted-child-united-states/your-new-childs-immigrant-visa.

———. "Your New Child's Immigrant Visa." *United States Citizenship and Immigration Services,* May 17, 2011. http://www.uscis.gov/adoption/bringing-your-internationally-adopted-child-unitedstates/your-new-childs-immigrant-visa.

———. "Your New Child's Immigrant Visa," U.S. Citizenship and Immigration Services, March 17, 2015. https://www.uscis.gov/adoption/bringing-your-internationally-adopted-child-united-states/your-new-childs-immigrant-visa.

Department of Justice. "Four Employees of Adoption Services Provider Charged with Conspiracy to Defraud the United States in Connection with Ethiopia Operations." News release, February 11, 2014. United States Department of Justice. http://www.justice.gov/opa/pr/2014/February/14-crm-149.html.

Derickson, Kate Driscoll. "The Racial Politics of Neoliberal Regulation in Post-Katrina Mississippi." *Annals of the Association of American Geographers* 104, no. 4 (2014): 889–902. doi:10.1080/00045608.2014.912542.

Docan-Morgan, Sara. "Cultural Differences and Perceived Belonging during Korean Adoptees' Reunions with Birth Families." *Adoption Quarterly* 19, no. 2 (2016): 99–118.

———. "'They Were Strangers Who Loved Me': Discussions, Narratives, and Rituals during Korean Adoptees' Initial Reunions with Birth Families." *Journal of Family Communication* 14, no. 4 (2014): 352–373.

Dokoupil, Tony. "What Adopting a White Girl Taught One Black Family." *Newsweek*, April 22, 2009. http://www.newsweek.com/what-adopting-white-girl-taught-one-black-family-77335.

Dorin Kobus, Amy Mee-Ran. "Hello Good-bye Hello." In *Voices from Another Place: A Collection of Works from a Generation Born in Korea and Adopted to Other Countries*, edited by Susan Soon-Keum Cox, 41–49. St. Paul: Yeong and Yeong Book, 1999.

Dorow, Sara K. *Transnational Adoption: A Cultural Economy of Race, Gender, and Kinship.* New York: New York University Press, 2006.

Dubinsky, Karen. *Babies without Borders: Adoption and Migration across the Americas.* New York: New York University Press, 2010.

———. "The Fantasy of the Global Cabbage Patch: Making Sense of Transnational Adoption." *Feminist Theory* 9, no. 3 (2008): 339–345. doi:10.1177/1464700108095855.

Duggan, Lisa. *The Twilight of Equality? Neoliberalism, Cultural Politics, and the Attack on Democracy.* Boston: Beacon Press, 2003.

Dunaway, David King, and Willa K. Baum, eds. *Oral History: An Interdisciplinary Anthology by Korean Adoptees.* Second ed. Lanham: Altamira Press, 1996.

Dunn, Elizabeth C. "Standards and Person-making in East Central Europe." In *Global Assemblages: Technology, Politics, and Ethics as Anthropological Problems*, edited by Aihwa Ong and Stephen J. Collier, 173–193. Malden, Mass.: Blackwell Publishing, 2005.

Edelman, Lee. *No Future: Queer Theory and the Death Drive.* Durham: Duke University Press, 2004.

———. "Queer Theory: Unstating Desire." *GLQ: A Journal of Lesbian and Gay Studies* 2, no. 4 (1995): 343–346.

Ehrenreich, Nancy. "Subordination and Symbiosis: Mechanisms of Mutual Support between Subordinating Systems." *UMKC Law Review* 71, no. 2 (2003): 251–324.

Eisenhower, Dwight D. "President Dwight D. Eisenhower's Farewell Address." Speech, Farewell Address, Washington D.C., 1961. http://ourdocuments.gov/doc.php?flash=true&doc=90&page=transcript.

Elam, Michelle. *The Souls of Mixed Folks: Race, Politics, and Aesthetics in the New Millennium.* Stanford: Stanford University Press, 2011.

Ellingboe, Meggan. "What Are Your Experiences as an Adoptee?" Minnesota Public Radio, July 10, 2012. http://minnesota.publicradio.org/collections/special/columns/daily_circuit/archive/2012/07/help-create-a-stronger-community-of-international-adoptees-and-families.shtml.

Elson, Diane. "From Survival Strategies to Transformation Strategies: Women's Needs and Structural Adjustment." In *Unequal Burden: Economic Crisis, Persistent Poverty, and Women's Work*, edited by Lourdes Benería and Shelley Feldman, 26–48. Oxford: Westview Press, 1992.

Embassy of the Republic of Korea in the USA. "Visa Issuance." http://usa.mofa.go.kr/english/am/usa/visa/visa/index.jsp.

Eng, David L. *The Feeling of Kinship: Queer Liberalism and the Racialization of Intimacy*. Durham: Duke University Press, 2010.

Eng, David L., and Alice Y. Hom, eds. *Q & A: Queer in Asian America*. Philadelphia: Temple University Press, 1998.

———. *The Curious Feminist: Searching for Women in a New Age of Empire*. Berkeley: University of California Press, 2004.

Enloe, Cynthia H. *Maneuvers: The International Politics of Militarizing Women's Lives*. Berkeley: University of California Press, 2000.

Ergas, Yasmine. "Are Children Today's Iron Ore? Russia's Adoption Ban and International Diplomacy." *Huffington Post* (web log), January 8, 2013. http://www.huffingtonpost.com/yasmine-ergas/russian-adoption-ban_b_2433606.html.

Espiritu, Yen Le. *Asian American Women and Men: Labor, Laws and Love*. Thousand Oaks: Sage Publications, 1997.

Eun, Elizabeth. "Where I Came From." *KoreAM*, February 7, 2011. http://iamkoream.com/where-i-come-from/.

Evan B. Donaldson Adoption Institute. *Intercountry Adoption in Emergencies: The Tsunami Orphans*. Issue brief, April 2005. http://www.adoptioninstitute.org/publications/2005_Brief_ICA_In_Emergencies_April.pdf.

Evans, Karin. *The Lost Daughters of China: Adopted Girls, Their Journey to America, and the Search for a Missing Past*. New York: Jeremy P. Tarcher/Penguin, 2008.

Evans, Stephen. "The 'Baby Box' Returns to Europe." BBC News, June 26, 2012. http://www.bbc.co.uk/news/magazine-18585020.

Ewing, Maura. "She'll Get US Citizenship 60 Years after Being Adopted, but Thousands More Must Still Wait." *PRI*, July 1, 2016. http://www.pri.org/stories/2016-07-01/shell-get-us-citizenship-60-years-after-being-adopted-thousands-more-must-still.

Fanon, Frantz. *Black Skin, White Masks*, translated by Richard Philcox. New York: Grove Press, 2008/1952.

———. *The Wretched of the Earth*, translated by Constance Farrington. London: Penguin Books, 2001/1961.

Fenkl, Heinz Insu. "The Future of Korean American Literature." In *The Sigur Center Asia Papers: Korean American Literature*, edited by Young-Key Kim-Renaud, R. Richard Grinker, and Kirk Larsen, 19–26. Washington, D.C.: Sigur Center for Asian Studies, 2004.

Fermi, Mark. "A Sense of Loss." In *Voices from Another Place: A Collection of Works from a Generation Born in Korea and Adopted to Other Countries*, edited by Susan Soon-Keum Cox, 20–23. St. Paul: Yeong and Yeong Book, 1999.

Fineman, Martha Albertson. *The Neutered Mother, The Sexual Family, and Other Twentieth Century Tragedies*. New York: Routledge, 1995.

First Person Plural. Directed by Deann Borshay Liem. San Francisco: Center for Asian American Media, 2000. DVD.

Fogg-Davis, Hawley Grace. *The Ethics of Transracial Adoption.* Ithaca: Cornell University Press, 2002.

Forzato, Jamie, and Jack Moore. "Md. Dad Who Killed Adopted Son Sentenced to 12 Years in Prison." *WTOP*, July 19, 2016. http://wtop.com/montgomery-county/2016/07/md-dad-admitted-killing-adopted-son-suffered-ptsd-colleagues-say/.

"Four Korean Adoptees Murdered in U.S." Chosun Ilbo. March 27, 2008. http://english.chosun.com/site/data/html_dir/2008/03/27/2008032761009.html.

Frailey, Mike. "Citizenship for ALL Adoptees." SignOn.org., 2013. http://signon.org/sign/citizenship-for-all-adoptees.

Frankenberg, Ruth. *White Women, Race Matters: The Social Construction of Whiteness.* Routledge: London, 1993.

Franklin, Sarah. "Biologization Revisited: Kinship Theory in the Context of the New Biologies." In *Relative Values: Reconfiguring Kinship Studies*, edited by Sarah Franklin and Susan McKinnon, 302–325. Durham: Duke University Press, 2001.

Franklin, Sarah, and Susan McKinnon, eds. *Relative Values: Reconfiguring Kinship Studies.* Durham: Duke University Press, 2001.

Freedman, Jessica. "Create Our Own Identification." In *I Didn't Know Who I Was*, edited by Korean Culture Network, 127–130. Seoul: Korean Culture Network, 2007.

Freundlich, Madelyn, and Joy Kim Lieberthal. *Survey of Adult Korean Adoptees: Report on the Findings.* Report. New York: Evan B. Donaldson Adoption Institute, 1999.

Friedman, May, and Silvia Schultermandl, eds. *Click and Kin: Transnational Identity and QuickMedia.* Toronto: University of Toronto Press, 2016.

Friedman, Susan Stanford. "Women's Autobiographical Selves: Theory and Practice." In *The Private Self: Theory and Practice of Women's Autobiographical Writings*, edited by Shari Benstock, 34–62. Routledge: London, 1988.

Fuchs, Chris. "Deported Adoptee's Death Heightens Calls for Citizenship Bill." *NBC News*, June 2, 2017. https://www.nbcnews.com/news/asian-america/deported-adoptee-s-death-heightens-calls-citizenship-bill-n767341.

Gambino, Lauren. "Trump Pans Immigration Proposal as Bringing People from 'Shithole Countries.'" *The Guardian*, January 11, 2018. https://www.theguardian.com/us-news/2018/jan/11/trump-pans-immigration-proposal-as-bringing-people-from-shithole-countries.

Gammage, Jeff. "A 'Normal' Family." *New York Times* (web log), December 2, 2007. http://relativechoices.blogs.nytimes.com/2007/12/02/a-normal-family/.

Gardner, Martha. *The Qualities of a Citizen: Women, Immigration, and Citizenship, 1870–1965.* Princeton: Princeton University Press, 2005.

Gates, Jeff. "I Was Taking Pictures of My Daughters. A Stranger Thought I Was Exploiting Them." *Washington Post*, August 29, 2014. https://www.washingtonpost.com/opinions/i-was-taking-pictures-of-my-daughters-but-a-stranger-thought-i-was-exploiting-them/2014/08/29/34831bb8–2c6c-11e4–994d-202962a9150c_story.html.

Gelb, Joyce, and Marian L. Palley, eds. *Women of Japan and Korea: Continuity and Change.* Philadelphia: Temple University Press, 1994.

Geok-Lim, Shirley, and Amy Ling. *Reading the Literatures of Asian America.* Philadelphia: Temple University Press, 1992.

Gerber, Marisa. "Adopted Russian Toddler's Death Ruled Accidental, Texas Officials Say." *Los Angeles Times,* March 1, 2013. http://www.latimes.com/news/nation/nationnow/la-na-nn-russian-toddler-texas-accidental-20130301,0,1489778.story.

Giffney, Noreen. "Denormatizing Queer Theory: More Than (Simply) Lesbian and Gay Studies." *Feminist Theory* 5, no. 1 (2004): 73–78.

Gilmore, Leigh. *Autobiographics: A Feminist Theory of Women's Self-representation.* Ithaca: Cornell University Press, 1994.

Goetz, Kaomi. "They Came to America as Adoptees but Were Never Made US Citizens." *PRI,* December 31, 2015. http://www.pri.org/stories/2015-12-31/they-came-america-adoptees-were-never-made-us-citizens.

Gonzalez, Rosita, Amanda Transue-Woolston, and Diane Rene Christian. *#FlipTheScript, Adult Adoptee Anthology.* Portland: The An-Ya Project, 2015.

Gordon, Linda. *The Great Arizona Orphan Abduction.* Cambridge: Harvard University Press, 1999.

Gotanda, Neil. "Exclusion and Inclusion: Immigration and American Orientalism." In *Across the Pacific: Asian Americans and Globalization,* edited by Evelyn Hu-DeHart, 129–151. Philadelphia: Temple University Press, 1999.

Gough, Ian. "Globalization and Regional Welfare Regimes: The East Asian Case." *Global Social Policy* 1, no. 2 (2001): 163–189.

Green, Michael Cullen. *Black Yanks in the Pacific: Race in the Making of American Military Empire after World War II.* Ithaca: Cornell University Press, 2010.

Greenhalgh, Susan. "Globalization and Population Governance in China." In *Global Assemblages: Technology, Politics, and Ethics as Anthropological Problems,* edited by Aihwa Ong and Stephen J. Collier, 354–372. Malden: Blackwell Pub., 2005.

Grice, Helena. *Negotiating Identities: An Introduction to Asian American Women's Writing.* Manchester: Manchester University Press, 2002.

"Growing Up on Asian Food vs. American Food!? W/Jenna Ushkowitz DANakaDAN+Sam Futerman-ASIAN-ISH EP2." YouTube Video, 14:59. Posted by "ISAtv," August 25, 2015. https://www.youtube.com/watch?v=BkexmBzoF-U.

Gruber, Xaque. "New Documentary Film, Twinsters, Shines a Light on Twins Separated at Birth." *Huffington Post,* July 19, 2015. http://www.huffingtonpost.com/xaque-gruber/new-documentary-film-twin_b_7829576.html.

Halberstam, J. Jack. *Female Masculinity.* Durham: Duke University Press, 1998.

———. *In a Queer Time and Place: Transgender Bodies, Subcultural Lives.* New York: New York University Press, 2005.

Hall, Christine C. Iijima. "Asian Eyes: Body Image and Eating Disorders of Asian and AsianAmerican Women." *Eating Disorders: The Journal of Treatment & Prevention* 3 no.1 (1995): 8–19.

Hallowell, A. Irving. "American Indians, White and Black: The Phenomenon of Trans-culturalization." *Current Anthropology* 4, no. 5 (December 1963): 519–531.

Han, Boonyoung. "Contextualizing Modern Korean Adoption Law." In *Proceedings of the First International Korean Adoption Studies Research Symposium*, edited by Kim Park Nelson, Eleana Kim, and Lene Myong Peterson. Myong, 37–54. Seoul: Dongguk University, 2007.

Han, Hyun Sook. *Many Lives Intertwined: A Memoir*. St. Paul: Yeong and Yeong Book, 2004.

Hansen, Jayme. Comment on "Minnesota Politics." *Land of Gazillion Adoptees* (web log), February 20, 2012. http://landofgazillionadoptees.com/2012/02/20/minnesota-politics/.

Hao, Karen. "YouTube Has Made Asian-Americans Impossible for Hollywood to Ignore." *How We Get to Next*, October 13, 2016. https://howwegettonext.com/youtube-has-made-asian-americans-impossible-for-hollywood-to-ignore-be9c110e2be#.es9666r2g.

Harding, Sandra. "Subjectivity, Experience, and Knowledge: An Epistemology from/for Rainbow Coalition Politics." In *Who Can Speak? Authority and Critical Identity*, edited by Judith Roof and Robyn Wiegman, 120–136. Urbana: University of Illinois Press, 1995.

Harper, Stephen. "Prime Minister Harper Offers Full Apology on Behalf of Canadians for the Indian Residential Schools System." Speech, June 11, 2008. http://www.pm.gc.ca/eng/media.asp?id=2149.

Harris, Cheryl I. "Whiteness as Property." In *Critical Race Theory: The Key Writings That Formed the Movement*, edited by Kimberlé Crenshaw, Neil Gotanda, Gary Peller, and Kendall Thomas, 276–291. New York: New Press, 1995.

Hartstock, Nancy C. "The Feminist Standpoint: Developing the Ground for a Specifically Feminist Historical Materialism." In *The Second Wave: A Reader in Feminist Theory*, edited by Linda J. Nicholson, 216–240. New York: Routledge, 1997.

Hatchard, Christine Jung. "Racial Experiences of Korean Adoptees: Do Adoptive Parents Make a Difference?" PhD diss., Chestnut College, Philadelphia, 2007.

Hawkesworth, Mary E. *Feminist Inquiry: From Political Conviction to Methodological Innovation*. New Brunswick: Rutgers University Press, 2006.

Heit, Shannon. "BUILD FAMILIES NOT BOXES!! REBLOG PLEASE!!! Stop ." Tales of Wonderlost, January 21, 2014. http://peaceshannon.tumblr.com/post/74058195003/build-families-not-boxes-reblog-please-stop.

Herman, Burt. "Olympic Skier Toby Dawson Reunites with Korean Family." *USA Today*, February 28, 2007. http://usatoday30.usatoday.com/sports/olympics/winter/2007-02-28-dawson-father_x.htm.

Herman, Ellen. *Kinship by Design: A History of Adoption in the Modern United States*. Chicago: University of Chicago Press, 2008.

Herzog, Jonathan P. *The Spiritual Industrial Complex: America's Religious Battle against Communism in the Early Cold War*. Oxford: Oxford University Press, 2011.

Hewitt, Scott. "International Adoptee Faces Deportation: Long-abused South Korean Adoptee Served Prison Time, May Get More Punishment." *The Columbian*, March 29, 2015. http://www.columbian.com/news/2015/mar/29/international-adoptee-deportation-korea/.

Higgins Swick, Becca. "Becca." In *Once They Hear My Name: Korean Adoptees and Their Journeys toward Identity*, edited by Ellen Lee, Marilyn Lammert, and Mary Anne Hess, 75–98. Silver Spring, Md.: Tamarisk Books, 2008.

Hill Collins, Patricia. *Black Feminist Thought: Knowledge, Consciousness, and the Politics of Empowerment*. New York: Routledge, 2000.

———. "It's All in the Family: Intersections of Gender, Race, and Nation." *Hypatia* 13, no. 3 (1998): 62–82.

Hing, Bill Ong. *Making and Remaking Asian America through Immigration Policy, 1850–1990*. Stanford: Stanford University Press, 1993.

Höhn, Maria, and Seungsook Moon, eds. *Over There: Living with the U.S. Military Empire from World War Two to the Present*. Durham: Duke University Press, 2010.

Holt Alumni Blog. "Senator Landrieu Passes Amendment to Help Adopted Children Secure Citizenship, Holt International, June 19, 2013. http://holtinternational.org/holtalumni/blog/?p=461.

Holt International. "Adoption Fees," 2018. http://www.holtinternational.org/adoption/fees.php.

Holt International. "Adoption Fees Overview," Adoption Fees and Financial Assistance, 2011. http://www.holtinternational.org/adoption/fees.php .

Holt International. "Adoption Fees Overview," *Holt International Children's Services*. http://www.holtinternational.org/adoption/fees.php.

Holt International. "Financial Assistance," *Holt International Children's Services*. http://www.holtinternational.org/adoption/assistance.shtml.

hooks, bell. *Black Looks: Race and Representation*. Boston: South End Press, 1992.

———. *Feminist Theory from Margin to Center*. Second ed. London: Pluto Press, 2000.

———. *Talking Back: Thinking Feminist, Thinking Black*. Boston: South End Press, 1989.

Howell, Signe. *Kinning of Foreigners: Transnational Adoption in a Global Perspective*. New York: Berghahn Books, 2006.

Hübinette, Tobias. *Comforting an Orphaned Nation: Representations of International Adoption and Adopted Koreans in Korean Popular Culture*. Seoul: Jimoondang, 2006.

———. "Disembedded and Free-floating Bodies Out-of-Place and Out-of-Control: Examining the Borderline Existence of Adopted Koreans." *Adoption & Culture* 1, no. 1 (2007): 129–162.

———. "From Orphan Trains to Babylifts: Colonial Trafficking, Empire Building, and Social Engineering." In *Outsiders Within: Writing on Transracial Adoption*, edited by Jane Jeong Trenka, Julia Sudbury, and Sun Yung Shin, 139–149. Cambridge: South End Press, 2006.

———. *The Korean Adoption Issue between Modernity and Coloniality: Transnational Adoption and Overseas Adoptees in Korean Popular Culture*. Sarrbrücken: Lambert Academic Press, 2009.

———. "The Orphaned Nation: Korea Imagined as an Overseas Adopted Child in Clon's Abandoned Child and Park Kwang-su's Berlin Report." *Inter-Asia Cultural Studies* 6, no. 2 (2005): 227–244.

Hübinette, Tobias, Indigo Willing, and Jenny Wills, eds., *Adoption & Discourses of Multiculturalism: Europe, the Americas and the Pacific* (Under Review).

Ignacio, Emily. *Building Diaspora: Filipino Community Formation on the Internet*. New Brunswick: Rutgers University Press, 2005.

Indo Asian News Service. "Ukraine to Probe Foreign Adoptions." *Yahoo News*, February 24, 2013. http://en-maktoob.news.yahoo.com/ukraine-probe-foreign-adoptions-234616018.html.

Internal Revenue Service. "Topic Number 607: Adoption Credit and Adoption Assistance Programs," *IRS*, 2018. https://www.irs.gov/taxtopics/tc607.

In the Matter of Cha Jung Hee. Directed by Deann Borshay Liem. Berkeley: Mu Films, 2010. DVD.

Jackson, Stevi. "Interchanges: Gender, Sexuality and Heterosexuality: The Complexity (and Limits) of Heteronormativity." *Feminist Theory* 7, no. 1 (2006): 105–121. doi:10.1177/1464700106061462.

Jacobs, Margaret D. *White Mother to a Dark Race: Settler Colonialism, Maternalism, and the Removal of Indigenous Children in the American West and Australia, 1880–1940*. Lincoln: University of Nebraska Press, 2009.

Jacobson, Heather. *Culture Keeping: White Mothers, International Adoption, and the Negotiation of Family Difference*. Nashville: Vanderbilt University Press, 2008.

Janine, "Janine's Story." Citizenship for All Adoptees, April 23, 2013. http://citizenship foralladoptees.tmblr.com/post/48711395713/janines-story.

Janowitz, Tama. "The Real Thing." *New York Times* (web log), November 12, 2007. http://relativechoices.blogs.nytimes.com/2007/11/12/the-real-thing.

Jerng, Mark C. *Claiming Others: Transracial Adoption and National Belonging*. Minneapolis: University of Minnesota Press, 2010.

Johnson, Dana, Maureen Warren, Jodi Harpstead, and David McKoskey. "Daily Circuit: International Adoption." Interview by Tom Weber, Minnesota Public Radio, July 9, 2012. http://minnesota.publicradio.org/display/web/2012/07/09/daily-circuit-international-adoption.

Jones, Maggie. "Adam Crapser's Bizarre Deportation Odyssey." *New York Times Magazine*, April 1, 2015. http://www.nytimes.com/2015/04/01/magazine/adam-crapsers-bizarre-deportationodyssey.html?_r=0.

———. "Why a Generation of Adoptees Is Returning to South Korea." *New York Times Magazine* (web log), January 14, 2015. http://www.nytimes.com/2015/01/18/magazine/why-a-generation-of-adoptees-isreturning-to-south-korea.html?_r=0.

Jones, Melissa L. "Portland's Korean Adoptees Help Others Uncover Old Roots and New." *Oregonian*, February 7, 2014. http://www.oregonlive.com/portland/index.ssf/2014/02/portlands_korean_adoptees_helhtml.

Jones, Nicola. "Mainstreaming Gender South Korean Women's Civic Alliances and Institutional Strategies, 1987–2002." PhD diss., University of North Carolina at Chapel Hill, 2003.

Jones, Steven G. "Information, Internet, and Community: Notes Toward an Understanding of Community in the Information Age." In *CyberSociety 2.0: Revisiting Computer-mediated Communication and Community*, edited by Steven G. Jones, 1–34. Thousand Oaks: Sage Publications, 1998.

Joo, Jaeseon. "Observing Change in the Status of Korean Women through Statistics." *Gender Studies and Policy Review* 1 (2008): 78–87.

Joyce, Kathryn. *The Child Catchers: Rescue, Trafficking, and the New Gospel of Adoption*. New York: PublicAffairs, 2013.

———. "The Evangelical Adoption Crusade." *The Nation*, April 21, 2011. http://www.thenation.com/article/160096/evangelical-adoption-crusade#.

———. "Why Adoption Plays Such a Big, Contentious Role in US-Russia Relations." *Vox*, July 22, 2017. https://www.vox.com/the-big-idea/2017/7/21/16005500/adoption-russia-us-orphans-abuse-trump.

Jung, Ha-won. "Korea's Welfare Expenditures Lag at 1/10 of GDP." *JoongAng Daily*, February 13, 2010. http://joongangdaily.joins.com/article/view.asp?aid=2916606.

Jung, Kyungja. "The Development of Women's Policy in South Korea." In *The Work of Policy: An International Survey*, edited by H. K. Colebatch, 109–132. Lanham: Rowman and Littlefield, 2006.

Kanstroom, Dan. *Deportation Nation: Outsiders in American History*. Cambridge: Harvard University Press, 2007.

Kaplan, Amy. *The Anarchy of Empire in the Making of U.S. Culture*. Cambridge: Harvard University Press, 2002.

Katz Rothman, Barbara. *Weaving a Family: Untangling Race and Adoption*. Boston: Beacon Press, 2005.

Kauffman, Ellwyn. "Bulgogi." In *Seeds from a Silent Tree: An Anthology by Korean Adoptees*, edited by Tonya Bishoff and Jo Rankin, 44–50. San Diego: Pandal Press, 1997.

Kaw, Eugenia. "Medicalization of Racial Features: Asian American Women and Cosmetic Surgery." *Medical Anthropology Quarterly* 7, no. 1 (1993): 74–89.

Kennedy, Randall. *Interracial Intimacies: Sex, Marriage, Identity, and Adoption*. New York: Vintage Books, 2003.

Kessel, Emily. "Over 70 Community Members Join Adoptee Citizenship Act Day of Action in DC and across the Country." *NAKASEC*, April 20, 2016. http://nakasec.org/5303/over-65-community-members-join-adoptee-citizenship-act-day-of-action-in-dc-and-across-the-country/.

Khazan, Olga. "Why Are Other Countries Wary of American Adoptions?" *Washington Post*, December 27, 2012. http://www.washingtonpost.com/blogs/worldviews/wp/2012/12/27/why-are-other-countries-wary-of-american-adoptions/.

Kim, Chin, and Timothy G. Carroll. "Intercountry Adoption of South Korean Orphans: A Lawyer's Guide." *Journal of Family Law* 14, no. 2 (1975): 223–253.

Kim, Do-hyun. "Overseas Adoption: Child Welfare for Abuse?" *Korea Times*, December 30, 2011. http://www.koreatimes.co.kr/www/news/opinon/2012/02/198_101917.html.

Kim, Dong Soo. "A Country Divided: Contextualizing Adoption from a Korean Perspective." In *International Korean Adoption: A Fifty-year History of Policy and Practice*, edited by Kathleen Ja Sook Bergquist, M. Elizabeth Vonk, Dong Soo Kim, and Marvin D. Feit, 3–24. New York: Haworth Press, 2007.

Kim, Elaine H. *American Autobiography: Retrospect and Prospect*, edited by Paul John Eakin. Madison: University of Wisconsin Press, 1991.

———. *Asian American Literature: An Introduction to the Writings and Their Social Contexts*. Philadelphia: Temple University Press, 1982.

———. "Defining Asian American Realities through Literature." *Cultural Critique* 6 (Spring 1987): 87–111.

———. "Korean American Literature." In *An Interethnic Companion to Asian American Literature*, edited by King-Kok Cheung, 156–191. Cambridge: Cambridge University Press, 1997.

———. "Roots and Wings: An Overview of Korean American Literature 1934–2003." In *The Sigur Center Asia Papers: Korean American Literature*, edited by Young-Key Kim-Renaud, R. Richard Grinker, and Kirk Larsen, 1–18. Washington, D.C.: Sigur Center for Asian Studies, 2004.

———. "These Bearers of a Homeland: An Overview of Korean American Literature, 1934–2001." *Korea Journal* 41, no. 3 (2001): 149–197.

Kim, Eleana J. *Adopted Territory: Transnational Korean Adoptees and the Politics of Belonging*. Durham: Duke University Press, 2010.

———. *The Origins of Korean Adoption: Cold War Geopolitics and Intimate Diplomacy*. Report, October 2009. http://uskoreainstitute.org/wp-content/uploads/2010/02/USKI_WP0909_KimAdoptee,pdf.

———. "Wedding Citizenship and Culture: Korean Adoptees and the Global Family of Korea." *Social Text* 21, no. 1 (Spring, 2003): 57–81. doi:10.1215/01642472–21–1_74–57.

Kim, Elizabeth. *Ten Thousand Sorrows: The Extraordinary Journey of a Korean War Orphan*. New York: Doubleday, 2000.

Kim, Heinsook. "Feminist Philosophy in Korea: Subjectivity of Korean Women." *Signs: Journal of Women in Culture and Society* 34, no. 2 (2009): 247–251. doi:10.1086/590977.

Kim, Hosu. *Birth Mothers and Transnational Adoption Practice in South Korea: Virtual Mothering*. New York: Palgrave Macmillan, 2016.

Kim, Jae Ran. "Adopted Chinese Daughters Seek Their Roots." *Racialicious* (web log), October 22, 2009. http://www.racialicious.com/2009/10/22/adopted-chinese-daughters-seek-their-roots/.

———. "Freaking Out over Freakonomics." *Racialicious* (web log), March 12, 2008. http://www.racialicious.com/2008/03/12/freaking-out-over-freakonomics/.

———. "I'm Tired of Adoptive Parent Confessionals." *Harlow's Monkey* (web log), April 16, 2010. http://harlowmonkey.typepad.com/harlows_monkey/2010/04/im-tired-of-adoptive-parent-confessionals.html.

———. "Is the Food Network the Whitest of the Cable Stations?" *Racialicious* (web log), February 6, 2008. http://www.racialicious.com/2008/02/06/is-the-food-network-the-whitest-of-the-cable-stations.

———. "*New York Times* aka 'the Adoption Police?'" *Harlow's Monkey* (web log), November 14, 2007. http://harlowmonkey.typepad.com/harlows_monkey/2007/11/new -york-time-3.html.

———. "Scattered Seeds: The Christian Influence on the Korean Adoption Phenomenon." In *Outsiders Within: Writing on Transracial Adoption*, edited by Jane Jeong Trenka, Julia Chinyere Oparah, and Sun Yung Shin, 151–162. Cambridge: South End Press, 2006.

———. "We Will Not Be Silenced." *Harlow's Monkey* (web log), November 14, 2007. http://harlowmonkey.typepad.com/harlows_monkey/2007/11/we-will-not-be-.html.

Kim, Jodi. *Ends of Empire: Asian American Critiques and the Cold War.* Minneapolis: University of Minnesota Press, 2010.

———. "'The Ending Is Not an Ending At All': On the Militarized and Gendered Diasporas of Korean Transnational Adoption and the Korean War." *positions: east asia cultures critique* 23, no. 4 (2015): 807–835.

Kim, Min-sang. "Adoptees Struggle with Uncertain Nationalities." *Korea Joongang Daily*, August 10, 2012. http://koreajoongangdaily.joinsmsn.com/news/article/article.aspx ?aid=2957703&cloc=joongangdaily|home|newslist1.

Kim, Nadia Y. *Imperial Citizens: Koreans and Race from Seoul to LA.* Stanford: Stanford University Press, 2008.

Kim, Sarah. "After 6 Months, a U-turn on Costly Free Day Care." *Korea Joongang Daily*, September 25, 2012. http://koreajoongangdaily.joinsmsn.com/news/article/article.aspx ?aid=2959958&cloc=rss|news|joongangdaily.

Kim, Sarah. "To Willow Janowitz: You're Not Alone. . . ." *Outside In . . . and Back Again* (web log), November 13, 2007. http://sarahkim.wordpress.com/2007/11/13/to-willow -janowitz-youre-not-alone/.

Kim, Sung-soo. "Adoptees Deported by US." *Korea Times*, March 4, 2012. http://www .koreatimes.co.kr/www/news/opinon/2012/03/137_106204.html.

Kim, Tae-jong. "Adoption Quota Causes Backlash." *Korea Times*, May 6, 2011. http:// www.koreatimes.co.kr/www/news/nation/2011/05/113_86561.html.

Kim, Wun Jung. "International Adoption: A Case Review of Korean Children." *Child Psychiatry and Human Development* 25, no. 3 (1995): 141–154.

Kim, Yeon-kwang. "Adoption Restrictions to Be Removed." *Chosun Ilbo*, March 7, 2000. http://english.chosun.com/site/data/html_dir/2000/03/07/2000030761392.html.

Kim-Cavicchi, Andrea. "Power, Resistance and Subjectivity: An Exploration of Overseas Korean Adoptees in Korea." Ends of Adoption Symposium, University of California-Irvine, Irvine, May 13, 2017.

Klein, Christina. *Cold War Orientalism: Asia in the Middlebrow Imagination, 1945–1961.* Berkeley: University of California Press, 2003.

Koch, Wendy. "Adoption Options Plummet as Russia Closes Its Doors." *USA Today* (web log), January 11, 2013. http://www.usatoday.com/story/news/nation/2013/01/10/ adoption-options-plummet-russia-closes-doors/1820853/.

Koh, Eunkang. "Gender Issues and Confucian Scriptures: Is Confucianism Incompatible with Gender Equality in South Korea?" *Bulletin of the School of Oriental and African Studies* 71, no. 02 (2008): 345–362.

Kollaboration. "Empowerment through Entertainment." *Kollaboration.org*. http:// kollaboration.org/about/5219/.

Kopacz, Elizabeth. "From Contingent Beginnings to Multiple Ends: DNA Technologies and the Korean Adoptee 'Cousin.'" *Adoption & Culture 6*, no. 2 (Forthcoming, 2018).

"Korean Adoptees Talk Korean Food! w /DANakaDAN, Sam Futerman, + Jenna Ushkowitz- ASIAN-ISH BONUS." YouTube Video, 7:25. Posted by "DANakaDan,"August 26, 2015. https://www.youtube.com/watch?v=D9oJ_BLibow.

Korean Focus Metro DC. "Citizenship for All US Intercountry Adoptees." Change.org., 2012. http://www.change.org/petitions/citizenship-for-all-us-intercountry-adoptees.

"Korean Intercountry Adoptees Support Birth Mother's Rights in South Korea." *The Hankyoreh*, July 15, 2009. http://english.hani.co.kr/arti/english_edition/e_international/ 354259.html.

Korean Unwed Mothers Support Network. *All Mothers Have the Right to Raise Their Own Children*. Seoul: Korean Unwed Mothers Support Network, 2011. http://www.kumsn .org/main/index.php?document_srl=10033.

———. "New Study Makes Recommendations on How to Improve Government Welfare Services for Unwed Mothers in Korea." News release, November 12, 2010. http://www .kumsn.org/main/index.php?document_srl=4260.

Korean Unwed Mothers Support Network and Korean Women's Development Institute. *Reviewing Issues on Unwed Mothers' Welfare in Korea: Intercountry Adoption, Related Statistics, and Welfare Policies in Developed Countries*. Report, May 2009. http://justice speaking.files.wordpress.com/2010/01/200905_reviewing-issues-on-unwed-mothers -welfare-in-korea.pdf.

KoRoot. "Build Families Not Boxes." KoRoot, January 24, 2014. http://www.koroot.org/ eng/bbs/bbs_view.asp?num=295&pos=295&boardid=13.

Kwak, Edward S. "Asian Cosmetic Facial Surgery." *Facial Plastic Surgery 26*, no. 2 (2010): 102–109.

Kwapisz, Todd D. "Perception vs. I Am." In *Voices from Another Place: A Collection of Works from a Generation Born in Korea and Adopted to Other Countries*, edited by Susan Soon-Keum Cox, 50–51. St. Paul: Yeong and Yeong Book, 1999.

Kwon Dobbs, Jennifer. "Korea to Haiti: Lessons in Overseas Adoption Corruption." *Conducive Magazine*, April/May 2010. http://www.conducivemag.com/2010/03/korea-to -haiti-lessons-in-overseas-adoption-corruption-2/.

Kwon Dobbs, Jennifer, Caitlin Kee, and Kristin R. Pak. "Deporting Adult Adoptees." *Foreign Policy in Focus*, July 4, 2012. http://www.fpif.org/articles/deporting_adult_adoptees.

Kwon, Hee-jung. "The Increase in the Number of Unwed Mothers Is Not Related to the Increase in Unwed Mothers' Social Welfare Expenditures." In *The Hankyoreh*, translated by Shannon Heit. http://www.kumsn.org/main/index.php?mid=kumsn_ resources_trnslation&document_srl=7556.

Kwon, Huck Ju. "Beyond European Welfare Regimes: Comparative Perspectives on East Asian Welfare Systems." *Journal of Social Policy 26*, no. 4 (1997): 467–484.

———. "Globalization, Unemployment and Policy Responses in Korea: Repositioning the State?" *Global Social Policy 1*, no. 2 (2001): 213–234. doi:10.1177/146801810100100204.

Kwon, Soonman, and Ian Holliday. "The Korean Welfare State: A Paradox of Expansion in an Era of Globalization and Economic Crisis." *International Journal of Social Welfare* 16, no. 3 (July 2007): 242–248.

Lally, Kathy, and Tara Bahrampour. "Death of Adopted Russian Child in U.S. Spurs Anger in Moscow." *Washington Post*, February 19, 2013. http://articles.washingtonpost.com/ 2013-02-19/world/37170339_1_american-adoptions-dima-yakovlev-russian-child.

Lam On, James. "The 'Drop Box' for Unwanted Babies Inspires Youngsters to Join South Korean Pastor Lee Jong-rak to Save Abandoned (VIDEO)." The Cross Map, January 10, 2014. http://crossmap.christianpost.com/news/the-drop-box-for-unwanted-babies-inspires -youngsters-to-join-south-korean-pastor-lee-jong-rak-to-save-abandoned-video-8380.

Larsen, Stevie. "Organizing without an Anchor: Race-making, Space-making, and the Many Trajectories of Korean Adoptee Politicization," Working Paper, Association for Asian American Studies Conference, 2015. http://aaastudies.org/wp-content/uploads/ 2015/03/Larson-AAAS-Working-Paper.docx.

Lau, Allison S. M., S. K. Lum, K. M. Chronister, and L. Forrest. "Asian American College Women's Body Image: A Pilot Study." *Cultural Diversity and Ethnic Minority Psychology* 12, no.2 (2006): 259–274.

Lau, William M. "Exploring the Lives of Asian American Men: Racial Identity, Male Role Norms, Gender Role Conflict, and Prejudicial Attitudes." *Psychology of Men &Masculinity* 3 no. 2 (2002): 107–118.

Lauber, Lynn. "Reunion." *New York Times* (web log), November 20, 2007. http://relative choices.blogs.nytimes.com/2007/11/20/reunion.

Lee, Claire. "Single Moms Denied Parental Allowance in South Korea." *Korea Herald*, March 8, 2016. http://m.koreaherald.com/view.php?ud=20160308000987#jyk.

Lee, Ellen, Marilyn Lammert, and Mary Anne Hess, eds. *Once They Hear My Name: Korean Adoptees and Their Journeys toward Identity*. Silver Spring, Md.: Tamarisk Books, 2008.

Lee, Erika, and Judy Yung. *Angel Island: Immigrant Gateway to America*. Oxford: Oxford University Press, 2010.

Lee, Jin-kyung. *Service Economies: Militarism, Sex Work, and Migrant Labor in South Korea*. Minneapolis: University of Minnesota Press, 2010.

Lee, Richard M. "The Transracial Adoption Paradox: History, Research, and Counseling Implications of Cultural Socialization." *Counseling Psychologist* 31, no. 6 (2003): 711–744.

Lee, Richard M., Hyung Chol Yoo, and Sara Roberts. "The Coming of Age of Korean Adoptees: Ethnic Identity Development and Psychological Adjustment." In *Korean-Americans: Past, Present, and Future*, edited by Ilpyong J. Kim, 203–224. Elizabeth, N.J.: Hollym International, 2004.

Lee, Robert G. *Orientals: Asian Americans in Popular Culture*. Philadelphia: Temple University Press, 1999.

Lee, Shelley, and Rick Baldoz. "Donald Trump Fails History: How the Right's Failure to Understand Japanese-American Internment Drives Anti-Muslim Hatred." Salon, December 28, 2015. https://www.salon.com/2015/12/28/donald_trump_fails_history_how_the _rights_failure_to_understand_japanese_american_internment_drives_anti_muslim _hatred/.

Lee, Tae-hoon. "Dual Citizenship to Be Allowed." *Korea Times*, April 21, 2010. http://www.koreatimes.co.kr/www/news/nation/2010/04/116_64629.html.

Lee, You-jin. "Single Moms' Day Shifts Focus to Family Preservation." *The Hankyoreh*, May 6, 2011. http://english.hani.co.kr/arti/english_edition/e_national/476672.html.

Lieberman, Kira. "The Process of Racial and Ethnic Identity Development and Search for Self in Adult Korean Transracial Adoptees." PhD diss., Massachusetts School of Professional Psychology, 1996.

Lim, Shirley Jennifer. *A Feeling of Belonging: Asian American Women's Public Culture, 1930–1960*. New York: New York University Press, 2005.

Lipsitz, George. *The Possessive Investment in Whiteness: How White People Profit from Identity Politics*. Philadelphia: Temple University Press, 2006.

Lister, Ruth. *Citizenship: Feminist Perspectives*. New York: New York University Press, 1997.

———. "Dilemmas in Engendering Citizenship." In *Gender and Citizenship in Transition*, edited by Barbara Hobson, 33–83. New York: Routledge, 2000.

Lo, B. K. "Korean Psych 101." In *Outsiders Within: Writing on Transracial Adoption*, edited by Jane Jeong Trenka, Julia Sudbury, and Sun Yung Shin, 167–176. Cambridge: South End Press, 2006.

Lowe, Lisa. *Immigrant Acts: On Asian American Cultural Politics*. Durham: Duke University Press, 1996.

Luhar, Monica. "Twin Adoptees Reunite In 'Twinsters' Documentary, Debuting This Summer." *NBC News*, June 18, 2015. http://www.nbcnews.com/news/asian-america/twin-adoptees-reunite-twinsters-documentary-debuting-summer-n372941.

Ma, Sheng-mei. *The Deathly Embrace: Orientalism and Asian American Identity*. Minneapolis: University of Minnesota Press, 2000.

MacMullan, Terrance. *Habits of Whiteness: A Pragmatist Reconstruction*. Bloomington: Indiana University Press, 2009.

Maggi, L., "Korea Closes Its Doors," *Ours* (January/February 1990): 48–49.

Maira, Sunaina. "Radical Deportation: Alien Tales from Lodi and San Francisco." In *The Deportation Regime: Sovereignty, Space, and the Freedom of Movement*, edited by Nicholas De Genova and Nathalie Peutz, 295–325. Chapel Hill: Duke University Press, 2010.

Mann, Leslie. "Foreign Adoption Comes with Obstacles, but Parents Advised to 'Stay the Course.'" *Chicago Tribune*, April 1, 2013. http://www.chicagotribune.com/news/local/ct-x-foreign-adoption-20130402,0,6301893.story.

Marcas, George E., and Erkan Saka. "Assemblage." *Theory, Culture, & Society* 23, no. 2–3 (2006): 101–106.

Marcotte, Amanda. "With El Salvador Decision, Trump's Immigration Policy Veers into White Nationalism." *Salon*, January 9, 2018. https://www.salon.com/2018/01/09/with-salvador-decision-trumps-immigration-policy-veers-into-white-nationalism/.

Marre, Diana, and Laura Briggs, eds., *International Adoption: Global Inequalities and the Circulation of Children*. New York: New York University Press, 2009.

Marshall, T. H., and Tom Bottomore. *Citizenship and Social Class*. London: Pluto Press, 1992.

Mashable. "'Avengers' Joke Ignites Online Protest by Adoption Community," May 14, 2012. http://mashable.com/2012/05/14/avengers-adoption-petition/.

McCauley Evans, Maureen. "Build Families, Not Boxes: Family Preservation in Korea." *Light of Day Stories,* January 21, 2014. http://lightofdaystories.com/2014/01/21/build-families-not-boxes-family preservation-in-korea/.

McClain DaCosta, Kimberly. "All in the Family: The Familial Roots of Racial Division." In *The Politics of Multiracialism: Challenging Racial Thinking,* edited by Heather M. Dalmage, 19–42. Albany: State University of New York Press, 2004.

McClintock, Anne. *Imperial Leather: Race, Gender and Sexuality in the Colonial Context.* London: Routledge, 1995.

McDonald, Stephanie. "Opinion Divided on the Merits of South Korean Pastor's 'Baby Box.'" SBS, February 11, 2014. http://www.sbs.com.au/news/article/2014/02/11/opinion-divided-merits-south-korean-pastors-baby-box.

McGinnis, Hollee. "Blood Ties and Acts of Love." *New York Times* (web log), December 4, 2007. http://relativechoices.blogs. nytimes.com/2007/12/04/blood-ties-and-acts-of-love/.

———. "South Korea and Its Children." *New York Times* (web log), November 27, 2007. http://relativechoices.blogs. nytimes.com/2007/11/27/south-korea-and-its-children.

———. "Who Are You Also Known As?" *New York Times* (web log), November 13, 2007. http://relativechoices. blogs.nytimes.com/2007/11/13/who-are-you-also-known-as.

McGinnis, Hollee, Susan Livingston Smith, Scott D. Ryan, and Jeanne A. Howard. *Beyond Culture Camp: Promoting Healthy Identity Formation in Adoption.* Report. November 2009. http://www.adoptioninstitute.org/publications/2009_11_BeyondCultureCamp.pdf.

McKee, Kimberly. "Adoption as Reproductive Justice." *Adoption & Culture* 6, No. 1 (June 2018): 74–93.

———. "An Open Letter: Why Co-opting 'Transracial' in the Case of Rachel Dolezal Is Problematic." Medium, June 16, 2015. https://medium.com/@Andy_Marra/an-open-letter-why-co-opting-transracial-in-the-case-of-rachel-dolezal-is-problematic-249f79f6d83c.

———. "Controlling Our Reproductive Destiny: Rethinking Adoption as the Better Option." *Gazillion Voices,* June 9, 2014. http://gazillionvoices.com/controlling-our-reproductive-destiny-rethinking-adoption-as-the-better-option/#.U6GhaC-T69F.

———. "Gendered Adoptee Identities: Performing Trans-Pacific Masculinity in the 21st Century." In *Gendering the Trans-Pacific World,* edited by Catherine Ceniza Choy and Judy Tzu-Chun Wu, 221–245. Leiden: Brill, 2017.

———. "Monetary Flows and the Movements of Children: The Transnational Adoption Industrial Complex." *Journal of Korean Studies* 21, no. 1 (2016): 137–178.

———. "*Real* versus *Fictive* Kinship: Legitimating the Adoptive Family." In *Critical Kinship Studies,* edited by Charlotte Kroløkke, Lene Myong, Stine Wilum Adrian, and Tine Tjørnhøj-Thomse, 221–336. London: Rowman and Littlefield International, 2015.

———. "Rewriting History: Adoptee Documentaries as a Site of Truth-telling." In *The Routledge Companion to Asian American Media*, eds. Lori K. Lopez and Vincent N. Pham, 119–130. New York: Routledge, 2017.

———. "Scenes of Misrecognition: The Absence of (Visible) Family Ties." *Kimberly McKee*, February 18, 2015. https://mckeekimberly.com/2015/02/18/scenes-of -misrecognition/.

———. "Why I #ThinkOutsidetheBabyBox: Let's #BuildFamiliesNotBoxes." *Kimberly McKee*, March 3, 2015. https://mckeekimberly.com/2015/03/05/why-i-thinkoutside thebabybox/.

McWhorter, Ladelle. *Racism and Sexual Oppression in Anglo-America: A Genealogy*. Bloomington: Indiana University Press, 2009.

Medefind, Jedd. "The Adoption Crusade: What a Misleading Article in 'The Nation' Can Teach Evangelicals." *Christianity Today*, April 27, 2011. http://www.christianitytoday. com/ct/2011/aprilweb-only/adoptioncrusade.html.

Meier, Dani I. "Cultural Identity and Place in Adult Korean-American Intercountry Adoptees." *Adoption Quarterly* 3, no. 1 (1999): 15–48. doi:10.1300/J145v03n01_03.

———. "Loss and Reclaimed Lives: Cultural Identity and Place in Korean American Intercountry Adoptees." PhD diss., University of Minnesota, 1998.

Melosh, Barbara. *Strangers and Kin: The American Way of Adoption*. Cambridge: Harvard University Press, 2002.

Miller, David. "Tightrope." In *Seeds from a Silent Tree: An Anthology by Korean Adoptees*, edited by Tonya Bishoff and Jo Rankin, 107. San Diego: Pandal Press, 1997.

Mills, Charles W. *The Racial Contract*. Ithaca: Cornell University Press, 1997.

Milroy, Jim. "The Stone Parable." In *Voices from Another Place: A Collection of Works from a Generation Born in Korea and Adopted to Other Countries*, edited by Susan Soon-Keum Cox, 58–59. St. Paul: Yeong and Yeong Book, 1999.

Min, Eun Kyung. "The Daughter's Exchange in Jane Jeong Trenka's 'The Language of Blood.'" *Social Text* 26, no. 1 (Spring 2008): 115–133.

Modell, Judith Schachter. *A Sealed and Secret Kinship: The Culture of Policies and Practices in American Adoption*. New York: Berghahn Books, 2002.

Mohanty, Chandra Talpade. *Feminism without Borders: Decolonizing Theory, Practicing Solidarity*. Durham: Duke University Press, 2003.

Mok, Teresa A. "Asian Americans and Standards of Attractiveness: What's in the Eye of the Beholder?" *Cultural Diversity and Mental Health* 4, no. 1 (1998): 1–18.

Moon, Seungsook. "Begetting the Nation: The Androcentric Discourse of National History and Tradition in South Korea." In *Dangerous Women: Gender and Korean Nationalism*, edited by Elaine H. Kim and Chungmoo Choi, 33–66. New York: Routledge, 1998.

———. "Economic Development and Gender Politics in South Korea (1963–1992)." PhD diss., Brandeis University, 1994.

———. *Militarized Modernity and Gendered Citizenship in South Korea*. Durham: Duke University Press, 2005.

Moosnick, Nora Rose. *Adopting Maternity: White Women Who Adopt Transracially or Transnationally*. Westport: Praeger, 2004.

Moraga, Cherríe, and Gloria Anzaldúa. *This Bridge Called My Back: Writings by Radical Women of Color*. New York: Kitchen Table, Women of Color Press, 1983.

Mu Films. "Geographies of Kinship—The Korean Adoption Story," Mu Films, 2015. http://www.mufilms.org/films/geographies-of-kinship-korean-adoption-story/#.Vl926d-rSRs.

Muñoz, José Esteban. *Cruising Utopia: The Then and There of Queer Futurity*. New York: NewYork University Press, 2009.

Muñoz, José Esteban. "Feeling Brown, Feeling Down: Latina Affect, the Performativity of Race, and the Depressive Position." *Signs* 31, no. 3 (2006): 675–688.

"My 1st Korean Birthday "DOL"—ASIAN*ISH Ep. 3." YouTube Video, 8:42. Posted by "ISAtv," December 1, 2015. https://youtu.be/PAAnJB30CuU?list=PLwf-CGTso19Tuyu-cRLjU4L5bOV_4tkiv.

Myers, Kit. "Race and the Violence of Love: Family and Nation in U.S. Adoptions from Asia." PhD diss., University of California San Diego, 2013.

———. "'Real' Families: The Violence of Low in New Media Adoption Discourse." *Critical Discourse Studies* 11, no. 2 (2014): 175–193.

Na, Jung, and Mugyeong Moon, *Early Childhood Education and Care Policies in the Republic of Korea*. Report, 2003. www.oecd.org/korea/27856763.pdf.

Nafzger, Ami Inja. "Ami." In *Once They Hear My Name: Korean Adoptees and Their Journeys toward Identity*, edited by Ellen Lee, Marilyn Lammert, and Mary Anne. Hess, 21–33. Silver Springs, Md.: Tamarisk Books, 2008.

Nagel, Joane. *Race, Ethnicity, and Sexuality: Intimate Intersections, Forbidden Frontiers*. Oxford: Oxford University Press, 2003.

Nakamura, Lisa. *Cybertypes: Race, Ethnicity, and Identity on the Internet*. New York: Routledge, 2002.

———. *Digitizing Race: Visual Cultures of the Internet*. Minneapolis: University of Minnesota Press, 2008.

NAKASEC. "Release: Halt Korean American Adoptee Adam Crasper's Pending Deportation." NAKASEC, April 13, 2015. http://nakasec.org/blog/3886/.

National Assembly of the Republic of Korea. "Constitution of the Republic of Korea." Constitution of the Republic of Korea, 2005. http://korea.assembly.go.kr/res/low_01_read.jsp?boardid=1000000035.

National Immigration Law Center. "DACA Renewal FAQ." Last modified December 18, 2014. https://nilc.org/dacarenewalprocess.html.

Navales, Ethal. "More on the 'Separated @ Birth' Twins Who Found Each Other on You Tube | Audrey Magazine." *Audrey Magazine*. http://audreymagazine.com/more-on-the-separated-birth-twins-who-found-each-other-on-youtube/.

Neff, Kelly. "The Rose." In *Voices from Another Place: A Collection of Works from a Generation Born in Korea and Adopted to Other Countries*, edited by Susan Soon-Keum Cox, 60–63. St. Paul: Yeong and Yeong Book, 1999.

Nelson, Hilde Lindemann. *Damaged Identities, Narrative Repair*. Ithaca: Cornell University Press, 2001.

Nelson-Erichsen, Jean. "Observations on Intercountry Adoption." In *Adoption Factbook III*, edited by Connaught Coyne Marshner. Washington, D.C.: National Council for Adoption, 1999.

Newcomb, Tim. "Tom Cruise at 50: Where Does the Newly Single Star Go from Here?" *Time*, July 3, 2012. http://entertainment.time.com/2012/07/03/tom-cruise-at -50-where-does-the-controversial-star-go-from-here/slide/the-brook-shields-debacle/.

Newton, Grace. "I Am Not My Dad's Girlfriend," *Red Thread Broken*, August 19, 2014. https://redthreadbroken.wordpress.com/2014/08/19/i-am-not-my-dads-girlfriend/.

Ngai, Mae M. *Impossible Subjects: Illegal Aliens and the Making of Modern America*. Princeton: Princeton University Press, 2004.

Ngai, Sianne. *Ugly Feelings*. Cambridge: Harvard University Press, 2005.

Niles, Su. "Obstacles and Challenges." In *Seeds from a Silent Tree: An Anthology by Korean Adoptees*, edited by Tonya Bishoff and Jo Rankin, 152–154. San Diego: Pandal Press, 1997.

Ning, Whitney Tae-Jin. "Returning…" In *Voices from Another Place: A Collection of Works from a Generation Born in Korea and Adopted to Other Countries*, edited by Susan Soon-Keum Cox, 127–130. St. Paul: Yeong and Yeong Book, 1999.

Ninh, erin Khuê. *Ingratitude: The Debt Bound Daughter in Asian American Literature*. New York: New York University Press, 2011.

Nissl, Jane. "Return to the Homeland." *New York Times* (web log), November 26, 2007. http://relativechoices.blogs.nytimes.com/2007/11/26/return-to-the-homeland/.

Obasogie, Osagie K. *Blinded by Sight: Seeing Race through the Eyes of the Blind*. Stanford, Calif.: Stanford University Press, 2013.

O'Brien, Eileen. *The Racial Middle: Latinos and Asian Americans Living beyond the Racial Divide*. New York: New York University Press, 2008.

O'Connor, Maureen. "Is Race Plastic? My Trip into the Ethnic Plastic Surgery Minefield." *NYMag.com*, July 27, 2014. http://nymag.com/thecut/2014/07/ethnic-plasticsurgery .html.

———. "Julie Chen Says Eyelid Surgery Saved Her Career." *NYMag.com.*, September 12, 2013. http://nymag.com/thecut/2013/09/julie-chen-says-eyelid-surgerysaved-her -career.html.

O'Dell, Keely E., Robert B. McCall, and Christina J. Groark. "Supporting Families throughout the International Special Needs Adoption Process." *Children and Youth Services Review* 59 (2015): 161–170.

Office of U.S. Senator Amy Klobuchar. "Klobuchar Calls on Colleagues to Support Adoptee Citizenship Act." *U.S. Senator Amy Klobuchar*, January 19, 2016. http://www.klobuchar .senate.gov/public/2016/1/klobuchar-calls-on-colleagues-to-support-adoptee -citizenship-act.

Official Website of the Department of Homeland Security. "Consideration of Deferred Action for Childhood Arrivals (DACA)." Last modified July 24, 2015. http://www.uscis .gov/humanitarian/consideration-deferred-action-childhood-arrivalsdaca.

Oh, Arissa. "A New Kind of Missionary Work: Christians, Christian Americanists, and the Adoption of Korean GI Babies, 1955–1961." *Women's Studies Quarterly* 33, no. 3/4 (Fall 2005): 161–188.

———. "From War Waif to Ideal Immigrant: The Cold War Transformation of the Korean Orphan." *Journal of American Ethnic History* 31, no. 4 (2012): 34–55.

———. *To Save the Children of Korea: The Cold War Origins of International Adoption.* Stanford: Stanford University Press, 2015.

Okihiro, Gary Y. *Margins and Mainstreams: Asians in American History and Culture.* Seattle: University of Washington Press, 1994.

———. "Oral History and the Writing of Ethnic History." In *Oral History: An Interdisciplinary Anthology,* edited by David K. Dunaway and Willa K. Baum, 199–214. Lanham: Altamira Press, 1996.

O'Loughlin, Paula. "A Comment about the Comments." *Heart, Mind and Seoul* (web log), November 14, 2007. http://heartmindandseoul.typepad.com/weblog/2007/11/a-comment-about-the-comments.html.

Omi, Michael, and Howard Winant. *Racial Formation in the United States: From the 1960s to the 1990s.* Second ed. New York: Routledge, 1994.

Ong, Aihwa. *Flexible Citizenship: The Cultural Logics of Transnationality.* Durham: Duke University Press, 1999.

Ong, Paul, and John M. Liu. "U.S. Immigration Policies and Asian Migration." In *Contemporary Asian America: A Multidisciplinary Reader,* edited by Min Zhou and James V. Gatewood, 155–174. New York: New York University Press, 2000.

Onishi, Norimitsu. "Korea Aims to End Stigma of Adoption and Stop 'Exporting' Babies." *New York Times,* October 8, 2008. http://www.nytimes.com/2008/10/09/world/asia/09adopt.html?_r=2&pagewanted=all.

Ortner, Sherry B. "Resistance and the Problem of Ethnographic Refusal." *Comparative Studies in Society and History* 37, no. 1 (1995): 173–193.

Owen, Jane. "It's a Wonderful Life!" In *Voices from Another Place: A Collection of Works from a Generation Born in Korea and Adopted to Other Countries,* edited by Susan Soon-Keum Cox, 67–68. St. Paul: Yeong and Yeong Book, 1999.

Palley, Marian L. "Feminism in a Confucian Society: The Women's Movement in Korea." In *Women of Japan and Korea: Continuity and Change,* edited by Joyce Gelb and Marian L. Palley, 274–294. Philadelphia: Temple University Press, 1994.

Palmer, John D. "Korean Adopted Young Women: Gender Bias, Racial Issues, and Educational Implications." *Research on the Education of Asian and Pacific Americans* (2001): 177–204.

———. *The Dance of Identities: Korean Adoptees and Their Journey toward Empowerment.* Honolulu: University of Hawai'i Press, 2011.

Palumbo-Liu, David. *Asian/American: Historical Crossings of a Racial Frontier.* Stanford: Stanford University Press, 1999.

Park, Chung-a. "Children Can Adopt Mother's Surname." *Korea Times,* June 3, 2007. http://www.koreatimes.co.kr/www/news/nation/2008/04/113_4064.html.

Park, Kyung-ae. "Political Representation and South Korean Women." *Journal of Asian Studies* 58, no. 2 (May 1999): 432–448.

Park, Shelley M. "Adoptive Maternal Bodies: A Queer Paradigm for Rethinking Mothering?" *Hypatia: A Journal of Feminist Philosophy* 21, no. 1 (2006): 201–226.

———. *Mothering Queerly, Queering Motherhood: Resisting Monomaternalism in Adoptive, Lesbian, Blended, and Polygamous Families.* Albany: State University of New York Press, 2013.

———. "Real (M)othering: The Metaphysics of Maternity in Children's Literature." In *Adoption Matters: Philosophical and Feminist Essays*, edited by Sally Anne Haslanger and Charlotte Witt, 171–194. Ithaca: Cornell University Press, 2005.

Park, Soon Ho. "Forced Child Migration Korea-born Intercountry Adoptees in the United States." PhD diss., University of Hawaii, 1994.

Park Dahlen, Sarah. Comment on "MPR, International Adoption, and Oh Wait . . . Where's the Adult Adoptee on the Adoption Panel?" Sarahpark.com (web log), July 9, 2012. http://readingspark.wordpress.com/2012/07/09/1212/.

Park Nelson, Kim. *Invisible Asians: Korean Adoptees, Asian American Experiences, and Racial Exceptionalism.* New Brunswick: Rutgers University Press, 2016.

———. "Korean Looks, American Eyes: Korean American Adoptees, Race, Culture and Nation." PhD diss., University of Minnesota, 2009.

———. "Loss Is More Than Sadness": Reading Dissent in Transracial Adoption Melodrama in The Language of Blood and First Person Plural." *Adoption and Culture* 1, no. 1 (2007): 101–128.

———. "Shopping for Children." In *Outsiders Within: Writing on Transracial Adoption*, edited by Jane Jeong Trenka, Julia Sudbury, and Sun Yung Shin, 89–104. Cambridge: South End Press, 2006.

Park Nelson, Kim, and Jae Ran Kim. "Special Edition: Talk to Me about Everything." Interview by Kevin Vollmers, *Land of Gazillion Adoptees* (audio blog), July 20, 2013. http://landofgazillionadoptees.com/2012/07/20/special-edition-talk-with-me-about -everything-featuring-dr-kim-park-nelson-and-jaeran-kim/.

Park Nelson, Kim, Jae Ran Kim, and Kelly Fern. "Roundtable: The Adoptee Experience." Interview by Tom Weber, *Minnesota Public Radio*, July 13, 2012. http://minnesota.public radio.org/display/web/2012/07/13/daily-circuit-roundtable-adoption.

Pate, Soojin. *From Orphan to Adoptee: U.S. Empire and Genealogies of Korean Adoption.* Minneapolis: University of Minnesota Press, 2014.

———. "Genealogies of Korean Adoption: American Empire, Militarization, and Yellow Desire." PhD diss., University of Minnesota, 2010.

Pateman, Carole. *The Sexual Contract.* Stanford: Stanford University Press, 1988.

Patterson, Orlando. *Slavery and Social Death: A Comparative Study.* Cambridge: Harvard University Press. 1982.

Patton, Sandra Lee. *Birth Marks: Transracial Adoption in Contemporary America.* New York: New York University Press, 2000.

Pearson, Holly. "Complicating Intersectionality through the Identities of a Hard of Hearing Korean Adoptee: An Autoethnography." *Equity & Excellence in Education* 43, no. 3 (2010): 341–356. doi:10.1080/10665684.2010.496642.

Pearson, Ruth. "Towards the Re-politicization of Feminist Analysis of the Global Economy." *International Feminist Journal of Politics* 6, no. 4 (2004): 603–622.

People's Republic of China. "New Criteria Spelt out for Adoption by Foreigners." Chinese Government's Official Web Portal, December 25, 2006. http://www.gov.cn/english/2006–12/25/content_477509.htm.

————. "Requirements for Adopters." Chinese Government's Official Web Portal, August 30, 2005. http://www.gov.cn/english/2005–08/30/content_26750.htm.

Perez, Jonathan. "Challenging the 'DREAMer' Narrative," *Huffington Post,* November 16, 2014. https://www.huffingtonpost.com/jonathan-perez/challenging-the-dreamerna_b_6163008.html.

Perry, Alyssa Jeong. "Korean Adoptee in Immigration Battle Fights to Remain in His Country." *The Guardian,* April 3, 2015. http://www.theguardian.com/us-news/2015/apr/03/adamcrapser-deportation-korean-adoption-system-immigration.

Perscheid, Margie. "#BuildFamiliesNotBoxes." *Third Mom,* January 21, 2014. http://third-mom.blogspot .com/2014/01/buildfamiliesnotboxes.html.

Pertman, Adam. "An Unnerving Reality: We're Deporting Adoptees." Editorial, *Huffington Post,* May 29, 2012. http://www.huffingtonpost.com/adam-pertman/an-unnerving -reality-were_b_1550747.html.

Phinney, Jean S. "Ethnic Identity in Adolescents and Adults: Review of Research. "*Psychological Bulletin* 108, no. 3 (1990): 499–514.

Poster, Mark. "Virtual Ethnicity: Tribal Identity in an Age of Global Communications." In *CyberSociety 2.0: Revisiting Computer-mediated Communication and Community,* edited by Steven G. Jones, 184–211. Thousand Oaks: Sage Publications, 1998.

Pound Pup Legacy. "Deportation Cases." Pound Pup Legacy, 2013. http://poundpuplegacy.org/deportation_cases.

Prébin, Elise. "Gifts and Money between Adoptees and Birth Families," edited by Kim Park Nelson, Tobias Hübinette, Eleana J. Kim, Jennifer Kwon Dobbs, Kim Langrehr, and Lene Myong, in *Proceedings of the Second International Symposium on Korean Adoption Studies.* Seoul: IKAA, Korea University, and the Presidential Council on National Branding, 2010.

————. *Meeting Once More: The Korean Side of Transnational Adoption.* New York: New York University Press, 2013.

Price, Rita. "Push On to Open Up Old Birth Certificates Records." *Columbus Dispatch,* January 27, 2013. http://www.dispatch.com/content/stories/local/2013/01/27/push-on -to-open-up-old-records.html.

Puar, Jasbir K. *Terrorist Assemblages: Homonationalism in Queer Times.* Durham: Duke University Press, 2007.

Raible, John. "Ally Parenting for Social Justice." In *Parenting as Adoptees,* edited by Kevin Ost Vollmers and Adam Chau, 84–104. Minneapolis: CQT Media and Publishing, 2012.

———. "Learning from Artyom's Plight." *John Raible Online* (web log), April 14, 2010. http://johnraible.wordpress.com/how-to-fix-adoption-first-respect-adult-adoptees/learning-from-artyoms-plight/.

———. "Sticking with a Wounded Child." *John Raible Online* (web log), April 18, 2010. http://johnraible.wordpress.com/how-to-fix-adoption-first-respect-adult-adoptees/sticking-with-a-wounded-child/.

———. "TRA Oppression: A Word about the New Blog Banner." *John Raible Online*(web log), August 13, 2011. https://johnraible.wordpress.com/2011/18/13/a-word-aboutthe new-blog-banner/.

———. "What Is Transracialization?" *John Raible Online* (web log), 2006. http://johnraible.wordpress.com/about-john-w-raible/what-is-transracialization/.

Raleigh, Elizabeth. *Selling Transracial Adoption: Families, Markets, and the Color Line.* Philadelphia: Temple University Press, 2018.

Ramesh, Randeep. "Spread of 'Baby Boxes' in Europe Alarms United Nations." *The Guardian,* June 11, 2012. http://www.theguardian.com/world/2012/jun/10/unitednations -europe-news.

Ramstad, Evan. "Organization Helps Korea's Single Moms." *Wall Street Journal,* February 11, 2011. http://blogs.wsj.com/korearealtime/2011/02/11/organization-helps-koreas -single-moms/.

Rapp-Hooper, Mira. "The Cataclysm that Would Follow a 'Bloody Nose' Strike in North Korea." *The Atlantic,* January 31, 2018. https://www.theatlantic.com/international/archive/2018/01/the-cataclysm-that-would-follow-a-bloody-nose-strike-in-north-korea/551924/.

Rasmussen, Kim Su, ed. "Editor's Note." *Journal of Korean Adoption Studies* 1, no. 1 (2009): 5.

Reinharz, Shulamit. *Feminist Methods in Social Research.* New York: Oxford Univ. Press, 1992.

Riben, Mirah. "Help Is Needed for International Adoptees Caught in a Legal—And Stateless—Quagmire." *Huffington Post,* June 30, 2016. http://www.huffingtonpost .com/mirah-riben/help-is-needed-for-intern_b_10726320.html.

———. *The Stork Market: America's Multi-billion Dollar Unregulated Adoption Industry.* Dayton: Advocate Publications, 2007.

Rich, Adrienne. "Notes toward a Politics of Location." In *Feminist Postcolonial Theory: A Reader,* edited by Reina Lewis and Sara Mills, 29–42. Edinburgh: Edinburgh University Press, 2003.

Ritchie, Donald A. *The Oxford Handbook of Oral History.* New York: Oxford University Press, 2011.

Rivas, Jorge. "Why You Should Stop Using the Term DREAMer," Splinter News, August 25, 2017. https://splinternews.com/why-you-should-stop-using-the-term-dreamer -1797908148.

Roberts, Dorothy E. *Shattered Bonds: The Color of Child Welfare.* New York: Basic Books, 2002.

Robinson, Katy. "Helping the Next Generation." *The New York Times* (web log), November 25, 2007. http://relativechoices.blogs.nytimes.com/2007/11/25/helping-the-next-generation/.

Robinson, Katy. *A Single Square Picture: A Korean Adoptee's Search for Her Roots.* New York: Berkeley Books, 2002.

———. "Helping the Next Generation." *New York Times* (web log), November 25, 2007. http://relativechoices.blogs.nytimes.com/2007/11/25/helping-the-next-generation/.

———. "Tracing My Roots Back to Korea." *New York Times* (web log), November 6, 2007. http://relativechoices.blogs.nytimes.com/2007/11/06/tracing-my-roots-back-to-korea/.

Roh, Mihye. "Women Workers in a Changing Korean Society." In *Women of Japan and Korea: Continuity and Change,* edited by Joyce Gelb and Marian L. Palley, 240–256. Philadelphia: Temple University Press, 1994.

Rojas, Leslie Berstein. "How Does an Adoptee Get Deported? More Easily Than One Might Think." *Southern California Public Radio,* May 29, 2012. http://www.scpr.org/blogs/multiamerican/2012/05/29/8304/how-does-an-adoptee-get-deported-more-easily-than-/.

Rollins, Lisa Marie. "Racist M/Paternalism at Its Best." *A Birth Project* (web log), November 13, 2007. http://birthproject.wordpress.com/2007/11/13/racist-mpaternalism-at-its-best/.

Roseneil, Sasha, and Shelley Budgeon. "Cultures of Intimacy and Care beyond 'the Family': Personal Life and Social Change in the Early 21st Century." *Current Sociology* 52, no. 2 (2004): 135–159. doi:10.1177/0011392104041798.

RT. "Russia Seeks Interpol Investigation of Deaths in Adoptive US Families." *RT,* March 20, 2013. http://rt.com/politics/russia-vows-to-prosecute-us-citizens-guilty-of-russian-kids-deaths-528/.

Ruth, Kari. "Dear Luuk." In *Seeds from a Silent Tree: An Anthology by Korean Adoptees,* edited by Tonya Bishoff and Jo Rankin, 143–144. San Diego: Pandal Press, 1997.

———. "Kimchee on White Bread." In *Voices from Another Place: A Collection of Works from a Generation Born in Korea and Adopted to Other Countries,* by Susan Soon-Keum Cox, 74–81. St. Paul: Yeong and Yeong Book, 1999.

Sachs, Dana. *The Life We Were Given: Operation Babylift, International Adoption, and the Children of War in Vietnam.* Boston: Beacon Press, 2010.

Salling, A. K. "Adoption Finalization Naturalization and Citizenship Deportation and Project." Paper presented at Building across Geographies: Current Adoptee Voices on the State of the Movement. KoRoot, Seoul, South Korea, August 2, 2016.

Sarri, Rosemary C., Yenoak Baik, and Marti Bombyk. "Goal Displacement and Dependency in South Korean-United States Intercountry Adoption." *Children and Youth Services Review* 20, no. 1–2 (1998): 87–114.

Schlosser, Eric. "The Prison-Industrial Complex." *The Atlantic,* December 1998. http://www.theatlantic.com/magazine/archive/1998/12/the-prison-industrial-complex/304669/.

Schwarzschild, Todd. "Red Flags Wave over Uganda's Adoption Boom." CNN, March 2, 2013. http://edition.cnn.com/2013/02/27/world/africa/wus-uganda-adoptions.

Schwekendiek, Daniel. "Happy Birthday? Official versus Chronological Age of Korean Adoptees." *Journal of Korean Adoption Studies* 1, no. 1 (2009): 25–39.

Seabrook, John. "The Joys and Struggles of International Adoption." Interview by Terry Gross, National Public Radio, May 13, 2010. http://www.npr.org/templates/story/story.php?storyId=126777059.

————. "The Last Babylift: Adopting a Child in Haiti." *New Yorker*, May 10, 2010. http://www.newyorker.com/reporting/2010/05/10/100510fa_fact_seabrook.

Seattle Human Rights Commission Letter to Honorable Judge John C. Odell, February 29, 2016. http://www.seattle.gov/Documents/Departments/SeattleHumanRights Commission/SHRC-Adam_Crapser-022916.pdf.

Sedgwick, Eve Kosofsky. *Tendencies*. Durham: Duke University Press, 1993.

"See That Box? That's Where They Put the Babies. And It's the Most Remarkable Thing You'll See All Week." Faithit, 2014. http://www.faithit.com/baby-box-rescue-seoul -south-korea-brave-pastor-disabilities/.

Seguino, Stephanie. "Accounting for Gender in Asian Economic Growth." *Feminist Economics* 6, no. 3 (2000): 27–58.

Selman, Peter. *Adoption Advocate* 44 (February 2012): 1–17. https://www.adoptioncouncil .org/images/stories/documents/NCFA_ADOPTION_ADVOCATE_NO44.pdf.

————. "Intercountry Adoption in the New Millennium: The 'Quiet Migration' Revisited." *Population Research and Policy Review* 22 (2002): 205–225.

————. "The Demographic History of Intercountry Adoption." In *Intercountry Adoption: Developments, Trends and Perspectives*, edited by Peter Selman, 15–39. London: British Agencies for Adoption and Fostering, 2000.

Shaw, Vivian, et al. "Collective Statement by Asian American Studies Scholars Regarding Japanese American 'Internment' and a Proposed Registry of Immigrants from Muslim-majority Countries," Medium, December 3, 2016. https://medium.com/ @vgshaw/collective-statement-by-asian-american-studies-scholars-regarding-japanese -american-internment-a7994c453a77.

Shiao, Jiannbin Lee, and Mia H. Tuan. "Korean Adoptees and the Social Context of Ethnic Exploration." *American Journal of Sociology* 113, no. 4 (2008): 1023–1066. doi:10.1086/522807.

Shifman, Limor. *Memes in Digital Culture*. Cambridge: MIT Press, 2014.

Shim, Sun-ah. "Dark Side of Inter-racial Adoption Surfaces with Arrivals of Grown-up Adoptees." *Yonhap News Agency*, October 10, 2012. http://english.yonhapnews.co.kr/n_feature/ 2012/10/10/5/4901000000AEN20121010008500315F.HTML.

Shin, Seung Woo. "Korean Woman, Adopted as Infant, Facing Deportation in Arizona," translated by Aruna Lee. *New American Media*, January 20, 2011. http://newamericamedia.org/2011/01/korean-woman-adopted-as-infant-facing-deportation-in-arizona.php.

Shin, Sung-sik, and Joo-young Jang. "Parents Take Full Advantage of Day Care." *Korea Joongang Daily*, January 9, 2013. http://koreajoongangdaily.joinsmsn.com/news/ article/article.aspx?aid=2965209&cloc=joongangdaily|home|newslist1.

Shoichet, Catherine E. "Americans Adopted Him; Now He's Facing Deportation." CNN.com, November 7, 2016. http://www.cnn.com/2016/11/04/us/adam-crapser-deportation/.

Sieck, Leah Kim. "A True Daughter." In *Voices from Another Place: A Collection of Works from a Generation Born in Korea and Adopted to Other Countries,* edited by Susan Soon-Keum Cox, 84–91. St. Paul: Yeong and Yeong Book, 1999.

Siegal, Erin. *Finding Fernanda: Two Mothers, One Child, and a Cross-border Search for Truth.* Oakland: Cathexis Press, 2011.

Siim, Birte. *Gender and Citizenship: Politics and Agency in France, Britain, and Denmark.* New York: Cambridge University Press, 2000.

Simon, Rita J., and Howard Altstein. *Adoption across Borders: Serving the Children in Transracial and Intercountry Adoptions.* Lanham: Rowman and Littlefield, 2000.

Simpson, Audra. "On Ethnographic Refusal: Indigeneity, 'Voice,' and Colonial Citizenship." *Junctures* 9 (2007): 67–80.

Smith, Linda Tuhiwai. *Decolonizing Methodologies: Research and Indigenous Peoples.* Dunedin, New Zealand: University of Otago Press, 1999.

Smith, Sidonie. *A Poetics of Women's Autobiography: Marginality and the Fictions of Self-representation.* Bloomington: Indiana University Press, 1987.

———. *Subjectivity, Identity, and the Body: Women's Autobiographical Practices in the Twentieth Century.* Bloomington: Indiana University Press, 1993.

Smolin, David M. "Of Orphans and Adoption, Parents and the Poor, Exploitation and Rescue: A Scriptural and Theological Critique of the Evangelical Christian Adoption and Orphan Care Movement." *Regent J. Int'l L* 8 (2011): 267–324.

Social Welfare Society, Inc. "Support for Families of Single Parents." Social Welfare Society, Inc., 2009. http://www.sws.or.kr/english/subo2d.php.

Solinger, Rickie. *Beggars and Choosers: How the Politics of Choice Shapes Adoption, Abortion, and Welfare in the United States.* New York: Hill and Wang, 2001.

Somewhere Between. Directed by Linda Goldstein Knowlton. New York: Long Shot Factory, 2011.

Song, Miri. *Choosing Ethnic Identity.* Cambridge: Polity Press, 2003.

Song, Sueyoung, and Richard Lee. "The Past and Present Cultural Experiences of Adopted Korean American Adults." *Adoption Quarterly* 12, no. 1 (2009): 19–36.

Spence-Chapin Adoption Services. "Korea | Adoption Programs | Spence-Chapin Adoption Services." Korea | Adoption Programs | Spence-Chapin Adoption Services,. 2011. http://www.spence-chapin.org/adoption-programs/countries/b3_korea.php.

Spickard, Paul R. *Mixed Blood: Intermarriage and Ethnic Identity in Twentieth-century America.* Madison: University of Wisconsin Press, 1989.

Stacey, Judith. *Brave New Families: Stories of Domestic Upheaval in Late Twentieth Century America.* Second ed. Berkeley: University of California Press, 1998.

———. "Can There Be a Feminist Ethnography?" *Women's Studies International Forum* 11, no. 1 (1988): 21–27.

———. *In the Name of the Family: Rethinking Family Values in the Postmodern Age.* Boston: Beacon Press, 1996.

———. *Unhitched: Love, Marriage, and Family Values from West Hollywood to Western China*. New York: New York University Press, 2011.

Staff. "The Wedding Industrial Complex." *The Week*, June 15, 2013. http://theweek.com/articles/463257/wedding-industrial-complex.

Stanley, Liz. "Feminist Auto/Biography and Feminist Epistemology." In *Out of the Margins: Women's Studies in the Nineties*, edited by Jane Aaron and Sylvia Walby, 204–219. London: Falmer Press, 1991.

State of California. "An Act to Protect Free White Labor against Competition from Chinese Coolie Labor, and to Discourage the Immigration of Chinese to the State of California." Protecting Free White Labor, January 31, 1998. http://academic.udayton.edu/race/02rights/statute1862.htm.

Stock, Kimberly Hee. "My Han." In *Voices from Another Place: A Collection of Works from a Generation Born in Korea and Adopted to Other Countries*, edited by Susan Soon-Keum Cox, 96–104. St. Paul: Yeong and Yeong Book, 1999.

———. "The Note." In *I Didn't Know Who I Was: A Collection of Essays and Poems by Korean Adoptees*, edited by Korean Culture Network, 10–13. Seoul: Korean Culture Network, 2007.

Stoler, Ann Laura. *Carnal Knowledge and Imperial Power: Race and the Intimate in Colonial Rule*. Second ed. Berkeley: University of California Press, 2010.

Sullivan, Nikki. *A Critical Introduction to Queer Theory*. Edinburgh: Edinburgh University Press, 2003.

Takaki, Ronald T. *Strangers from a Different Shore: A History of Asian Americans*. Boston: Little, Brown and Company, 1989.

Terrell, John, and Judith Modell. "Anthropology and Adoption." *American Anthropologist* 96, no. 1 (1994): 155–161.

The Adoption Guide. "The Adoption Guide: Getting Started on China Adoption." The Adoption Guide, 2013. http://www.theadoptionguide.com/options/adoption-from-china.

The Adoption History Project. "Adoption History: Confidentiality and Sealed Records." Adoption History: Confidentiality and Sealed Records, February 22, 2012. http://darkwing.uoregon.edu/~adoption/topics/confidentiality.htm.

The Dying Rooms. Produced by Lauderdale Productions. Directed by Kate Blewett and Brian Woods. London: British Broadcasting Company, 1995.

Thomas, Mary E. *Multicultural Girlhood: Racism, Sexuality, and the Conflicted Spaces of American Education*. Philadelphia: Temple University Press, 2011.

Ting, Jennifer. "Bachelor Society: Deviant Heterosexuality and Asian American Historiography." In *Privileging Positions: The Sites of Asian American Studies*, edited by Gary Y. Okihiro, Marilyn Alquizola, Dorothy Fujita Rony, and K. Scott Wong, 271–279. Pullman: Washington State University Press, 1995.

"To Market, to Market." *Sex and the City*. HBO, June 22, 2003.

Tooley, Heather. "South Korean Adoptee Deportation: American Parents Abused Adopted Son, Now He Faces Deportation as Adult." *Inquisitr*, April 1, 2015. http://www.inquisitr.com/1973071/south-korean-adoptee-deportation-american-parents-abused-adopted-son-now-he-faces-deportation-as-adult/.

Tracy, Michelle, and Kathleen Guidroz, eds. *The Intersectional Approach: Transforming the Academy through Race, Class, and Gender*. Chapel Hill: University of North Carolina Press, 2010.

Trenka, Jane Jeong. *Fugitive Visions: An Adoptee's Return to Korea*. Saint Paul: Graywolf Press, 2009.

———. "How to Stop Languishing and Get Yourself Adopted." Editorial, *Minnesota Public Radio*, January 14, 2013. http://minnesota.publicradio.org/display/web/2013/01/14/trenka.

———. "No Rubber-stamp Court for Int'l Adoptions." *Korea Times*, March 20, 2013. http://www.koreatimes.co.kr/www/news/opinon/2013/03/197_132426.html.

———. *The Language of Blood: A Memoir*. St. Paul: Graywolf Press, 2003.

Trenka, Jane Jeong, Julia Sudbury, and Sun Yung Shin, eds. *Outsiders Within: Writing on Transracial Adoption*. Cambridge, Mass.: South End Press, 2006.

Trepagnier, Barbara. *Silent Racism, Expanded Edition: How Well-Meaning White People Perpetuate the Racial Divide*. Second ed. Boulder: Paradigm Publishers, 2010.

Triseliotis, John. "Intercountry Adoption: Global Trade or Global Gift?" *Adoption & Fostering* 24 no. 2 (2000): 45–54. doi. 10.1177/030857590002400207.

Tuan, Mia. *Forever Foreigners or Honorary Whites? The Asian Ethnic Experience Today*. New Brunswick: Rutgers University Press, 1998.

Tuan, Mia, and Jiannbin Lee Shiao. *Choosing Ethnicity, Negotiating Race: Korean Adoptees in America*. New York: Russell Sage Foundation, 2011.

Turkle, Sherry. *Life on the Screen: Identity in the Age of the Internet*. New York: Simon and Schuster, 1995.

Turner, Kat. "Planted in the West: The Story of an American Girl." In *Voices from Another Place: A Collection of Works from a Generation Born in Korea and Adopted to Other Countries*, edited by Susan Soon-Keum Cox, 132–137. St. Paul: Yeong and Yeong Book, 1999.

Turner, William B. *A Genealogy of Queer Theory*. Philadelphia: Temple University Press, 2005.

Turner Strong, Pauline. "To Forget Their Tongue, Their Name, and Their Whole Relation: Captivity, Extra-Tribal Adoption, and the Indian Child Welfare Act." In *Relative Values: Reconfiguring Kinship Studies*, edited by Sarah Franklin and Susan McKinnon, 468–493. Durham: Duke University Press, 2001.

Twine, France Winddance. "Brown Skinned White Girls: Class, Culture and the Construction of White Identity in Suburban Communities." *Gender, Place and Culture: A Journal of Feminist Geography* 3, no. 2 (1996): 205–224. doi:10.1080/09663699650021891.

Twohey, Megan, Ryan McNeill, and Robin Respaut. "Reuters Investigates." *Reuters*, October 8, 2013. http://www.reuters.com/investigates/adoption/.

United States Census Bureau. *Income and Poverty in the United States: 2016*, Report Number P60–259, by Jessica L. Semega, Kayla R. Fontenot, and Melissa A. Kollar. Washington D.C.: United States Bureau of the Census, 2017. https://www.census.gov/data/tables/2017/demo/income-poverty/p60–259.html.

———. *Income, Poverty, and Health Insurance Coverage in the United States 2010*, by Carmen DeNavas-Walt, Bernadette D. Proctor, and Jessica C. Smith. Washington, D.C.: United States Bureau of the Census, 2011.

———. U.S. Department of Justice. Office of Justice Programs. *Family Violence Statistics: Including Statistics on Strangers and Acquaintances.*, by Matthew Durose, Caroline Wolf Harlow, Patrick A. Langan, Mark Motivans, Ramona R. Rantala, and Erica L. Smith, June 2005. bjs.gov/content/pub/pdf/fvs02.pdf.

USAID. "Working without a Net: Women and the Asian Financial Crisis." *Gender Matters Quarterly* 2 (2000): 1–8.

Vance, Jeannine Joy. *Twins Found in a Box: Adapting to Adoption.* Bloomington, Ind.: AuthorHouse, 2003.

Vance, Mary Lee. "Who Do I Resemble?" In *Voices from Another Place: A Collection of Works from a Generation Born in Korea and Adopted to Other Countries,* edited by Susan Soon-Keum Cox, 114–117. St. Paul: Yeong and Yeong Book, 1999.

Vasilyeva, Nataliya. "Russian Boy Adopted by Americans Returns to Russia." *MSN News,* March 27, 2013. http://news.msn.com/world/russian-boy-adopted-by-americans-returns-to-russia.

Volkman, Toby Alice, ed. *Cultures of Transnational Adoption.* Durham: Duke University Press, 2005.

Vollmers, Kevin. Interview with Adam Crapser, Gazillion Voices Radio, SoundCloud, March 2015. https://soundcloud.com/gazillion-voices/adam-crapser-gazillion-voices-radio.

———. "The Most Satisfying Unsatisfying Show." *Land of Gazillion Adoptees* (web log), July 13, 2012. http://landofgazillionadoptees.com/2012/07/13/the-most-satisfying-unsatisfying-show/.

———. "Top Seven Reasons Why Adoption Fundraisers Are Problematic." *Land of Gazillion Adoptees,* November 14, 2014. http://landofgazillionadoptees.com/2014/11/11/top-seven-reasons-why-adoption-fundraisers-are-problematic/.

Wang, Francis Kai-Hwa. "A Push to Protect Adult Adoptees from Deportation." *NBC News.*, March 12, 2015. http://www.nbcnews.com/news/asian-america/retroactive-citizenshipadult-adoptees-n318581.

———. "Bill Would Provide Retroactive Citizenship for All International Adoptees." *NBC News,* November 13, 2015. http://www.nbcnews.com/news/asian-america/bill-would-provide-retroactive-citizenship-all-international-adoptees-n462151.

Warner, Michael. "Introduction: Fear of a Queer Planet." *Social Text* 29 (1991): 3–17.

———. *Publics and Counterpublics.* New York: Zone Books, 2005.

Watson, Julia. "Toward an Anti-Metaphysics of Autobiography." In *The Culture of Autobiography: Constructions of Self-representation,* edited by Robert Folkenflik, 57–79. Stanford: Stanford University Press, 1993.

Weaver, Ray. "Social Minister Stops Adoptions from Ethiopian Orphanage." *Copenhagen Post,* March 1, 2013. http://cphpost.dk/international/social-minister-stops-adoptions-ethiopian-orphanage.

Weaver, SuLyn. "An Adoptee at the Baby Box." *Gazillion Voices,* January 2014. http://gazillionvoices.com/guest-post-by-sulyn-weaver-an-adoptee-at-the-baby-box/#.Uvf UOPYnvFs.

Wei, Lu. "Filter Blogs vs. Personal Journals: Understanding the Knowledge Production Gap on the Internet." *Journal of Computer-Mediated Communication* 14, no. 3 (2009): 532–558. doi:10.1111/j.1083–6101.2009.01452.x.

Weir, Fred. "Adopted Toddler's Alleged Death-by-Abuse in Texas Inflames Russia." *Christian Science Monitor*, February 19, 2013. http://www.csmonitor.com/World/Europe/2013/0219/Adopted-toddler-s-alleged-death-by-abuse-in-Texas-inflames-Russia.

Wells, Loey Werking. "Native 'Korean' American: Or, How a Korean Adoptee Searched for an Identity She Could Call Her Own." In *Voices from Another Place: A Collection of Works from a Generation Born in Korea and Adopted to Other Countries*, edited by Susan Soon-Keum Cox, 120–124. St. Paul: Yeong and Yeong Book, 1999.

Wesolowski Kim, Paul. "Ethnic Identity Development of Korean, International, Transracial Adoptees." PhD diss., Wright Institute, 1996.

Wheeler, Jacob. *Between Light and Shadow: A Guatemalan Girl's Journey through Adoption*. Lincoln: University of Nebraska Press, 2011.

Wickes, Kevin L., and John R. Slate. "Transracial Adoption of Koreans: A Preliminary Study of Adjustment." *International Journal for the Advancement of Counseling* 19 (1996): 187–195.

Wilkinson, Hei Sook Park, and Nancy Fox, eds. *After the Morning Calm: Reflections of Korean Adoptees*. Bloomfield Hills: Sunrise Ventures, 2002.

Wilson, Samuel M., and Leighton C. Peterson. "The Anthropology of Online Communities." *Annual Review of Anthropology* 31, no. 1 (2002): 449–467. doi:10.1146/annurev.anthro.31.040402.085436.

Winnubst, Shannon. "Review Essay. No Future: Queer Theory and the Death Drive." *Environment and Planning D: Society and Space* 28, no. 1 (2010): 178–183. doi:10.1068/d445re.

Witt, Charlotte. "Family Resemblances: Adoption, Personal Identity and Genetic Essentialism." In *Adoption Matters: Philosophical and Feminist Essays*, by Sally Anne. Haslanger and Charlotte Witt, 135–145. Ithaca: Cornell University Press, 2005.

Wong, Sau-Ling C. "Immigrant Autobiography: Some Questions of Definition and Approach." In *American Autobiography: Retrospect and Prospect*, edited by Paul John Eakin, 142–170. Madison: University of Wisconsin Press, 1991.

Woo, Myungsook. *The Politics of Social Welfare Policy in South Korea: Growth and Citizenship*. Lanham: University Press of America, 2004.

World Entertainment News Network. "Tom Cruise Slams Brooke Shields' Drug Use." Hollywood.com, May 25, 2005. http://www.hollywood.com/news/brief/2440860/tom-cruise-slams-brooke-shields-drug-use?page=all.

World Wide News Ukraine. "Ukraine Tracks the Fate of Ukrainian Children Adopted Abroad." *World Wide News Ukraine*, April 2, 2013. http://wnu-ukraine.com/news/culture-lifestyle/?id=2844.

Wright, Kristin. "Md. Father Charged with Adopted Son's Death." NBC4 Washington, February 19, 2014. http://www.nbcwashington.com/news/local/Father-Charged-With-Adopted-Sons-Death—245972321.html.

Wright, Michelle M. *Becoming Black: Creating Identity in the African Diaspora.* Durham: Duke University Press, 2004.

Yim, Seung-hye. "Korea Passes Law to Change Adoption Policy." *Korea Joongang Daily,* July 1, 2011. http://koreajoongangdaily.joinsmsn.com/news/article/article.aspx?aid=2938312.

Yngvesson, Barbara. *Belonging in an Adopted World: Race, Identity, and Transnational Adoption.* Chicago: University of Chicago Press, 2010.

———. "Placing the 'Gift Child' in Transnational Adoption." *Law & Society Review* 36, no. 2 (2002).

Yngvesson, Barbara, and Maureen A. Mahoney. "'As One Should, Ought and Wants to Be': Belonging and Authenticity in Identity Narratives." *Theory, Culture & Society* 17, no. 6 (2000): 77–110. doi:10.1177/02632760022051509.

Yokoyama, Kayoko. "The Double Binds of Our Bodies." *Women & Therapy* 30, no. 3–4 (2007): 177–192.

Yonhap News. "13 Korean Adoptees Obtain Dual Citizenship." *Korea Herald,* April 19, 2011. http://www.koreaherald.com/view.php?ud=20110419000739.

Yoo Soo-Sun. "A Sad Ending for Deported Adoptee." *Korea Times,* May 24, 2017. http://www.koreatimes.co.kr/www/nation/2017/05/119_229975.html.

Yoshihara, Mari. *Embracing the East: White Women and American Orientalism.* Oxford: Oxford University Press, 2003.

YoungHee. "Laurel." In *Seeds from a Silent Tree: An Anthology by Korean Adoptees,* edited by Tonya Bishoff and Jo Rankin, 86–88. San Diego: Pandal Press, 1997.

Yu, Jae Eon. "The Use of Deleauze's Theory of Assemblage for Process-Oriented Methodology." *Historical Social Research* 38, no. 2 (2013): 197–217.

Yu, Phil. "God Bless Trump. We're Going to Nuke You Guys," *Angry Asian Man,* January 30, 2018. http://blog.angryasianman.com/2018/01/god-bless-trump-were-going-to-nuke-you.html.

Yuh, Ji-Yeon. *Beyond the Shadow of Camptown: Korean Military Brides in America.* New York: New York University Press, 2002. "'

Y U NO' Guy." Know Your Meme News, 2014. http://knowyourmeme.com/memes/y-u-no-guy.

Zack, Naomi. *Race and Mixed Race.* Philadelphia: Temple University Press, 1993.

Zahara, Alex. "Refusal as Research Method in Discard Studies." *Discard Studies,* March 21, 2016. https://discardstudies.com/2016/03/21/refusal-as-research-method-in-discard-studies/.

Zhou, Min, and James V. Gatewood, eds. *Contemporary Asian America: A Multidisciplinary Reader.* New York: New York University Press, 2000.

Zia, Helen. *Asian American Dreams: The Emergence of an American People.* New York: Farrar, Straus, and Giroux, 2000.

Index

adoptee killjoys, 60, 104, 121, 150; and adoptee legibility, 77; alienation of, 92; as angry, 11–12, 95, 130–131, 140, 144; and gratitude, 11–12, 82, 144; as knowledge producers, 140; as people of color, 65, 74; political activism of, 27, 102, 130, 140. *See also* adoptees, adult; every adoptee

Adoptee Rights Campaign, 52–53, 165n56

adoptees: birth records of, 155n47; commodification of, 2, 3, 8, 27, 35, 160n74; as gifts, 77; and gratitude, 27, 129; heterogeneity of, 95, 104; knowledge production of, 78; natal details of, 28; performativity of, 62–63; rehoming of, 110, 151; social death of, 28, 68; undocumented, 40–41, 58–60, 69, 105–107

adoptees, adult, 14, 155n47; activism of, 5, 50–56, 119–120, 123–125, 131, 133–144, 149; as adoption experts, 79, 80, 102–103, 131, 134, 137, 140; agency of, 78–79, 81, 99, 106, 141; as angry, 9–11, 77, 95, 104, 121, 124, 127–131, 140, 142, 144; as Asian American, 79; autobiographical narratives of, 14–15, 78–100, 125, 141; belonging, 93; birth records of, 28; and citizenship of, 50–51, 53–60, 113–114, 122, 147; counterpublic of, 5–6, 16, 104, 118, 141, 144; diversity of, 101, 104, 119–120; and family, 114–118; and gratefulness, 27, 90, 94, 99, 104, 108, 116–117, 121–122, 124, 127–128, 140, 144; and happiness, 94–95, 117, 121, 124–125, 128, 131, 140, 144; and internalized racism, 94; kinship among, 118–121; as knowledge producers, 102, 122, 125, 140; as Korean diaspora, 121–122; Korean nationalism of, 148–149; legibility of, 78, 114; memes, use of, 141–144; networks among, 121, 123–124, 133, 175n53; oral histories of, 101–122, 125; and passing, 119; pathologizing of, 81, 97, 117, 120–121, 125, 128, 140, 145; as people of color, 40; as perpetual children, 80, 123, 125, 155n47; and racism, 71, 79, 105; re-racialization of, 72; and retroactive citizenship, 103, 106–110, 113, 122; on returning to Korea, 79, 90–93, 110; silencing of, 127–128, 133, 140–141, 176n13; subjectivity of, 123, 141; transculturalization of, 72, 105, 110; transraciality of, 123; voices of, 123, 127, 140, 152. *See also* adoptee killjoys; every adoptee adoptees, Korean, 2; agency of, 85, 99; and American democracy, 33; Americanness of, 54–55, 71, 86, 106–109, 129; as Americans, 106–109; as Asian Americans, 6, 12, 81, 83, 96, 114, 153n5; of Asian families, 169n68; and assimilation, 112; and belonging, 63, 76, 81, 89, 93, 97, 103; birth family reunions of, 12, 137, 148–149; of Black families, 169n68; citizenship of, 23, 50–51, 103, 106–110, 113, 149–150, 161n97; as consumers, 148; and cultural authenticity, 82, 91–94, 95, 97, 111–112; as cultural whites, 44, 83, 84, 91, 108, 118; deportation of, 66, 122; as diasporic, 6–7, 12, 50, 91, 98; double agency of, 92–93; and erasure, 27, 78, 107, 111, 113, 116–117; exceptional status of, 40, 43, 53, 57, 60, 69, 107; and family, 81, 103–104; and happiness, 92; heterogeneity of, 95, 104; identity formation of, 29, 69–71, 81, 83, 86, 94–100, 104, 108, 112–114, 121, 129, 145; as "immediate relatives," 44; as immigrants, 44, 107, 109; and impersonation, 83; as interchangeable, 29, 30; and kinship, 61, 104; and Korean language, 72, 74, 111–112; Koreanness of, 91; legibility of, 73–74, 84, 90, 92; and loss, 105; marketing of, 30, 32, 142 fig. 4; natal records of, 29–30, 37, 113–114; naturalization of, 22, 40, 45–50, 107–109; as neoliberal subjects, 148, 149; and passing, 83, 119; as people of color, 66, 73, 74; racial construction of, 40; racial performativity of, 63; racial salience of, 83, 171n25; re/birth of, 82–86, 106, 129; re-racialization of, 71–72; returning to Korea, 5, 12, 37, 79, 90–93, 129, 147–148; self-expression of, 5; social death of, 27–28, 86, 91, 102, 104–105, 112–114, 158n52; "special needs," 161n97; subjectivity of, 112–113; transculturalization of, 71–73, 108, 110; transraciality of, 69–70, 86, 93, 95–99; undocumented, 60, 106–107, 109, 165n56; and whiteness, 44, 60, 73–74, 83–84, 86, 87–90, 94, 96, 114, 168n64, 171n25; and white privilege, 5, 40, 41, 44, 71, 83, 108. *See also* adoptees, transnational; adoption, Korean; adoption, transnational

adoptees, mixed race, 24, 35, 47, 48; and citizenship, 7, 21–22. *See also* mixed race children

adoptees, transnational, 131; as acceptable aliens, 39; Americanness of, 54–55; citizenship of, 40, 45–53; deportation of, 15, 49, 122; derivative citizenship of, 40, 44, 51, 58, 60, 106–107; as diasporic, 5–6; erasure of, 54; identity formation of, 126–127; as lucky, 129–130; marketing of, 142 fig. 4; naturalization of, 40, 45–50, 109; objectification of, 30; racialization of, 15; retroactive citizenship of, 55–57, 59–60, 69, 103, 106–110, 113, 122; social death of, 77–78; and U.S. imperialism, 40; and U.S. militarism, 40; and white heteronormative families, 58; and whiteness, 60; and white privilege, 51, 60. *See also* adoptees, adult; adoptees, Korean; adoption, Korean; adoption, transnational

Adoptees Have Answers, 176n14

Adoptee Solidarity Korea (ASK), 27, 135, 138

Adoptee Solidarity Korea—Los Angeles (ASK-LA), 138, 139 fig. 3

adoptees without citizenship, 14, 51; as term, 40–41, 51; versus "undocumented adoptees," 40–41, 59. *See also* undocumented adoptees

adoption: and belonging, 3–4; of children of color, 4; as child rescue, 1, 5–6, 10–11, 16, 19–20; discourse of, 9, 144; domestic, 169n65; everyday practices of, 1; family narrative of, 1; in film and TV, 116; forever family discourse, 6, 40, 51, 108–110, 150; as "gift," 10, 17, 31, 48; and gratefulness, 9–13; humanitarian ideals of, 3, 11, 16, 81; love narrative of, 1; monetization of, 149; naturalization of, 1; and neoliberalism, 3–4, 124; of mixed race children, 20–21, 161n97; politics of, 8; post-adoption services, 151–152; and racism, 21, 161n97; as reproductive justice issue, 8; transracial, 131, 169n65

adoption, Korean, 1–2; and airline companies, 148, 177n1; and American Dream, 19; and American Orientalism, 19; and assemblage theory, 23; and "child laundering," 159n63; as child rescue, 47, 100, 129, 135; and Christian Americanism, 4, 19, 44, 55, 125; and Cold War rhetoric, 6–8, 13–15, 32–33, 34 fig. 1; and communism, 22, 32; as de facto social welfare

KIMBERLY D. MCKEE is an assistant professor of liberal studies at Grand Valley State University.

THE ASIAN AMERICAN EXPERIENCE

The University of Illinois Press
is a founding member of the
Association of American University Presses.

University of Illinois Press
1325 South Oak Street
Champaign, IL 61820-6903
www.press.uillinois.edu